Influence

Science and Practice

Fourth Edition

Robert B. Cialdini
Arizona State University

Allyn and Bacon
Boston • London • Toronto • Sydney • Tokyo • Singapore

Series Editor: Carolyn Merrill
Developmental Editor: Jodi Devine
Editorial Assistant: Lara M. Zeises
Production Editor: Joe Sweeney
Editorial-Production Service: Omegatype Typography, Inc.
Composition and Prepress Buyer: Linda Cox
Manufacturing Buyer: Megan Cochran
Cover Administrator: Linda Knowles
Electronic Composition: Omegatype Typography, Inc.
Photo Research: Sue C. Howard

Library of Congress Cataloging-in-Publication Data

Cialdini, Robert B.
      Influence : science and practice / Robert B. Cialdini.—4th ed.
         p.   cm.
      Includes bibliographical references and index.
      ISBN 0-321-01147-3 (alk. paper)
      1. Influence (Psychology)   2. Persuasion (Psychology)   3. Compliance.   I. Title.

   BF774 .C53 2001
   153.8'52—dc21   00-026647

Printed in the United States of America

10   9   8   7   05   04   03   02

Contents

Preface vii

Introduction ix

Chapter 1 Weapons of Influence 1
Click, Whirr 3
Betting the Shortcut Odds 6
The Profiteers 10
Jujitsu 12
Summary 16
Study Questions 17

Chapter 2 Reciprocation: The Old Give and Take . . . and Take 19
How the Rule Works 21
The Rule Is Overpowering 22
Politics 26
The Not-So-Free Sample 27
The Rule Enforces Uninvited Debts 30
The Rule Can Trigger Unequal Exchanges 33
Reciprocal Concessions 36
Rejection-Then-Retreat 38
Reciprocal Concessions, Perceptual Contrast, and the
Watergate Mystery 40
Damned If You Do, Damned If You Don't 43
Here's My Blood, and Do Call Again 44
The Sweet, Secret Side Effects 44
Responsibility 45
Satisfaction 45
Defense 46
Rejecting the Rule 46
Smoking Out the Enemy 47
Summary 50
Study Questions 51

Chapter 3 Commitment and Consistency: Hobgoblins of the Mind 52
Whirring Along 54
The Quick Fix 55

The Foolish Fortress   55
Seek and Hide   58
Commitment Is the Key   *61*
Hearts and Minds   67
The Magic Act   68
    The Public Eye   72
    The Effort Extra   75
The Inner Choice   80
Growing Legs to Stand On   84
Standing Up for the Public Good   87
Defense   *90*
Stomach Signs   91
Heart-of-Hearts Signs   93
Summary   *95*
Study Questions   *96*

Chapter 4   Social Proof: Truths Are Us   98
The Principle of Social Proof   *100*
People Power   101
After the Deluge   104
Cause of Death: Uncertain(ty)   *111*
A Scientific Approach   115
Devictimizing Yourself   117
Monkey Me, Monkey Do   *119*
Monkey Die   121
Monkey Island   130
Defense   *134*
Sabotage   134
Looking Up   137
Summary   *140*
Study Questions   *141*

Chapter 5   Liking: The Friendly Thief   143
Making Friends to Influence People   *147*
Why Do I Like You? Let Me List the Reasons   *148*
Physical Attractiveness   148
Similarity   150
Compliments   152
Contact and Cooperation   154
    Off to Camp   156
    Back to School   158
Conditioning and Association   *161*
Does the Name Pavlov Ring a Bell?   167
From the News and Weather to the Sports   168

Defense   174
Summary   176
Study Questions   176

Chapter 6   Authority: Directed Deference   178
             The Power of Authority Pressure   180
             The Allures and Dangers of Blind Obedience   185
             Connotation Not Content   188
                  Titles   188
                  Clothes   193
                  Trappings   195
             Defense   196
                  Authoritative Authority   196
                  Sly Sincerity   197
             Summary   200
             Study Questions   201

Chapter 7   Scarcity: The Rule of the Few   203
             Less Is Best and Loss Is Worst   204
                  Limited Numbers   205
                  Time Limits   207
             Psychological Reactance   208
                  Adult Reactance: Love, Guns, and Suds   212
                  Censorship   215
             Optimal Conditions   218
                  New Scarcity: Costlier Cookies and Civil Conflict   219
                  Competition for Scarce Resources: Foolish Fury   223
             Defense   228
             Summary   231
             Study Questions   231

Chapter 8   Instant Influence: Primitive Consent
             for an Automatic Age   233
             Primitive Automaticity   234
             Modern Automaticity   236
             Shortcuts Shall Be Sacred   238
             Summary   239
             Study Questions   240

References   241

Index   257

About the Author

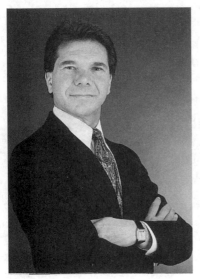

Robert B. Cialdini is Regents' Professor of Psychology at Arizona State University, where he has also been named Graduate Distinguished Research Professor. He received undergraduate, graduate, and postgraduate training in psychology from the University of Wisconsin, the University of North Carolina, and Columbia University, respectively. He is past president of the Society of Personality and Social Psychology.

He attributes his long-standing interest in the intricacies of social influence to the fact that he was raised in an entirely Italian family, in a predominantly Polish neighborhood, in a historically German city (Milwaukee), in an otherwise rural state.

Preface

The initial version of *Influence* was designed for the popular reader, and as such, an attempt was made to write it in an engaging style. In the subsequent versions, that style is retained, but in addition, I present the research evidence for my statements, recommendations, and conclusions. Although they are dramatized and corroborated through such devices as interviews, quotes, and systematic personal observations, the conclusions of *Influence* are based on controlled, psychological research. This fact allows the instructor, the student, and the popular reader to feel confident that the book is not "pop" psychology but represents work that is scientifically grounded. The subsequent versions also provide new and updated material, chapter summaries, and study questions to enhance its classroom utility.

A potentially attractive feature of the present version of *Influence* lies in its ability to serve as an enjoyable, practical, yet scientifically documented text for both students and the general reader. For students, one way to view the book, then, is to see it as a refreshing change of pace (from standard text material) that does not retreat from scientific respectability. In a related vein, for both students and the general reader, the book might be seen as a way to demonstrate that, properly presented, what often seems like dry science can actually prove to be lively, useful, and relevant to all readers' personal lives.

COMMENT ON THE FOURTH EDITION OF *INFLUENCE: SCIENCE AND PRACTICE*

It has been some time since *Influence* was last published. In the interim, some things have happened that deserve a place in this new edition. First, we now know more about the influence process than before. The study of persuasion, compliance, and change has advanced, and the pages that follow have been adapted to reflect that progress. In addition to an overall update of the material, I have expanded a feature that was stimulated by the responses of prior readers.

This feature highlights the experiences of individuals who have read *Influence*, recognized how one of the principles worked on (or for) them in a particular instance, and wrote to me describing the event. Their descriptions, which appear in the "Reader's Reports" in each chapter, illustrate how easily and frequently we can fall victim to the influence process in our everyday lives.

An array of people deserve and have my appreciation for their aid in making *Influence* possible. Several of my academic colleagues read and provided perceptive comments on the entire manuscript in its initial draft form, greatly strengthening the subsequent version. They are Gus Levine, Doug Kenrick, Art Beaman, and Mark Zanna. In addition, the first draft was read by a few family members and friends—

Richard and Gloria Cialdini, Bobette Gorden, and Ted Hall—who offered not only much-needed emotional support but insightful substantive commentary as well.

A second, larger group provided helpful suggestions for selected chapters or groups of chapters: Todd Anderson, Sandy Braver, Catherine Chambers, Judi Cialdini, Nancy Eisenberg, Larry Ettkin, Joanne Gersten, Jeff Goldstein, Betsy Hans, Valerie Hans, Joe Hepworth, Holly Hunt, Ann Inskeep, Barry Leshowitz, Darwyn Linder, Debbie Littler, John Mowen, Igor Pavlov, Janis Posner, Trish Puryear, Marilyn Rall, John Reich, Peter Reingen, Diane Ruble, Phyllis Sensenig, Roman Sherman, and Henry Wellman.

Certain people were instrumental at the beginning stages. John Staley was the first publishing professional to recognize the project's potential. Jim Sherman, Al Goethals, John Keating, Dan Wagner, Dalmas Taylor, Wendy Wood, and David Watson provided early, positive reviews that encouraged author and editors alike. My editors at Allyn and Bacon, Carolyn Merrill and Jodi Devine, were consistently congenial, helpful, and insightful. I would like to thank the following users of the third edition for their feedback during a telephone survey: Emory Griffin, Wheaton College; Robert Levine, California State, Fresno; Jeffrey Lewin, Georgia State University; David Miller, Daytona Beach Community College; Lois Mohr, Georgia State University; and Richard Rogers, Daytona Beach Community College. The third edition benefited substantially from the reviews of Assaad Azzi, Yale University; Robert M. Brady, University of Arkansas; Brian M. Cohen, University of Texas at San Antonio; Christian B. Crandall, University of Florida; Catherine Goodwin, University of Alaska; Robert G. Lowder, Bradley University; James W. Michael, Jr., Virginia Polytechnic Institute and State University; Eugene P. Sheehan, University of Northern Colorado; Jefferson A. Singer, Connecticut College; and Sandi W. Smith, Michigan State University.

Finally, throughout the project, no one was more on my side than Bobette Gorden, who lived every word with me.

I wish to thank the following individuals who—either directly or through their course instructors—contributed the "Reader's Reports" used in this edition: Pat Bobbs, Annie Carto, William Cooper, Alicia Friedman, William Graziano, Mark Hastings, Endayehu Kendie, Danuta Lubnicka, James Michaels, Steven Moysey, Paul Nail, Alan J. Resnik, Daryl Retzlaff, Geofrey Rosenberger, Dan Swift, and Karla Vasks.

I would also like to invite new readers to contribute similar "Reports" for possible publication in a future edition. They can be sent to me at the Department of Psychology, Arizona State University, Tempe, AZ 85287-1104 or Robert.Cialdini@ASU.EDU. Finally, more influence-relevant information can be obtained at Influenceatwork.com.

R.B.C.

Introduction

I can admit it freely now. All my life I've been a patsy. For as long as I can recall, I've been an easy mark for the pitches of peddlers, fund-raisers, and operators of one sort or another. True, only some of these people have had dishonorable motives. The others—representatives of certain charitable agencies, for instance—have had the best of intentions. No matter. With personally disquieting frequency, I have always found myself in possession of unwanted magazine subscriptions or tickets to the sanitation workers' ball. Probably this long-standing status as sucker accounts for my interest in the study of compliance: Just what are the factors that cause one person to say yes to another person? And which techniques most effectively use these factors to bring about such compliance? I have wondered why it is that a request stated in a certain way will be rejected, but a request that asks for the same favor in a slightly different fashion will be successful.

So in my role as an experimental social psychologist, I began to research the psychology of compliance. At first the research took the form of experiments performed, for the most part, in my laboratory and on college students. I wanted to find out which psychological principles influenced the tendency to comply with a request. Right now, psychologists know quite a bit about these principles—what they are and how they work. I have characterized such principles as weapons of influence and will be discussing some of the most important of them in this book.

After a time, though, I began to realize that the experimental work, while necessary, wasn't enough. It didn't allow me to judge the importance of the principles in the world beyond the psychology building and the campus where I was examining them. It became clear that if I was to understand fully the psychology of compliance, I would need to broaden my scope of investigation. I would need to look to the compliance professionals—the people who had been using the principles on me all my life. They know what works and what doesn't; the law of survival of the fittest assures it. Their business is to make us comply, and their livelihoods depend on it. Those who don't know how to get people to say yes soon fall away; those who do, stay and flourish.

Of course, the compliance professionals aren't the only ones who know about and use these principles to help them get their way. We all employ them and fall victim to them to some degree in our daily interactions with neighbors, friends, lovers, and family. But the compliance practitioners have much more than the vague and amateurish understanding of what works than the rest of us have. As I thought about it, I knew that they represented the richest vein of information about compliance available to me. For nearly three years, then, I combined my experimental studies with a decidedly more entertaining program: I systematically immersed myself in the world of compliance professionals—salespeople, fund-raisers, advertisers, and others.

My purpose was to observe, from the inside, the techniques and strategies most commonly and effectively used by a broad range of compliance practitioners. That

program of observation sometimes took the form of interviews with the practitioners themselves and sometimes with the natural enemies (for example, police bunco-
squad officers, consumer agencies) of certain of the practitioners. At other times, it
involved an intensive examination of the written materials by which compliance techniques are passed down from one generation to another—sales manuals and the like.

Most frequently, though, it took the form of participant observation. Participant
observation is a research approach in which the researcher becomes a spy of sorts.
With disguised identity and intent, the investigator infiltrates the setting of interest
and becomes a full-fledged participant in the group to be studied. So when I wanted
to learn about the compliance tactics of encyclopedia (or vacuum cleaner, or por-
trait photography, or dance lesson) sales organizations, I would answer a newspaper ad for sales trainees and have them teach me their methods. Using similar but
not identical approaches, I was able to penetrate advertising, public relations, and
fund-raising agencies to examine their techniques. Much of the evidence presented
in this book, then, comes from my experience posing as a compliance professional,
or aspiring professional, in a large variety of organizations dedicated to getting us
to say yes.

One aspect of what I learned in this three-year period of participant observation
was most instructive. Although there are thousands of different tactics that compliance practitioners employ to produce yes, the majority fall within six basic categories. Each of these categories is governed by a fundamental psychological principle
that directs human behavior and, in so doing, gives the tactics their power. This book
is organized around these six principles. The principles—reciprocation, consistency,
social proof, liking, authority, and scarcity—are each discussed in terms of their function in the society and in terms of how their enormous force can be commissioned
by a compliance professional who deftly incorporates them into requests for purchases, donations, concessions, votes, or assent.[1]

Finally, each principle is examined as to its ability to produce a distinct kind of
automatic, mindless compliance from people, that is, a willingness to say yes without thinking first. The evidence suggests that the ever-accelerating pace and informational crush of modern life will make this particular form of unthinking compliance
more and more prevalent in the future. It will be increasingly important for the society, therefore, to understand the how and why of automatic influence.

---

[1]It is worth noting that I have not included among the six principles the simple rule of material self-interest: that people want to get the most and pay the least for their choices. This omis-
sion does not stem from any perception on my part that the desire to maximize benefits and
minimize costs is unimportant in driving our decisions. Nor does it come from any evidence
that I have that compliance professionals ignore the power of this rule. Quite the opposite: in
my investigations, I frequently saw practitioners use (sometimes honestly, sometimes not) the
compelling "I can give you a good deal" approach. I chose not to treat the material self-interest
rule separately in this book because I see it as a motivational given, as a goes-without-saying
factor that deserves acknowledgment, but not extensive description.

Weapons of Influence

*Civilization advances by extending the number
of operations we can perform without thinking
about them.*

—ALFRED NORTH WHITEHEAD

I got a phone call one day from a friend who had recently opened an Indian jewelry store in Arizona. She was giddy with a curious piece of news. Something fascinating had just happened, and she thought that, as a psychologist, I might be able to explain it to her. The story involved a certain allotment of turquoise jewelry she had been having trouble selling. It was the peak of the tourist season, the store was unusually full of customers, the turquoise pieces were of good quality for the prices she was asking; yet they had not sold. My friend had attempted a couple of standard sales tricks to get them moving. She tried calling attention to them by shifting their location to a more central display area; no luck. She even told her sales staff to "push" the items hard—again without success.

Finally, the night before leaving on an out-of-town buying trip, she scribbled an exasperated note to her head saleswoman, "Everything in this display case, price × ½," hoping just to be rid of the offending pieces, even if at a loss. When she returned a few days later, she was not surprised to find that every article had been sold. She was shocked, though, to discover that, because the employee had read the "½" in her scrawled message as a "2," the entire allotment had sold at twice the original price!

That's when she called me. I thought I knew what had happened but told her that, if I were to explain things properly, she would have to listen to a story of mine. Actually, it isn't my story; it's about mother turkeys, and it belongs to the relatively new science of ethology—the study of animals in their natural settings. Turkey mothers are good mothers—loving, watchful, and protective. They spend much of their time tending, warming, cleaning, and huddling their young beneath them; but there is something odd about their method. Virtually all of this mothering is triggered by one thing: the "cheep-cheep" sound of young turkey chicks. Other identifying features of the chicks, such as their smell, touch, or appearance, seem to play minor roles in the mothering process. If a chick makes the cheep-cheep noise, its mother will care for it; if not, the mother will ignore or sometimes kill it.

The extreme reliance of maternal turkeys upon this one sound was dramatically illustrated by animal behaviorist M. W. Fox (1974) in his description of an experiment involving a mother turkey and a stuffed polecat. For a mother turkey, a polecat is a natural enemy whose approach is to be greeted with squawking, pecking, clawing rage. Indeed, the experiments found that even a stuffed model of a polecat, when drawn by a string to a mother turkey, received an immediate and furious attack. When, however, the same stuffed replica carried inside it a small recorder that played the cheep-cheep sound of baby turkeys, the mother not only accepted the oncoming polecat but gathered it underneath her. When the machine was turned off, the polecat model again drew a vicious attack.

CLICK, WHIRR

How ridiculous a mother turkey seems under these circumstances: She will embrace a natural enemy just because it goes cheep-cheep and she will mistreat or murder one of her chicks just because it does not. She acts like an automaton whose maternal instincts are under the automatic control of that single sound. The ethologists tell us that this sort of thing is far from unique to the turkey. They have begun to identify regular, blindly mechanical patterns of action in a wide variety of species.

Called *fixed-action patterns*, they can involve intricate sequences of behavior, such as entire courtship or mating rituals. A fundamental characteristic of these patterns is that the behaviors comprising them occur in virtually the same fashion and in the same order every time. It is almost as if the patterns were recorded on tapes within the animals. When a situation calls for courtship, a courtship tape gets played; when a situation calls for mothering, a maternal behavior tape gets played. *Click* and the appropriate tape is activated; *whirr* and out rolls the standard sequence of behaviors.

The most interesting aspect of all this is the way the tapes are activated. When an animal acts to defend its territory for instance, it is the intrusion of another animal of the same species that cues the territorial-defense tape of rigid vigilance, threat, and if need be, combat behaviors; however, there is a quirk in the system. It is not the rival as a whole that is the trigger; it is, rather, some specific feature, the *trigger feature*. Often the trigger feature will be just one tiny aspect of the totality that is the approaching intruder. Sometimes a shade of color is the trigger feature. The experiments of ethologists have shown, for instance, that a male robin, acting as if a rival robin had entered its territory, will vigorously attack nothing more than a clump of robin red breast feathers placed there. At the same time, it will virtually ignore a perfect stuffed replica of a male robin *without* red breast feathers (Lack, 1943). Similar results have been found in another species of bird, the bluethroat, where it appears that the trigger for territorial defense is a specific shade of blue breast feathers (Peiponen, 1960).

Before we enjoy too smugly the ease with which trigger features can trick lower animals into reacting in ways wholly inappropriate to the situation, we should realize two things. First, the automatic, fixed-action patterns of these animals work very well most of the time. For example, because only normal, healthy turkey chicks make the peculiar sound of baby turkeys, it makes sense for mother turkeys to respond maternally to that single cheep-cheep noise. By reacting to just that one stimulus, the average mother turkey will nearly always behave correctly. It takes a trickster like a scientist to make her tapelike response seem silly. The second important thing to understand is that we, too, have our preprogrammed tapes; and, although they usually work to our advantage, the trigger features that activate them can dupe us into playing the tapes at the wrong times.[1]

This parallel form of human automaticity is aptly demonstrated in an experiment by social psychologist Ellen Langer and her co-workers (Langer, Blank, & Chanowitz, 1978). A well-known principle of human behavior says that when we ask someone to do us a favor we will be more successful if we provide a reason. People simply like to have reasons for what they do. Langer demonstrated this unsurprising fact by asking a small favor of people waiting in line to use a library copying machine: "Excuse me, I have five pages. May I use the Xerox machine because I'm in a rush?" The effectiveness of this request plus-reason was nearly total: 94 percent of those asked let her skip ahead of them in line. Compare this success rate to the results when she made the request only: "Excuse me, I have five pages. May I use the Xerox machine?" Under those circumstances only 60 percent of those asked complied. At first glance, it appears that the crucial difference between the two requests was the additional information provided by the words *because I'm in a rush.* However, a third type of request tried by Langer showed that this was not the case. It seems that it was not the whole series of words, but the first one, *because,* that made the difference. Instead of including a real reason for compliance, Langer's third type of request used the word *because* and then, adding nothing new, merely restated the obvious: "Excuse me, I have five pages. May I use the Xerox machine because I have to make some copies?" The result was that once again nearly all (93 percent) agreed, even though no real reason, no new information was added to justify their compliance. Just as the cheep-cheep sound of turkey chicks triggered an automatic mothering response from mother turkeys, even when it emanated from a stuffed polecat, so the word *because* triggered an automatic compliance response from Langer's subjects, even when they were given no subsequent reason to comply. *Click, whirr.*[2]

Although some of Langer's additional findings show that there are many situations in which human behavior does not work in a mechanical, tape-activated way, she is convinced that most of the time it does (Langer, 1989). For instance, consider the strange behavior of those jewelry store customers who swooped down on an allotment of turquoise pieces only after the items had been mistakenly offered at double their original price. I can make no sense of their behavior unless it is viewed in *click, whirr* terms.

---

[1]Although several important similarities exist between this kind of automaticity in humans and lower animals, there are some important differences as well. The automatic behavior patterns of humans tend to be learned rather than inborn, more flexible than the lock-step patterns of the lower animals, and responsive to a larger number of triggers.

[2]Perhaps the common "because . . . just because" response of children asked to explain their behavior can be traced to their shrewd recognition of the unusual amount of power adults appear to assign to the word *because.*

DOUG DISCOVERS THAT ELLEN, TOO, IS AN ORNITHOLOGIST, AND THE MATING RITUAL BEGINS...

Cluck-Whirr

Human mating rituals aren't actually as rigid as animals'. Still, researchers have uncovered impressive regularities in courtship patterns across many human cultures (Kenrick & Keefe, 1992). For instance, in personals ads around the world, women describe their physical attractiveness while men trumpet their material wealth (Buss & Kenrick, 1998).

Cartoon © 1996 Creators Syndicate/Dave Coverly.

The customers, mostly well-to-do vacationers with little knowledge of turquoise, were using a standard principle—a stereotype—to guide their buying: expensive = good. Much research shows that people who are unsure of an item's quality often use this stereotype (for a review, see Olson, 1977). Thus the vacationers, who wanted "good" jewelry, saw the turquoise pieces as decidedly more valuable and desirable when nothing about them was enhanced but the price. Price alone had become a trigger feature for quality, and a dramatic increase in price alone had led to a dramatic increase in sales among the quality-hungry buyers.[3]

READER'S REPORT 1.1

From a Management Doctoral Student

A man who owns an antique jewelry store in my town tells a story of how he learned the expensive = good lesson of social influence. A friend of his wanted a special birthday present for his fiancée. So, the jeweler picked out a necklace that would have sold in his store for $500 but that he was willing to let his friend have for $250. As soon as he saw it, the friend was enthusiastic about the piece. But when the jeweler quoted the $250 price, the man's face fell, and he began backing away from the deal because he wanted something "really nice" for his intended bride.

When a day later it dawned on the jeweler what had happened, he called his friend and asked him to come back to the store because he had another necklace to show him. This time, he introduced the new piece at its regular $500 price. His friend liked it enough to buy it on the spot. But before any money was exchanged, the jeweler told him that, as a wedding gift, he would drop the price to $250. The man was thrilled. Now, rather than finding the $250 sales price offensive, he was overjoyed—and grateful—to have it.

Author's note: Notice that, as in the case of the turquoise jewelry buyers, it was someone who wanted to be assured of good merchandise who disdained the low-priced item. I'm confident that besides the "expensive = good" rule, there's a flip side, "inexpensive = bad" rule that applies to our thinking as well. After all, in English, the word cheap doesn't just mean inexpensive; it has come to mean inferior, too.

BETTING THE SHORTCUT ODDS

It is easy to fault the tourists for their foolish purchase decisions, but a close look offers a kinder view. These were people who had been brought up on the rule, "You

---

[3]In marketing lore, the classic case of this phenomenon is that of Chivas Regal Scotch Whiskey, which had been a struggling brand until its managers decided to raise its price to a level far above its competitors. Sales skyrocketed, even though nothing was changed in the product itself (Aaker, 1991).

get what you pay for" and who had seen that rule borne out over and over in their lives. Before long, they had translated the rule to mean expensive = good. The expensive = good stereotype had worked quite well for them in the past, since normally the price of an item increases along with its worth; a higher price typically reflects higher quality. So when they found themselves in the position of wanting good turquoise jewelry but not having much knowledge of turquoise, they understandably relied on the old standby feature of cost to determine the jewelry's merits (Rao & Monroe, 1989).

Although they probably did not realize it, by reacting solely to the price of the turquoise, they were playing a shortcut version of betting the odds. Instead of stacking all the odds in their favor by trying painstakingly to master each feature that indicates the worth of turquoise jewelry, they were counting on just one— the one they knew to be usually associated with the quality of any item. They were betting that price alone would tell them all they needed to know. This time, because someone mistook a "½" for a "2," they bet wrong. In the long run, over all the past and future situations of their lives, betting those shortcut odds may represent the most rational approach possible.

In fact, automatic, stereotyped behavior is prevalent in much human action, because in many cases, it is the most efficient form of behaving (Gigerenzer & Goldstein, 1996), and in other cases it is simply necessary (Bodenhausen, Macrae, & Sherman, 1999; Fiske & Neuberg, 1990). You and I exist in an extraordinarily complicated environment, easily the most rapidly moving and complex that has ever existed on this planet. To deal with it, we *need* shortcuts. We can't be expected to recognize and analyze all the aspects in each person, event, and situation we encounter in even one day. We haven't the time, energy, or capacity for it. Instead, we must very often use our stereotypes, our rules of thumb, to classify things according to a few key features and then to respond without thinking when one or another of these trigger features is present.

Sometimes the behavior that unrolls will not be appropriate for the situation, because not even the best stereotypes and trigger features work every time. We will accept their imperfections since there is really no other choice. Without these features we would stand frozen—cataloging, appraising, and calibrating—as the time for action sped by and away. From all indications, we will be relying on these stereotypes to an even greater extent in the future. As the stimuli saturating our lives continue to grow more intricate and variable, we will have to depend increasingly on our shortcuts to handle them all.[4]

---

[4]Take, by way of illustration, the case (Zimmatore, 1983) of the automatic, mindless consumer response to a standard trigger for buying in our society—the discount coupon. A tire company found that mailed-out coupons which, because of a printing error, offered no savings to recipients produced just as much customer response as did the error-free coupons that offered substantial savings.

Psychologists have recently uncovered a number of mental shortcuts that we employ in making our everyday judgments (Chaiken & Trope, 1999; Kahneman, Slovic, & Tversky, 1982). Termed *judgmental heuristics*, these shortcuts operate in much the same fashion as the expensive = good rule, allowing for simplified thinking that works well most of the time but leaves us open to occasional, costly mistakes. Especially relevant to this book are those heuristics that tell us when to believe or do what we are told. Consider, for example, the shortcut rule that goes, "If an expert said so, it must be true." As we will see in Chapter 6, there is an unsettling tendency in our society to accept unthinkingly the statements and directions of individuals who appear to be authorities on the topic. That is, rather than thinking about an expert's arguments and being convinced (or not), we frequently ignore the arguments and allow ourselves to be convinced just by the expert's status as "expert." This tendency to respond mechanically to one piece of information in a situation is what we have been calling automatic or *click, whirr* responding; the tendency to react on the basis of a thorough analysis of all of the information can be referred to as *controlled responding* (Chaiken & Trope, 1999).

"Perhaps Monsieur would care for something more expensive?"

Expensive = Good (Taste)

Quite a lot of laboratory research has shown that people are more likely to deal with information in a controlled fashion when they have both the desire and the ability to analyze it carefully; otherwise, they are likely to use the easier *click, whirr* approach (for reviews, see Chen & Chaiken, 1999; Petty & Wegener, 1999). For instance, in one study (Petty, Cacioppo, & Goldman, 1981), students at the University of Missouri listened to a recorded speech that supported the idea of requiring all seniors to pass comprehensive examinations before they would be allowed to graduate. The issue affected some of them personally, because they were told that the exams could go into effect in the next year—before they had the chance to graduate. Of course, this news made them want to analyze the arguments carefully. However, for other subjects in the study, the issue had little personal importance—because they were told that the exams would not begin until long after they had graduated; consequently, they had no strong need to carefully consider the argument's validity. The study's results were quite straightforward: Those subjects with no personal stake in the topic were primarily persuaded by the speaker's expertise in the field of education; they used the "If an expert said so, it must be true" rule, paying little attention to the strength of the speaker's arguments. Those subjects for whom the issue mattered personally, on the other hand, ignored the speaker's expertise and were persuaded primarily by the quality of the speaker's arguments.

So, it appears that when it comes to the dangerous business of *click, whirr* responding, we give ourselves a safety net: We resist the seductive luxury of registering and reacting to just a single (trigger) feature of the available information when an issue is important to us. No doubt this is often the case (Leippe & Elkin, 1987). Yet, I am not fully comforted. Recall that earlier we learned that people are likely to respond in a controlled, thoughtful fashion only when they have both the desire *and* the ability to do so. I have recently become impressed by evidence suggesting that the form and pace of modern life is not allowing us to make fully thoughtful decisions, even on many personally relevant topics (Cohen, 1978; Milgram, 1970). That is, sometimes the issues may be so complicated, the time so tight, the distractions so intrusive, the emotional arousal so strong, or the mental fatigue so deep that we are in no cognitive condition to operate mindfully. Important topic or not, we have to take the shortcut.[5]

Perhaps nowhere is this last point driven home more dramatically than in the life-and-death consequences of a phenomenon that airline industry officials have labeled *Captainitis* (Foushee, 1984). Accident investigators from the Federal Aviation

---

[5]It's instructive that even though we often don't take a complex approach to personally important topics, we wish our advisors—our physicians, accountants, lawyers, and brokers—to do precisely that for us (Kahn & Baron, 1995). When feeling overwhelmed by a complicated and consequential choice, we still want a fully considered, point-by-point analysis of it—an analysis we may not be able to achieve except, ironically enough, through a shortcut: reliance on an expert.

Administration have noted that, frequently, an obvious error made by a flight captain was not corrected by the other crew members and resulted in a crash. It seems that, despite the clear and strong personal importance of the issues, the crew members were using the shortcut "If an expert says so, it must be true" rule in failing to attend or respond to the captain's disastrous mistake (Harper, Kidera, & Cullen, 1971).

An account by John Watson, Jr., the former chairman of IBM, offers graphic evidence of the phenomenon. During World War II, he was assigned to investigate plane crashes in which high-ranking officers were killed or injured. One case involved a famous air force general named Uzal Ent whose copilot got sick before a flight. Ent was assigned a replacement who felt honored to be flying alongside the legendary general. During takeoff, Ent began singing to himself, nodding in time to a song in his head. The new copilot interpreted the gesture as a signal to him to lift the wheels. Even though they were going much too slowly to fly, he raised the landing gear, causing the plane to drop immediately onto its belly. In the wreck, a propeller blade sliced into Ent's back, severing his spine and rendering him a paraplegic. Watson (1990) described the copilot's explanation for his action:

> When I took the copilot's testimony, I asked him, "If you knew the plane wasn't going to fly, why did you put the gear up?"
> He said, "I thought the general wanted me to." He was stupid. (p. 117)

Stupid? In that singular set of circumstances, yes. Understandable? In the shortcut-demanding maze of modern life, also yes.

THE PROFITEERS

It is odd that despite their current widespread use and looming future importance, most of us know very little about our automatic behavior patterns. Perhaps that is so precisely because of the mechanistic, unthinking manner in which they occur. Whatever the reason, it is vital that we clearly recognize one of their properties. They make us terribly vulnerable to anyone who *does* know how they work.

To understand fully the nature of our vulnerability, let us take another glance at the work of the ethologists. It turns out that these animal behaviorists with their recorded cheep-cheeps and their clumps of colored breast feathers are not the only ones who have discovered how to activate the behavior tapes of various species. One group of organisms, often termed *mimics,* copy the trigger features of other animals in an attempt to trick these animals into mistakenly playing the right behavior tapes at the wrong times. The mimics then exploit this altogether inappropriate action for their own benefit.

Take, for example, the deadly trick played by the killer females of one genus of firefly (*Photuris*) on the males of another firefly genus (*Photinus*). Understandably, the *Photinus* males scrupulously avoid contact with the bloodthirsty *Photuris* females. However, through centuries of natural selection, the *Photuris* female hunters have located a weakness in their prey—a special blinking courtship code by which members of the victims' species tell one another they are ready to mate. By mimicking the flashing mating signals of her prey, the murderess is able to feast on the bodies of males whose triggered courtship tapes cause them to fly mechanically into death's, not love's, embrace (Lloyd, 1965).[6]

In the struggle for survival, nearly every form of life has its mimics—right down to some of the most primitive pathogens. By adopting certain critical features of useful hormones or nutrients, these clever bacteria and viruses can gain entry into a healthy host cell. The result is that the healthy cell eagerly and naively sweeps into itself the causes of such diseases as rabies, mononucleosis, and the common cold (Goodenough, 1991).[7] It should come as no surprise, then, that there is a strong but sad parallel in the human jungle. We too have profiteers who mimic trigger features for our own brand of automatic responding. Unlike the mostly instinctive response sequences of nonhumans, however, our automatic tapes usually develop from psychological principles or stereotypes we have learned to accept. Although they vary in their force, some of these principles possess a tremendous ability to direct human action. We have been subjected to them from such an early point in our lives, and they have moved us about so pervasively since then, that you and I rarely perceive their power. In the eyes of others, though, each such principle is a detectable and ready weapon, a weapon of automatic influence.

There are some people who know very well where the weapons of automatic influence lie and who employ them regularly and expertly to get what they want. They go from social encounter to social encounter, requesting others to comply with their wishes; their frequency of success is dazzling. The secret of their effectiveness lies in the way that they structure their requests, the way that they arm themselves with one or another of the weapons of influence that exist is the social environment. To do this may take no more than one correctly chosen word that engages a strong psychological principle and sets rolling one of our automatic behavior tapes. Trust the

---

[6]Apparently, the tendency of males to be bamboozled by powerful mating signals extends to humans. Two University of Vienna biologists, Astrid Juette and Karl Grammer secretly exposed young men to airborne chemicals (called copulins) that mimic human vaginal scents. The men then rated the attractiveness of women's faces. Exposure to the copulins increased the judged attractiveness of all the women and masked the genuine physical attractiveness differences among them ("For Women," 1999).

[7]As exploitative as these creatures seem, they are topped in this respect by an insect known as the rove beetle. By using a variety of triggers involving smell and touch, the rove beetles get two species of ants to protect, groom, and feed them as larvae and to harbor them for the winter as adults. Responding mechanically to the beetles' trick trigger features, the ants treat the beetles as though they were fellow ants. Inside the ant nests, the beetles respond to their hosts' hospitality by eating ant eggs and young; yet they are never harmed (Holldobler, 1971).

human profiteers to learn quickly exactly how to benefit from our tendency to respond mechanically according to these principles.

Remember my friend the jewelry store owner? Although she benefited by accident the first time, it did not take her long to begin exploiting the expensive = good stereotype regularly and intentionally. Now during the tourist season, she first tries to speed the sale of an item that has been difficult to move by increasing its price substantially. She claims that this is marvelously cost-effective. When it works on the unsuspecting vacationers—as it frequently does—it results in an enormous profit margin.

And even when it is not initially successful, she can then mark the article "Reduced" and sell it to bargain-hunters at its original price while still taking advantage of their expensive = good reaction to the inflated figure.

By no means is my friend original in this last use of the expensive = good rule to snare those seeking a bargain. Culturist and author Leo Rosten gives the example of the Drubeck brothers, Sid and Harry, who owned a men's tailor shop in Rosten's neighborhood in the 1930s. Whenever Sid had a new customer trying on suits in front of the shop's three-sided mirror, he would admit to a hearing problem and repeatedly request that the man speak more loudly to him. Once the customer had found a suit he liked and asked for the price, Sid would call to his brother, the head tailor, at the back of the room, "Harry, how much for this suit?" Looking up from his work—and greatly exaggerating the suit's true price—Harry would call back, "For that beautiful, all wool suit, forty-two dollars." Pretending not to have heard and cupping his hand to his ear, Sid would ask again. Once more Harry would reply, "Forty-two dollars." At this point, Sid would turn to the customer and report, "He says twenty-two dollars." Many a man would hurry to buy the suit and scramble out of the shop with his expensive = good bargain before poor Sid discovered the "mistake."

JUJITSU

A woman employing the Japanese martial art form called jujitsu would use her own strength only minimally against an opponent. Instead, she would exploit the power inherent in such naturally present principles as gravity, leverage, momentum, and inertia. If she knows how and where to engage the action of these principles she can easily defeat a physically stronger rival. And so it is for the exploiters of the weapons of automatic influence that exist naturally around us. The profiteers can commission the power of these weapons for use against their targets while exerting little personal force. This last feature of the process gives the profiteers an enormous additional benefit—the ability to manipulate without the appearance of manipulation. Even the victims themselves tend to see their compliance as a result of the action of natural forces rather than the designs of the person who profits from that compliance.

An example is in order. There is a principle in human perception, the contrast principle, that affects the way we see the difference between two things that are presented one after another. Simply put, if the second item is fairly different from the first, we will tend to see it as *more* different than it actually is. So if we lift a light object first and then lift a heavy object, we will estimate the second object to be heavier than if we had lifted it without first lifting the light one. The contrast principle is well established in the field of psychophysics and applies to all sorts of perceptions besides weight. If we are talking to a very attractive individual at a party and are then joined by an unattractive individual, the second will strike us as less attractive than he or she actually is.[8]

Another demonstration of perceptual contrast is sometimes employed in psychophysics laboratories to introduce students to the principle. Each student takes a turn sitting in front of three pails of water—one cold, one at room temperature, and one hot. After placing one hand in the cold water and one in the hot water, the student is told to place both hands in the room-temperature water simultaneously. The look of amused bewilderment that immediately registers tells the story: Even though both hands are in the same bucket, the hand that has been in the cold water feels as if it is now in hot water, while the one that was in the hot water feels as if it is now in cold water. The point is that the same thing—in this instance, room-temperature water—can be made to seem very different depending on the nature of the event that precedes it.

Be assured that the nice little weapon of influence provided by the contrast principle does not go unexploited. The great advantage of this principle is not only that it works but also that it is virtually undetectable. Those who employ it can cash in on its influence without any appearance of having structured the situation in their favor. Retail clothiers are a good example. Suppose a man enters a fashionable men's store and says that he wants to buy a three-piece suit and a sweater. If you were the salesperson, which would you show him first to make him likely to spend the most money? Clothing stores instruct their sales personnel to sell the costly item first. Common sense might suggest the reverse: If a man has just spent a lot of money to purchase a suit, he may be reluctant to spend much more on the purchase of a sweater; but the clothiers know better. They behave in accordance with what the contrast principle would suggest: Sell the suit first, because when it comes time to look at sweaters, even expensive ones, their prices will not *seem* as high in comparison. The same principle applies to a man who wishes to buy the accessories (shirt, shoes, belt) to go along with his new suit. Contrary to the commonsense view, the evidence supports the contrast principle prediction. According to sales motivation analysts

---

[8]Some researchers warn that the unrealistically attractive people portrayed in the popular media (actors, actresses, models) may cause us to be less satisfied with the looks of the genuinely available romantic possibilities around us. For instance, one study demonstrated that exposure to the exaggerated sexual attractiveness of nude pinup bodies (in such magazines as *Playboy* and *Playgirl*) causes people to become less pleased with the sexual desirability of their current spouse or live-in mate (Kenrick, Gutierres, & Goldberg, 1989).

SHOE

Perceptual Contrast
A bright idea

Whitney, Hubin, and Murphy (1965), "The interesting thing is that even when a man enters a clothing store with the express purpose of purchasing a suit, he will almost always *pay more* for whatever accessories he buys if he buys them after the suit purchase than before."

It is much more profitable for salespeople to present the expensive item first; to fail to do so will lose the influence of the contrast principle and will also cause the principle to work actively against them. Presenting an inexpensive product first and following it with an expensive one will make the expensive item seem even more costly as a result—hardly a desirable consequence for most sales organizations. So, just as it is possible to make the same bucket of water appear to be hotter or colder depending on the temperature of previously presented water, it is possible to make the price of the same item seem higher or lower depending on the price of a previously presented item.

Clever use of perceptual contrast is by no means confined to clothiers. (See Figure 1.1.) I came across a technique that engaged the contrast principle while I was investigating, undercover, the compliance tactics of real estate companies. To "learn the ropes," I accompanied a salesman on a weekend of showing houses to prospective home buyers. The salesman—we can call him Phil—was to give me tips to help me through my break-in period. One thing I quickly noticed was that whenever Phil began showing a new set of customers potential buys, he would start with a couple of undesirable houses. I asked him about it, and he laughed. They were what he called "setup" properties. The company maintained a run-down house or two on its lists at inflated prices. These houses were not intended to be sold to customers but only to be shown to them, so that the genuine properties in the company's inventory would benefit from the comparison. Not all the sales staff made use of the setup houses, but Phil did. He said he liked to watch his prospects' "eyes light up" when

Dear Mother and Dad,

Since I left for college I have been remiss in writing and I am sorry for my thoughtlessness in not having written before. I will bring you up to date now, but before you read on, please sit down. You are not to read any further unless you are sitting down, okay?

Well, then, I am getting along pretty well now. The skull fracture and the concussion I got when I jumped out the window of my dormitory when it caught on fire shortly after my arrival here is pretty well healed now. I only spent two weeks in the hospital and now I can see almost normally and only get those sick headaches once a day. Fortunately, the fire in the dormitory, and my jump, was witnessed by an attendant at the gas station near the dorm, and he was the one who called the Fire Department and the ambulance. He also visited me in the hospital and since I had nowhere to live because of the burnt-out dormitory, he was kind enough to invite me to share his apartment with him. It's really a basement room, but it it's kind of cute. He is a very fine boy, and we have fallen deeply in love and are planning to get married. We haven't set the exact date yet, but it will be before my pregnancy begins to show.

Yes, Mother and Dad, I am pregnant. I know how much you are looking forward to being grandparents and I know you will welcome the baby and give it the same love and devotion and tender care you gave me when I was a child. The reason for the delay in our marriage is that my boyfriend has a minor infection which prevents us from passing our premarital blood tests and I carelessly caught it from him. I know that you will welcome him into our family with open arms. He is kind and, although not well educated, he is ambitious.

Now that I have brought you up to date, I want to tell you that there was no dormitory fire, I did not have a concussion or skull fracture, I was not in the hospital, I am not pregnant, I am not engaged, I am not infected, and there is no boyfriend. However, I am getting a "D" in American History and an "F" in Chemistry, and I want you to see those marks in their proper perspective.

Your loving daughter,

Sharon

FIGURE 1.1   Perceptual Contrast and the College Coed
Sharon may be failing chemistry, but she'd get an "A" in psychology.

he showed the places he really wanted to sell them after they had seen the rundown houses. "The house I got them spotted for looks really great after they've first looked at a couple of dumps."

Automobile dealers use the contrast principle by waiting until the price of a car has been negotiated before suggesting one option after another. In the wake of a many-thousand-dollar deal, the hundred or so dollars extra for a nicety like a CD player seems almost trivial in comparison. The same will be true of the added expense of accessories like tinted windows, dual side-view mirrors, better tires, or special trim that the dealer might suggest in sequence. The trick is to bring up the options independently of one another so that each small price will seem petty when compared to the already determined much larger price. As veteran car buyers can attest, many a budget-sized final price figure has ballooned out of proportion from the addition of all those seemingly little options. While the customers stand, signed contract in hand, wondering what happened and finding no one to blame but themselves, the car dealer stands smiling the knowing smile of the jujitsu master.

READER'S REPORT 1.2

From a University of Chicago Business School Student

While waiting to board a flight at O'Hare, I heard a desk agent announce that the flight was overbooked and that, if passengers were willing to take a later plane, they would be compensated with a voucher worth $10,000! Of course, this exaggerated amount was a joke. It was supposed to make people laugh. It did. But I noticed that when he then revealed the *actual* offer (a $200 voucher), there were no takers. In fact, he had to raise the offer twice, to $300 and then $500, before he got any volunteers.

I was reading your book at the time, and I realized that, although he got his laugh, according to the contrast principle he screwed up. He'd arranged things so that compared to $10,000, a couple hundred bucks seemed like a pittance. That was an expensive laugh. It cost his airline an extra $300 per volunteer.

Author's note: Any ideas on how the desk agent could have used the contrast principle to his advantage rather than his detriment? Perhaps he could have started with a $5 joke offer and then revealed the true (and now much more attractive-sounding) $200 amount. Under those circumstances, I'm pretty sure he would have secured his laugh and his volunteers.

SUMMARY

- Ethologists, researchers who study animal behavior in the natural environment, have noticed that among many animal species behavior often occurs in rigid and mechanical patterns. Called **fixed-action patterns,** these mechanical behavior sequences are noteworthy in their similarity to certain automatic (*click, whirr*) responding by humans. For both humans and subhumans, the automatic behavior patterns tend to be triggered by a single feature of the relevant information in the situation. This single feature, or trigger feature, can often prove very valuable by allowing an individual to decide on a correct course of action without having to analyze carefully and completely each of the other pieces of information in the situation.

- The advantage of such shortcut responding lies in its efficiency and economy; by reacting automatically to a usually informative trigger feature, an individual preserves crucial time, energy, and mental capacity. The disadvantage of such responding lies in its vulnerability to silly and costly mistakes; by reacting to only a piece of the available information (even a normally predictive piece), an individual increases the chances of error, especially when responding in an automatic, mindless fashion. The chances of error increase even further when other individuals seek to profit by arranging (through manipulation of trigger features) to stimulate a desired behavior at inappropriate times.

- Much of the compliance process (wherein one person is spurred to comply with another person's request) can be understood in terms of a human tendency for automatic, shortcut responding. Most individuals in our culture have developed a set of trigger features for compliance, that is, a set of specific pieces of information that normally tell us when compliance with a request is likely to be correct and beneficial. Each of these trigger features for compliance can be used like a weapon (of influence) to stimulate people to agree to requests.

STUDY QUESTIONS

Content Mastery

1. What are fixed-action patterns among animals? How are they similar to some types of human functioning? How are they different?

2. What makes automatic responding in humans so attractive? So dangerous?

3. What are the three components of a weapon of automatic influence?

Critical Thinking

1. Suppose you were an attorney representing a woman who broke her leg in a department store and was suing the store for $10,000 in damages. Knowing only what you do about perceptual contrast, what could you do during the trial to make the jury see $10,000 as a reasonable, even small, award?

2. The charity request card in Figure 1.2 seems rather ordinary except for the odd sequencing of the donation request amounts. Explain why, according to the contrast principle, placing the smallest donation figure between two larger figures is an effective tactic to prompt more and larger donations.

3. What points do the following quotes make about the dangers of *click-whirr* responding?
   "Everything should be made as simple as possible, but not simpler." Albert Einstein
   "The greatest lesson in life is to know that even fools are sometimes right." Winston Churchill

4. How does the ad that opens this chapter reflect the topic of the chapter?

Society for the Prevention of CRABGRASS

Unsightly crabgrass can be conquered—but only with the help of concerned citizens like you. Your generous contribution makes research possible to reach our goal of a crabgrass-free world. Please join us and make your donation payable to the Society for the Prevention of Crabgrass. A return envelope has been provided for your convenience!

Yes, I want to further the Society's efforts for a crabgrass-free world.
   Enclosed is my contribution in the amount of:
   ☐ $25   ☐ $10   ☐ $5   ☐ $15   ☐ $_____

Name _____

Address _____

City _____ State _____ Zip _____

Society for the Prevention of Crabgrass
P.O. Box 5-CG
Lawn City, USA 12345

FIGURE 1.2   Charity Request Card

2 | *Reciprocation*

The Old Give and Take
. . . and Take

LIFE INSURANCE ISN'T
FOR THE PEOPLE WHO DIE.
IT'S FOR THE PEOPLE
WHO LIVE.

"My husband Ron was every-thing — president, salesman, manager, buyer, and warehouse worker. The only thing he wasn't, was immortal."

Mary Vandenbroek's husband Ron had a highly successful wine brokerage business. But at age 49, he discovered he had something else—terminal cancer.

Fortunately, he also had foresight. Though he knew his business could be sold if he died, his life insurance provided Mary with the money to keep the business and run it. Today, employees still have their jobs; cus-tomers still have their fine wines; and Mary is keeping Ron's dream alive.

Are you prepared? Without insur-ance, your financial plan may be just a savings and investment pro-gram that dies when you do. An insurance agent or other financial professional can help you create a plan that will continue to provide for the ones you love.

To learn more call 1-800-LIFE-777, or visit www.life-line.org.

Mary Vandenbroek

LIFE
LIFE AND HEALTH INSURANCE FOUNDATION FOR EDUCATION
A NONPROFIT ORGANIZATION

> *Pay every debt, as if God wrote the bill.*
> —RALPH WALDO EMERSON

Several years ago, a university professor tried a little experiment. He sent Christmas cards to a sample of perfect strangers. Although he expected some reaction, the response he received was amazing—holiday cards addressed to him came pouring back from people who had never met nor heard of him. The great majority of those who returned cards never inquired into the identity of the unknown professor. They received his holiday greeting card, *click*, and *whirr*, they automatically sent cards in return (Kunz & Woolcott, 1976).

While small in scope, this study shows the action of one of the most potent of the weapons of influence around us—the rule of reciprocation. The rule says that we should try to repay, in kind, what another person has provided us. If a woman does us a favor, we should do her one in return; if a man sends us a birthday present, we should remember his birthday with a gift of our own; if a couple invites us to a party, we should be sure to invite them to one of ours. By virtue of the reciprocity rule, then, we are *obligated* to the future repayment of favors, gifts, invitations, and the like. So typical is it for indebtedness to accompany the receipt of such things that a phrase like "much obliged" has become a synonym for "thank you," not only in the English language but in others as well.

The impressive aspect of reciprocation with its accompanying sense of obligation is its pervasiveness in human culture. It is so widespread that, after intensive study, Alvin Gouldner (1960), along with other sociologists, report that all human societies subscribe to the rule.[1] Within each society it seems pervasive also; it permeates exchanges of every kind. Indeed, it may well be that a developed system of indebtedness flowing from the rule of reciprocation is a unique property of human culture. The noted archaeologist Richard Leakey ascribes the essence of what makes us human to the reciprocity system. He claims that we are human because our ancestors learned to share food and skills "in an honored network of obligation" (Leakey & Lewin, 1978). Cultural anthropologists view this "web of indebtedness" as a unique adaptive mechanism of human beings, allowing for the division of labor, the exchange of diverse forms of goods and different services, and the creation of

---

[1]Certain societies have formalized the rule into ritual. Consider for example the Vartan Bhanji, an institutionalized custom of gift exchange common to parts of Pakistan and India. In commenting upon the Vartan Bhanji, Gouldner (1960) remarks:

> *It is . . . notable that the system painstakingly prevents the total elimination of outstanding obligations. Thus, on the occasion of a marriage, departing guests are given gifts of sweets. In weighing them out, the hostess may say, "These five are yours," meaning "These are a repayment for what you formerly gave me," and then she adds an extra measure, saying, "These are mine." On the next occasion, she will receive these back along with an additional measure which she later returns, and so on. (p. 175)*

interdependencies that bind individuals together into highly efficient units (Ridley, 1997; Tiger & Fox, 1989).

It is a sense of future obligation that is critical to produce social advances of the sort described by Tiger and Fox. A widely shared and strongly held feeling of future obligation made an enormous difference in human social evolution because it meant that one person could give something (for example, food, energy, care) to another with confidence that the gift was not being lost. For the first time in evolutionary history, one individual could give away any of a variety of resources without actually giving them away. The result was the lowering of the natural inhibitions against transactions that must be *begun* by one person's providing personal resources to another. Sophisticated and coordinated systems of aid, gift giving, defense, and trade became possible, bringing immense benefits to the societies that possessed them. With such clearly adaptive consequences for the culture, it is not surprising that the rule for reciprocation is so deeply implanted in us by the process of socialization we all undergo.

I know of no better illustration of the way reciprocal obligations can reach long and powerfully into the future than the perplexing story of $5,000 of relief aid that was exchanged between Mexico and Ethiopia. In 1985, Ethiopia could justly lay claim to the greatest suffering and privation in the world. Its economy was in ruin. Its food supply had been ravaged by years of drought and internal war. Its inhabitants were dying by the thousands from disease and starvation. Under these circumstances, I would not have been surprised to learn of a $5,000 relief donation from Mexico to that wrenchingly needy country. I remember my feeling of amazement, though, when a brief newspaper item I was reading insisted that the aid had gone in the opposite direction. Native officials of the Ethiopian Red Cross had decided to send the money to help the victims of that year's earthquakes in Mexico City.

It is both a personal bane and a professional blessing that whenever I am confused by some aspect of human behavior, I feel driven to investigate further. In this instance, I was able to track down a fuller account of the story. Fortunately, a journalist who had been as bewildered as I by the Ethiopians' actions had asked for an explanation. The answer he received offered eloquent validation of the reciprocity rule: Despite the enormous needs prevailing in Ethiopia, the money was being sent to Mexico because, in 1935, Mexico had sent aid to Ethiopia when it was invaded by Italy ("Ethiopian Red Cross," 1985). So informed, I remained awed, but I was no longer puzzled. The need to reciprocate had transcended great cultural differences, long distances, acute famine, many years, and immediate self-interest. Quite simply, a half-century later, against all countervailing forces, obligation triumphed.

HOW THE RULE WORKS

Make no mistake, human societies derive a truly significant competitive advantage from the reciprocity rule and, consequently, they make sure their members are trained to comply with and believe in it. Each of us has been taught to live up to the rule, and each of us knows the social sanctions and derision applied to anyone who violates it. Because there is a general distaste for those who take and make no effort to give in return, we will often go to great lengths to avoid being considered a moocher, ingrate, or freeloader. It is to those lengths that we will often be taken and, in the process, be "taken" by individuals who stand to gain from our indebtedness.

To understand how the rule of reciprocation can be exploited by one who recognizes it as the weapon of influence it certainly is, we might closely examine an experiment conducted by psychologist Dennis Regan (1971). A subject who participated in the study rated, along with another subject, the quality of some paintings as part of an experiment on "art appreciation." The other rater—we can call him Joe—was only posing as a fellow subject and was actually Dr. Regan's assistant. For our purposes, the experiment took place under two different conditions. In some cases, Joe did a small, unsolicited favor for the true subject. During a short rest period, Joe left the room for a couple of minutes and returned with two bottles of Coca-Cola, one for the subject and one for himself, saying "I asked him [the experimenter] if I could get myself a Coke, and he said it was OK, so I bought one for you, too." In other cases, Joe did not provide the subject with a favor; he simply returned from the two-minute break empty-handed. In all other respects, however, Joe behaved identically.

Later on, after the paintings had all been rated and the experimenter had momentarily left the room, Joe asked the subject to do *him* a favor. He indicated that he was selling raffle tickets for a new car and that if he sold the most tickets, he would win a $50 prize. Joe's request was for the subject to buy some raffle tickets at 25 cents apiece: "Any would help, the more the better." The major finding of the study concerns the number of tickets subjects purchased from Joe under the two conditions. Without question, Joe was more successful in selling his raffle tickets to the subjects who had received his earlier favor. Apparently feeling that they owed him something, these subjects bought twice as many tickets as the subjects who had not been given the prior favor. Although the Regan study represents a fairly simple demonstration of the workings of the rule of reciprocation, it illustrates several important characteristics of the rule that, upon further consideration, help us to understand how it may be profitably used.

The Rule Is Overpowering

One of the reasons reciprocation can be used so effectively as a device for gaining another's compliance is its power. The rule possesses awesome strength, often producing a yes response to a request that, except for an existing feeling of indebtedness, would have surely been refused. Some evidence of how the rule's force can overpower the influence of other factors that normally determine compliance with a request can be seen in a second result of the Regan study. Besides his interest in the impact of the reciprocity rule on compliance, Regan was also investigating how liking for a person affects the tendency to comply with that person's request. To measure how liking toward Joe affected the subjects' decisions to buy his raffle tickets, Regan had them fill out several rating scales indicating how much they had liked Joe. He then compared their liking responses with the number of tickets they had purchased from Joe. There was a significant tendency for subjects to buy more raffle tickets from Joe the more they liked him. This alone is hardly a startling finding, since most of us would have guessed that people are more willing to do a favor for someone they like.

The interesting finding of the Regan experiment, however, was that the relationship between liking and compliance was completely wiped out in the condition under which subjects had been given a Coke by Joe. For those who owed him a favor, it made no difference whether they liked him or not; they felt a sense of obligation to repay him, and they did. The subjects who indicated that they disliked Joe bought just as many of his tickets as did those who indicated that they liked him. The rule for reciprocity was so strong that it simply overwhelmed the influence of a factor— liking for the requester—that normally affects the decision to comply.

Think of the implications. People we might ordinarily dislike—unsavory or unwelcome sales operators, disagreeable acquaintances, representatives of strange or unpopular organizations—can greatly increase the chance that we will do what they wish merely by providing us with a small favor prior to their requests. Let's take a recent historical example. The Hare Krishna Society is an Eastern religious sect with centuries-old roots traceable to the Indian city of Calcutta. Its spectacular modern-day story occurred in the 1970s when it experienced a remarkable growth, not only in followers, but also in wealth and property. The economic growth was funded through a variety of activities, the principal and most visible of which was society members' requests for donations from passersby in public places. During the early history of the group in this country, the solicitation for contributions was attempted in a fashion memorable for anyone who saw it. Groups of Krishna devotees—often with shaved heads, and wearing ill-fitting robes, leg wrappings, beads, and bells— would canvass a city street, chanting and bobbing in unison while begging for funds.

Although highly effective as an attention-getting technique, this practice did not work especially well for fund-raising. The average American considered the Krishnas weird, to say the least, and was reluctant to provide money to support them. It quickly became clear to the society that it had a considerable public-relations problem. The people being asked for contributions did not like the way the members looked, dressed, or acted. Had the society been an ordinary commercial organization, the solution would have been simple—change the things the public does not like. The Krishnas are a religious organization, however, and the way members look, dress, and act is partially tied to religious factors. Since religious factors are typically resistant to change because of worldly considerations, the Krishna leadership was faced with a real dilemma. On the one hand were beliefs, modes of dress, and hairstyles that had religious significance. On the other, and threatening the organization's financial welfare, were the less-than-positive feelings of the American public toward these things. What's a sect to do?

The Krishnas' resolution was brilliant. They switched to a fund-raising tactic that made it unnecessary for their targets to have positive feelings toward the fund-raisers. They began to employ a donation-request procedure that engaged the rule for reciprocation, which, as demonstrated by the Regan study, was strong enough to overcome dislike for the requester. The new strategy still involved the solicitation of contributions in public places with much pedestrian traffic (airports were a favorite), but, before a donation was requested, the target person was given a "gift"—a book

Kriss Krishna
Taking disguise to its limits but still employing the reciprocity rule as an ally, these Krishna members were arrested for soliciting without a license when they pressed candy canes on Christmas shoppers and then made requests for donations.

(usually the *Bhagavad Gita*), the *Back to Godhead* magazine of the society, or, in the most cost-effective version, a flower. The unsuspecting passersby who suddenly found flowers pressed into their hands or pinned to their jackets were under no circumstances allowed to give them back, even if they asserted that they did not want them. "No, it is our gift to you," said the solicitor, refusing to take it back. Only after the Krishna member had thus brought the force of the reciprocation rule to bear on the situation was the target asked to provide a contribution to the society. This benefactor-before-beggar strategy was wildly successful for the Hare Krishna Society, producing large-scale economic gains and funding, the ownership of temples, businesses, houses, and property in 321 centers in the United States and abroad.

As an aside, it is instructive that the reciprocation rule has outlived its usefulness for the Krishnas, not because the rule itself has become any less potent societally, but because we have found ways to prevent the Krishnas from using it on us. After once falling victim to their tactic, many travelers became alert to the presence of robed Krishna Society solicitors in airports and train stations, adjusting their paths to avoid an encounter and preparing beforehand to ward off a solicitor's "gift." Although the society tried to counter this increased vigilance by instructing members to be dressed and groomed in modern styles to avoid immediate recognition when soliciting (some actually carried flight bags or suitcases), even disguise did not work especially well for the Krishnas. Too many individuals now know better than to accept unrequested offerings in public places such as airports. In addition, after a flood of complaints, airports began banning the Society's fund-raising efforts from their premises.

As a result, the Krishnas experienced a severe financial reversal. In North America, nearly 30 percent of their temples have been closed for economic reasons, and the number of devotees staffing the remaining temples has plummeted from a high of 5,000 to an estimated 800. The Krishnas are a resilient group, though. Officials admit that the organization is struggling to maintain its long-standing presence in North America, but they report that it is thriving in the newly opened "markets" of Eastern Europe—where, apparently, people haven't yet caught on to the Krishnas' strategic benevolence.

Although the Krishnas have moved on to "greener" pastures, we would be foolish to think that they've taken all the effective reciprocation tactics with them. Survey researchers have discovered that sending a monetary gift (a silver dollar or a $5 check) in an envelope with a mailed questionnaire greatly increases survey completion rates, compared to offering the same monetary amount as an after-the-fact reward (Church, 1993; Warriner, Goyder, Gjertsen, Horner, & McSpurren, 1996). Indeed, one study showed that mailing a $5 "gift" check along with an insurance survey was twice as effective as offering a $50 payment for sending back a completed survey (James & Bolstein, 1992). Similarly, food servers have learned that simply giving customers a candy or mint along with their bill significantly increases tips (Lynn & McCall, 1998). In general, business operators have found that, after accepting a gift, customers are willing to purchase products and services they would have otherwise declined (Gruner, 1996).

It appears that the give-and-take of social interaction is recognized well before adulthood. One fifth-grade teacher wrote to me about a test she gives her students on the proper use of the past, present, and future tenses. To the question, The future of "I give" is _____?, one enterprising young man wrote, "I take." He may have gotten that particular grammatical rule wrong, but he got a larger societal rule precisely right.

Politics

Politics is another arena in which the power of the reciprocity rule shows itself. Reciprocation tactics appear at every level:

- At the top, elected officials engage in "logrolling" and the exchange of favors that makes politics the place of strange bedfellows, indeed. The out-of-character vote of one of our elected representatives on a bill or measure can often be understood as a favor returned to the bill's sponsor. Political analysts were amazed at Lyndon Johnson's success in getting so many of his programs through Congress during his early administration. Even members of Congress who were thought to be strongly opposed to the proposals were voting for them. Close examination by political scientists has found the cause to be not so much Johnson's political savvy as the large score of favors he had been able to provide to other legislators during his many years of power in the House and Senate. As president, he was able to produce a truly remarkable amount of legislation in a short time by calling in those favors. It is interesting that this same process may account for the problems Jimmy Carter had in getting his programs through Congress during his early administration, despite heavy Democratic majorities in both the House and Senate. Carter came to the presidency from outside the Capitol Hill establishment. He campaigned on his outside-Washington identity, saying that he was indebted to no one. Much of his legislative difficulty upon arriving may be traced to the fact that no one there was indebted to *him*. Much the same may be said about the first-term legislation record of Washington outsider Bill Clinton.
- At another level, we can see the recognized strength of the reciprocity rule in the desire of corporations and individuals to provide judicial and legislative officials with gifts and favors and in the series of legal restrictions against such gifts and favors. Even with legitimate political contributions, the stockpiling of obligations often underlies the stated purpose of supporting a favorite candidate. One look at the lists of companies and organizations that contribute to the campaigns of *both* major candidates in important elections gives evidence of such motives. A skeptic, requiring direct evidence of the *quid pro quo* expected by political contributors, might look to the remarkably bald-faced admission by businessman Roger Tamraz at congressional hearings on campaign finance reform. When asked if he felt he received a good return on his contribution of $300,000, he smiled and replied, "I think next time, I'll give $600,000."

Honesty of this sort is rare in politics. For the most part, the givers and takers join voices to dismiss the idea that campaign contributions, free trips, and Super Bowl tickets would bias the opinions of "sober, conscientious" government officials. As the head of one lobbying organization insisted, there is no cause for concern because "These [government officials] are smart, mature, sophisticated men and women at the top of their professions, disposed by training to be discerning, critical, and alert" (Barker, 1998). And, of course, the politicians concur. Regularly, we hear them proclaiming total independence from the feelings of obligation that influence everyone else. One of my own state representatives left no room for doubt when describing his accountability to gift-givers, "It gets them exactly what it gets everybody else: nothing" (Foster, 1991).

Excuse me if I, as a scientist, laugh. Sober, conscientious scientists know better. One reason they know better is that these "smart, mature, sophisticated men and women at the top of their [scientific] professions" have found themselves to be as susceptible as anyone else to the process. Take the case of the medical controversy surrounding the safety of calcium-channel blockers, a class of drugs for heart disease. One study discovered that 100 percent of the scientists who found and published results supportive of the drugs had received prior support (free trips, research funding, or employment) from the pharmaceutical companies; but only 37 percent of those critical of the drugs had received any such prior support (Stelfox, Chua, O'Rourke, & Detsky, 1998). If scientists, "disposed by training to be discerning, critical, and alert," can be swayed by the insistent undertow of exchange, we should fully expect that politicians will be, too. Elected and appointed officials often see themselves as immune to the rules that apply to rest of us—parking regulations and the like. But, to indulge them in this conceit when it comes to the rule of reciprocity is not only laughable, it's dangerous.

The Not-So-Free Sample
Of course, the power of reciprocity can be found in the merchandising field as well. Although the number of examples is large, let's examine a pair of familiar ones. As a marketing technique, the free sample has a long and effective history. In most instances, a small amount of the relevant product is given to potential customers to see if they like it. Certainly this is a legitimate desire of the manufacturer—to expose the public to the qualities of the product. The beauty of the free sample, however, is that it is also a gift and, as such, can engage the reciprocity rule. In true jujitsu fashion, a promoter who provides free samples can release the natural indebting force inherent in a gift, while innocently appearing to have only the intention to inform.

A favorite place for free samples is the supermarket, where customers are frequently given small amounts of a certain product to try. Many people find it difficult to accept samples from the always smiling attendant, return only the toothpicks or cups, and walk away. Instead, they buy some of the product, even if they might not have liked it very much. A highly effective variation on this marketing procedure is

Buenos Nachos
Some food manufacturers no longer wait until the customers are in
the store to provide them with free samples.

illustrated in the case, cited by Vance Packard in *The Hidden Persuaders* (1957), of
the Indiana supermarket operator who sold an astounding 1,000 pounds of cheese in
a few hours one day by putting out the cheese and inviting customers to cut off sliv-
ers for themselves as free samples.

A different version of the free-sample tactic is used by the Amway Corporation,
a rapid-growth company that manufactures and distributes household and personal-

care products in a vast national network of door-to-door neighborhood sales. The company, which has grown from a basement-run operation to a $1.5 billion yearly sales business, makes use of the free sample in a device called the BUG. The BUG consists of a collection of Amway products—bottles of furniture polish, detergent, or shampoo, spray containers of deodorizers, insect killers, or window cleaners—carried to a customer's home in a specially designed tray or just a polyethylene bag. The confidential Amway Career Manual then instructs the salesperson to leave the BUG with the customer "for 24, 48, or 72 hours, at no cost or obligation to her. Just tell her you would like her to try the products. . . . That's an offer no one can refuse." At the end of the trial period, the Amway representative is to return and pick up orders for the products the customer wishes to purchase. Since few customers use up the entire contents of even one of the product containers in such a short time, the salesperson may then take the remaining product portions in the BUG to the next potential customer down the line or across the street and start the process again. Many Amway representatives have several BUGS circulating in their districts at one time.

Of course, by now you and I know that the customer who has accepted and used the BUG products has been trapped by the reciprocity rule. Many such customers yield to a sense of obligation to order the products that they have tried and partially consumed—and, of course, by now the Amway Corporation knows that to be the case. Even in a company with as excellent a growth record as Amway, the BUG device has created a big stir. Reports by state distributors to the parent company record a remarkable effect:

> *Unbelievable! We've never seen such excitement. Product is moving at an unbelievable rate, and we've only just begun. . . . Local distributors took the BUGS, and we've had an unbelievable increase in sales [from Illinois distributor]. The most fantastic retail idea we've ever had! . . . On the average, customers purchased about half the total amount of the BUG when it is picked up. . . . In one word, tremendous! We've never seen a response within our entire organization like this [from Massachusetts distributor].*

The Amway distributors appear to be bewildered—happily so, but nonetheless bewildered—by the startling power of the BUG. Of course, by now you and I should not be.

The reciprocity rule governs many situations of a purely interpersonal nature where neither money nor commercial exchange is at issue. Perhaps my favorite illustration of the enormous force available from the reciprocation weapon of influence comes from such a situation. The European scientist Eibl-Eibesfeldt (1975) provides the account of a German soldier during World War I whose job was to capture enemy soldiers for interrogation. Because of the nature of the trench warfare at that time, it was extremely difficult for armies to cross the no-man's-land between opposing front lines, but it was not so difficult for a single soldier to crawl across and slip into an enemy trench position. The armies of the Great War had experts who regularly did so to capture enemy soldiers, who would then be brought back for questioning. The German expert had often successfully completed such missions in the past and was sent on another. Once again, he skillfully negotiated the area between fronts and surprised a lone enemy soldier in his trench. The unsuspecting soldier, who had been eating at the time, was easily disarmed. The frightened captive, with only a piece of bread in his hand, then performed what may have been the most important act of his life. He gave his enemy some of the bread. So affected was the German by this gift that he could not complete his mission. He turned from his benefactor and recrossed the no-man's-land empty-handed to face the wrath of his superiors.

An equally compelling point regarding the power of reciprocity comes from an account of a woman who saved her own life, not by *giving* a gift as did the captured soldier, but by *refusing* a gift and the powerful obligations that went with it. In November 1978 Jim Jones the leader of Jonestown, Guyana, called for the mass suicide of all residents, most of whom compliantly drank and died from a vat of poison-laced Kool-Aid. Diane Louie, a resident, however, rejected Jones's command and made her way out of Jonestown and into the jungle. She attributes her willingness to do so to her earlier refusal to accept special favors from him when she was in need. She turned down his offer of special food while she was ill, because "I knew once he gave me those privileges, he'd have me. I didn't want to owe him nothin' " (Anderson & Zimbardo, 1984).

The Rule Enforces Uninvited Debts

Earlier we suggested that the power of the reciprocity rule is such that, by first doing us a favor, strange, disliked, or unwelcome others can enhance the chance that we will comply with one of their requests. However, there is another aspect of the rule, in addition to its power, that allows this phenomenon to occur. A person can trigger a feeling of indebtedness by doing us an uninvited favor (Paese & Gilin, 2000). Recall that the rule states only that we should provide to others the kind of actions they have provided us; it does not require us to have asked for what we have received in order to feel obligated to repay. For instance, the American Disabled Veterans organization reports that its simple mail appeal for donations produces a response rate of about 18 percent. But when the mailing also includes an unsolicited gift (gummed, individualized address labels), the success rate nearly doubles to 35 percent. This is not to say that we might not feel a stronger sense of obligation to return a favor we have requested, but such a request is not necessary to produce our feeling of indebtedness.

If we reflect for a moment about the social purpose of the reciprocity rule, we can see why this is the case. The rule was established to promote the development of reciprocal relationships between individuals so that one person could *initiate* such a relationship without the fear of loss. If the rule is to serve that purpose, then an uninvited first favor must have the ability to create an obligation. Recall, also, that reciprocal relationships confer an extraordinary advantage upon cultures that foster them and that, consequently, there will be strong pressures to ensure that the rule does serve its purpose. Little wonder, then, that influential French anthropologist Marcel Mauss (1954), in describing the social pressures surrounding the gift-giving process in human culture, says that there is an obligation to give, an obligation to receive, and an obligation to repay.

Although an obligation to repay constitutes the essence of the reciprocity rule, it is the obligation to receive that makes the rule so easy to exploit. An obligation to receive reduces our ability to choose those to whom we wish to be indebted and puts the power in the hands of others. Let's reexamine a pair of earlier examples to see how the process works. First, in the Regan study, we find that the favor causing subjects to double the number of raffle tickets purchased from Joe was not one they had requested. Joe had voluntarily left the room and returned with one Coke for himself and one for the subject. There was not a single subject who refused the Coke. It is easy to see why it would have been awkward to turn down Joe's favor: Joe had already spent his money; a soft drink was an appropriate favor in the situation, especially since Joe had one himself; it would have been considered impolite to reject Joe's thoughtful action. Nevertheless, receipt of that Coke produced a feeling of indebtedness that became clear when Joe announced his desire to sell some raffle tickets. Notice the important asymmetry here—all the genuinely free choices were Joe's. He chose the form of the initial favor, and he chose the form of the return favor. Of course, one could say that the subject had the choice of refusing both of Joe's offers, but those would have been tough choices. To have said no at either point would have required the subject to go against the natural cultural forces favoring reciprocation.

The extent to which even an unwanted favor, once received, can produce indebtedness is aptly illustrated in the soliciting technique of the Hare Krishna Society. During systematic observation of the Krishnas' soliciting strategy, I recorded a variety of responses from target persons. One of the most regular was as follows:

An airport visitor—a businessman—is hurriedly walking along through a densely peopled area. The Krishna solicitor steps in front of him and hands him a flower. The man, reacting with surprise, takes it.[2] Almost immediately,

---

[2]Surprise is an effective compliance producer in its own right. People who are surprised by a request will often comply because they are momentarily unsure of themselves and, consequently, influenced easily. For example, social psychologists Stanley Milgram and John Sabini (1975) have shown that people riding on the New York subway were twice as likely to give up their seats to a person who surprised them with the request, "Excuse me. May I have your seat?" than to one who forewarned them first by mentioning to a fellow passenger that he or she was thinking of asking for someone's seat (56 versus 28 percent).

he tries to give it back, saying he does not want the flower. The Krishna member responds that it is a gift from the Krishna Society and that it is the man's to keep . . . however, a donation to further the Society's good works would be appreciated. Again the target protests, "I don't want this flower. Here, take it." And again the solicitor refuses, "It's our gift to you, sir." There is visible conflict on the businessman's face. Should he keep the flower and walk away without giving anything in return, or should he yield to the pressure of the deeply ingrained reciprocity rule and provide a contribution? By now, the conflict has spread from his face to his posture. He leans away from his benefactor, seemingly about to break free, only to be drawn back again by the pull of the rule. Once more his body tilts away, but it's no use; he cannot disengage. With a nod of resignation, he fishes in his pocket and comes up with a dollar or two that is graciously accepted. Now he can walk away freely, and he does, "gift" in hand, until he encounters a waste container—where he throws the flower, with force.

Purely by accident, I happened to witness a scene that demonstrates that the Krishnas know very well how frequently their gifts are unwanted by the people who receive them. While spending a day observing a soliciting Krishna group at Chicago's O'Hare International Airport a few years ago, I noticed that one of the group members would frequently leave the central area and return with more flowers to resupply her companions. As it happened, I had decided to take a break just as she was leaving on one of her supply missions. Having nowhere to go, I followed her. Her journey turned out to be a garbage route. She went from trash can to trash can beyond the immediate area to retrieve all the flowers that had been discarded by Krishna targets. She then returned with the cache of recovered flowers (some that had been recycled who knows how many times) and distributed them to be profitably cycled through the reciprocation process once more. What really impressed me about all this was that most of the discarded flowers had brought donations from the people who had cast them away. The nature of the reciprocity rule is such that a gift so unwanted that it was thrown away at the first opportunity had nonetheless been effective and exploitable.

The ability of uninvited gifts to produce feelings of obligation is recognized by a variety of organizations besides the Krishnas. How many times has each of us received small gifts through the mail—personalized address labels, greeting cards, key rings—from charitable agencies that ask for funds in an accompanying note? I have received five in just the past year, two from disabled veterans' groups and the others from missionary schools and hospitals. In each case, there was a common thread in the accompanying message. The goods that were enclosed were to be considered a gift from the organization; and money I wished to send should not be regarded as payment but rather as a return offering. As the letter from one of the missionary programs stated, the packet of greeting cards I had been sent was not to be directly paid for but was designed "to encourage your [my] kindness." If we look past the obvious tax advantage, we can see why it would be beneficial for the organization to have the cards viewed as a gift instead of merchandise: There is a strong cultural pressure to reciprocate a gift, even an unwanted one; but there is no such pressure to purchase an *unwanted* commercial product.

The Rule Can Trigger Unequal Exchanges

There is yet another feature of the reciprocity rule that allows it to be exploited for profit. Paradoxically, although the rule developed to promote equal exchanges between partners, it can be used to bring about decidedly unequal results. The rule demands that one sort of action be reciprocated with a similar sort of action. A favor is to be met with another favor; it is not to be met with neglect and certainly not with attack; however, considerable flexibility is allowed. A small initial favor can produce a sense of obligation to agree to a substantially larger return favor. Since, as we have already seen, the rule allows one person to choose the nature of the indebting first favor *and* the nature of the debt-canceling return favor, we could easily be manipulated into an unfair exchange by those who might wish to exploit the rule.

Once again, we turn to the Regan experiment for evidence. Remember in that study, Joe gave one group of subjects a bottle of Coca-Cola as an initiating gift and later asked all subjects to buy some of his raffle tickets at 25 cents apiece. What I have so far neglected to mention is that the study was done in the late 1960s, when the price of a Coke was a dime. On the average, subjects who had been given a 10-cent drink bought two of Joe's raffle tickets, although some bought as many as seven. Even if we look just at the average, though, we can tell that Joe made quite a deal. A 500 percent return on investment is respectable indeed!

In Joe's case, though, even a 500 percent return amounted to only 50 cents. Can the reciprocity rule produce meaningfully large differences in the sizes of the exchanged favors? Under the right circumstances, it certainly can. Take, for instance, the account of a student of mine concerning a day she remembers ruefully.

> *About one year ago, I couldn't start my car. As I was sitting there, a guy in the parking lot came over and eventually jump-started the car. I said thanks, and he said you're welcome; as he was leaving, I said that if he ever needed a favor to stop by. About a month later, the guy knocked on my door and asked to borrow my car for two hours as his was in the shop. I felt somewhat obligated but uncertain, since the car was pretty new and he looked very young. Later, I found out that he was underage and had no insurance. Anyway, I lent him the car. He totaled it.*

How could it happen that an intelligent young woman would agree to turn over her new car to a virtual stranger (and a youngster at that) because he had done her a small favor a month earlier? Or, more generally, why should it be that small first favors often stimulate larger return favors? One important reason concerns the clearly unpleasant character of the feeling of indebtedness. Most of us find it highly disagreeable to be in a state of obligation. It weighs heavily on us and demands to be removed. It is not difficult to trace the source of this feeling. Because reciprocal arrangements are so vital in human social systems, we have been conditioned to feel uncomfortable when beholden. If we were to ignore the need to return another's initial favor, we would stop one reciprocal sequence dead and make it less likely that our benefactor would do such favors in the future. Neither event is in the best interests of society. Consequently, we are trained from childhood to chafe, emotionally, under the saddle of obligation. For this reason alone, then, we may be willing to agree to perform a larger favor than the one we received, merely to relieve ourselves of the psychological burden of debt.

There is another reason as well. A person who violates the reciprocity rule by accepting without attempting to return the good acts of others is disliked by the social group. The exception, of course, occurs when a person is prevented from repayment by reasons of circumstance or ability. For the most part, however, there is a genuine distaste for an individual who fails to conform to the dictates of the reciprocity rule.[3] Moocher and ingrate are unsavory labels to be scrupulously shunned. So undesirable are they that people will sometimes agree to an unequal exchange in order to dodge them.

In combination, the reality of internal discomfort and the possibility of external shame can produce a heavy psychological cost. When seen in the light of this cost, it is not so puzzling that, in the name of reciprocity, we will often give back more than we have received. Neither is it so odd that we will often avoid asking for a needed favor if we will not be in a position to repay it (De Paulo, Nadler, & Fisher, 1983; Greenberg & Shapiro, 1971; Riley & Eckenrode, 1986). The psychological cost may simply outweigh the material loss.

The risk of still other kinds of losses may also persuade people to decline certain gifts and benefits. Women frequently comment on the uncomfortable sense of obligation they can feel to return the favors of a man who has given them an expensive present or paid for a costly evening out. Even something as small as the price of a drink can produce a feeling of debt. A student in one of my classes expressed it quite plainly in a paper she wrote: "After learning the hard way, I no longer let a guy I meet in a club buy me a drink because I don't want either of us to feel that I am obligated sexually." Research suggests that there is a basis for her concern. If, in-

---

[3]Interestingly enough, a cross-cultural study has shown that those who break the reciprocity rule in the reverse direction—by giving without allowing the recipient an opportunity to repay—are also disliked for it. This result was found to hold for each of the three nationalities investigated—Americans, Swedes, and Japanese (Gergen, Ellsworth, Maslach, & Seipel, 1975).

off the mark   by Mark Parisi

Guilt-Edged Exchange
Even the stingiest people feel the pull of the reciprocity rule.

Atlantic Feature © 1991 Mark Parisi.

stead of paying for them herself, a woman allows a man to buy her drinks, she is immediately judged (by both men and women) as more sexually available to him (George, Gournic, & McAfee, 1988).

The rule for reciprocity applies to most relationships; however, in its purest form reciprocity is unnecessary and undesirable in certain long-term relationships such as families or established friendships. In these "communal" relationships (Clark & Mills, 1979; Mills & Clark, 1982), what is exchanged reciprocally is the willingness to provide what the other needs, when it is needed (Clark, Mills, & Corcoran, 1989). Under this form of reciprocity, it is not necessary to calculate who has given more or less but only whether both parties are living up to the more general rule (Clark, 1984; Clark & Waddell, 1985; Clark, Mills, & Powell, 1986). Still, it appears that persistent inequities can lead to dissatisfactions, even in friendships.

READER'S REPORT 2.1

From a State of Oregon Employee

The person who used to have my job told me during my training that I would like working for my boss because he is a very nice and generous person. She said that he always gave her flowers and other gifts on different occasions. She decided to stop working because she was going to have a child and wanted to stay home; otherwise I am sure she would have stayed on at this job for many more years.

I have been working for this same boss for six years now, and I have experienced the same thing. He gives me and my son gifts for Christmas and gives me presents on my birthday. It has been over two years since I have reached the top of my classification for a salary increase. There is no promotion for the type of job I have and my only choice is to take a test with the state system and reapply to move to another department or maybe find another job in a private company. But I find myself resisting trying to find another job or move to another department. My boss is reaching retirement age and I am thinking maybe I will be able to move out after he retires because for now I feel obligated to stay since he has been so nice to me.

Author's note: I am struck by this reader's language in describing her current employment options, saying that she "will be able" to move to another job only after her boss retires. It seems that his small kindnesses have nurtured a binding sense of obligation that has made her unable *to seek a better paying position. There is an obvious lesson here for managers wishing to instill loyalty in employees. But there is a larger lesson for all of us, as well: Little things are not always little—not when they link to the* big *rules of life, like reciprocity.*

RECIPROCAL CONCESSIONS

There is a second way to employ the reciprocity rule to get someone to comply with a request. It is more subtle than the direct route of providing that person with a favor and then asking for one in return, yet in some ways it is much more effective. A personal experience I had a few years ago gave me firsthand evidence of just how well this compliance technique works.

I was walking down the street when I was approached by an 11- or 12-year-old boy. He introduced himself and said he was selling tickets to the annual Boy Scouts Circus to be held on the upcoming Saturday night. He asked if I wished to buy any tickets at $5 apiece. Since one of the last places I wanted to spend Saturday evening was with the Boy Scouts, I declined. "Well," he said, if you don't want to buy any tickets, how about buying some of our chocolate bars? They're only $1 each." I bought a couple and, right away, realized that something noteworthy had happened. I knew that to be the case because (a) I do not like chocolate bars; (b) I do like dollars; (c) I was standing there with two of his chocolate bars; and (d) he was walking away with two of my dollars.

To try to understand precisely what had happened, I went to my office and called a meeting of my research assistants. In discussing the situation, we began to see how the reciprocity rule was implicated in my compliance with the request to buy the candy bars. The general rule says that a person who acts in a certain way toward us is entitled to a similar return action. We have already seen that one consequence of the rule is an obligation to repay favors we have received. Another consequence of the rule, however, is an obligation to make a concession to someone who has made a concession to us. As my research group thought about it, we realized that was exactly the position the Boy Scout had put me in. His request that I purchase some $1 chocolate bars had been put in the form of a concession on his part; it was presented as a retreat from his request that I buy some $5 tickets. If I were to live up to the dictates of the reciprocation rule, there had to be a concession on my part. As we have seen, there was such a concession: I changed from noncompliant to compliant when he moved from a larger to a smaller request, even though I was not really interested in *either* of the things he offered.

It was a classic example of the way a weapon of influence can infuse a compliance request with its power. I had been moved to buy something, not because of any favorable feelings toward the item, but because the purchase request had been presented in a way that drew force from the reciprocity rule. It had not mattered that I do not like chocolate bars; the Boy Scout had made a concession to me, *click,* and *whirr,* I responded with a concession of my own. Of course, the tendency to reciprocate with a concession is not so strong that it will work in all instances on all people; none of the weapons of influence considered in this book is that strong. However, in my exchange with the Boy Scout, the tendency had been sufficiently powerful to leave me in mystified possession of a pair of unwanted and overpriced candy bars.

Why should I feel obliged to reciprocate a concession? The answer rests once again in the benefit of such a tendency to the society. It is in the interest of any human group to have its members working together toward the achievement of common goals. However, in many social interactions the participants begin with requirements and demands that are unacceptable to one another. Thus, the society must arrange to have these initial, incompatible desires set aside for the sake of socially beneficial cooperation. This is accomplished through procedures that promote compromise. Mutual concession is one important such procedure.

The reciprocation rule brings about mutual concession in two ways. The first is obvious; it pressures the recipient of an already-made concession to respond in kind. The second, while not so obvious, is pivotally important. Because of a recipient's obligation to reciprocate, people are freed to make the *initial* concession and, thereby, to begin the beneficial process of exchange. After all, if there were no social obligation to reciprocate a concession, who would want to make the first sacrifice? To do so would be to risk giving up something and getting nothing back. However, with the rule in effect, we can feel safe making the first sacrifice to our partner, who is obligated to offer a return sacrifice.

REJECTION-THEN-RETREAT

Because the rule for reciprocation governs the compromise process, it is possible to use an initial concession as part of a highly effective compliance technique. The technique is a simple one that we will call the rejection-then-retreat technique, although it is also known as the door-in-the-face technique. Suppose you want me to agree to a certain request. One way to increase the chances that I will comply is first to make a larger request of me, one that I will most likely turn down. Then, after I have refused, you make the smaller request that you were really interested in all along. Provided that you structured your requests skillfully, I should view your second request as a concession to me and should feel inclined to respond with a concession of my own—compliance with your second request.

Was that the way the Boy Scout got me to buy his candy bars? Was his retreat from the $5 request to the $1 request an artificial one that was intentionally designed to sell candy bars? As one who has still refused to discard even his first Scout merit badge, I genuinely hope not. Whether or not the large-request-then-small-request sequence was planned, its effect was the same. It worked! Because it works, the rejection-then-retreat technique can and will be used *purposely* by certain people to get their way. First let's examine how this tactic can be used as a reliable compliance device. Later we will see how it is already being used. Finally we can turn to a pair of little-known features of the technique that make it one of the most influential compliance tactics available.

Remember that after my encounter with the Boy Scout, I called my research assistants together to try to understand what had happened to me—and, as it turned out, to eat the evidence. Actually, we did more than that. We designed an experiment to test the effectiveness of the procedure of moving to a desired request after a larger preliminary request had been refused. We had two purposes in conducting the experiment. First, we wanted to see whether this procedure worked on people besides me. (It certainly seemed that the tactic had been effective on me earlier in the day, but then I have a history of falling for compliance tricks of all sorts.) So the question remained, "Does the rejection-then-retreat technique work on enough people to make it a useful procedure for gaining compliance?" If so, it would definitely be something to be aware of in the future. Our second reason for doing the study was to determine how powerful a compliance device the technique was. Could it bring about compliance with a genuinely sizable request? In other words, did the *smaller* request to which the requester retreated have to be a *small* request? If our thinking about what caused the technique to be effective was correct, the second request did not actually have to be small; it only had to be smaller than the initial one. It was our suspicion that the critical aspect of a requester's retreat from a larger to a smaller favor was its appearance as a concession. So the second request could be an objectively large one—as long as it was smaller than the first request—and the technique would still work.

After a bit of thought, we decided to try the technique on a request that we felt few people would agree to perform. Posing as representatives of the "County Youth Counseling Program," we approached college students walking on campus and asked if they would be willing to chaperon a group of juvenile delinquents on a day trip to the zoo. This idea of being responsible for a group of juvenile delinquents of unspecified age for hours in a public place without pay was hardly an inviting one for these students. As we expected, the great majority (83 percent) refused. Yet we obtained very different results from a similar sample of college students who were asked the very same question with one difference. Before we invited them to serve as unpaid chaperons on the zoo trip, we asked them for an even larger favor—to spend two hours per week as counselors to juvenile delinquents for a minimum of two years. It was only after they refused this extreme request, as all did, that we made the small, zoo-trip request. But presenting the zoo trip as a retreat from our initial request, our success rate increased dramatically. Three times as many of the students approached in this manner volunteered to serve as zoo chaperons (Cialdini, Vincent, Lewis, Catalan, Wheeler, & Darby, 1975).

Be assured that any strategy able to triple the percentage of compliance with a substantial request (from 17 to 50 percent in our experiment) will be used often in a variety of natural settings. Labor negotiators, for instance, often use the tactic of making extreme demands that they do not expect to win but from which they can retreat and draw real concessions from the opposing side. It would appear, then, that the procedure would be more effective the larger the initial request, since there would be more room available for illusory concessions. This is true only up to a point, however. Research conducted at BarIlan University in Israel on the rejection-then-retreat technique shows that if the first set of demands is so extreme as to be seen as unreasonable, the tactic backfires (Schwarzwald, Raz, & Zvibel, 1979). In such cases, the party who has made the extreme first request is not seen to be bargaining in good faith. Any subsequent retreat from that wholly unrealistic initial position is not viewed as a genuine concession and, thus, is not reciprocated. The truly gifted negotiator, then, is one whose initial position is exaggerated just enough to allow for a series of small reciprocal concessions and counteroffers that will yield a desirable final offer from the opponent (Thompson, 1990).

I witnessed another form of the rejection-then-retreat technique in my investigations of door-to-door sales operations. These organizations used a less engineered, more opportunistic version of the tactic. Of course, the most important goal for a door-to-door salesperson is to make the sale. However, the training programs of each of the companies I investigated emphasized that a second important goal was to obtain from prospects the names of referrals—friends, relatives, or neighbors, on whom the salesperson could call. For a variety of reasons, which we will discuss in Chapter 5, the percentage of successful door-to-door sales increases impressively when the

Calvin and Hobbes

by Bill Watterson

Right and wrong ways to use the rejection-then-retreat tactic
The extreme request has to go first, and it can't be too extreme.

sales representative is able to mention the name of a familiar person who "recommended" the sales visit.

Never as a sales trainee was I taught to get the sales pitch refused so that I could then retreat to a request for referrals. In several such programs, though, I was trained to take advantage of the opportunity to secure referrals offered by a customer's purchase refusal: "Well, if it is your feeling that a fine set of encyclopedias is not right for you at this time, perhaps you could help me by giving me the names of some others who might wish to take advantage of our company's great offer. What would be the names of some of these people you know?" Many individuals who would not otherwise subject their friends to a high-pressure sales presentation do agree to supply referrals when the request is presented as a concession from a purchase request they have just refused.

Reciprocal Concessions, Perceptual Contrast, and the Watergate Mystery

We have already discussed one reason for the success of the rejection-then-retreat technique—its incorporation of the reciprocity rule. This larger-then-smaller-request strategy is effective for a pair of other reasons as well. The first concerns the perceptual contrast principle we encountered in Chapter 1. That principle accounted for, among other things, the tendency of a man to spend more money on a sweater *following* his purchase of a suit than before: After being exposed to the price of the larger item, he sees the price of the less expensive item as *appearing* smaller by comparison. In the same way, the larger-then-smaller request procedure uses the contrast principle to make the smaller request look even smaller by comparison with the larger one. If I want you to lend me $5, I can make the request seem smaller than it is by first asking you to lend me $10. One of the beauties of this tactic is that, by first requesting $10 and then retreating to $5, I will have simultaneously engaged the force of both the reciprocity rule and the contrast principle. Not only will my $5 request be viewed as a concession to be reciprocated, it will also look like a smaller request than if I had just asked for $5 straightaway.

In combination, the influences of reciprocity and perceptual contrast can present a fearsomely powerful force. Embodied in the rejection-then-retreat sequence, they are jointly capable of genuinely astonishing effects. It is my feeling that they provide the only really plausible explanation of one of the most baffling political actions of our time: the decision to break into the Watergate offices of the Democratic National Committee that led to the ruin of Richard Nixon's presidency. One of the participants in that decision, Jeb Stuart Magruder, upon hearing that the Watergate burglars had been caught, responded with appropriate bewilderment, "How could we have been so stupid?" Indeed, how?

To understand how enormously ill-conceived an idea it was for the Nixon administration to undertake the break-in, let's review a few facts:

- The idea was that of G. Gordon Liddy, who was in charge of intelligence-gathering operations for the Committee to Re-elect the President (CREEP). Liddy had gained a reputation among administration higher-ups as "flaky," and there were questions about his stability and judgment.
- Liddy's proposal was extremely costly, requiring a budget of $250,000 in untraceable cash.
- In late March, when the proposal was approved in a meeting of the CREEP director, John Mitchell, and his assistants Magruder and Frederick LaRue, the outlook for a Nixon victory in the November election could not have been brighter. Edmund Muskie, the only announced candidate the early polls had given a chance of unseating the president, had done poorly in the primaries. It looked very much as though the most defeatable candidate, George McGovern, would win the Democratic nomination. A Republican victory seemed assured.
- The break-in plan itself was a highly risky operation requiring the participation and discretion of ten men.
- The Democratic National Committee and its chairman, Lawrence O'Brien, whose Watergate office was to be burglarized and bugged, had no information damaging enough to defeat the incumbent president. Nor were the Democrats likely to get any, unless the administration did something *very, very* foolish.

Despite the obvious counsel of the previously mentioned reasons, the expensive, chancy, pointless, and potentially calamitous proposal of a man whose judgment was known to be questionable was approved. How could it be that intelligent, accomplished men such as Mitchell and Magruder would do something so *very, very* foolish? Perhaps the answer lies in a little-discussed fact: The $250,000 plan they approved was not Liddy's first proposal. In fact, it represented a significant concession on his part from two earlier proposals of immense proportions. The first of these plans, made two months earlier in a meeting with Mitchell, Magruder, and John Dean, described a $1 million program that included (in addition to the bugging of the Watergate) a specially equipped communications "chase plane," break-ins, kidnapping and mugging squads, and a yacht featuring "high-class call girls" to blackmail Democratic politicians. A second Liddy plan, presented a week later to the same group of Mitchell, Magruder, and Dean, eliminated some of the program and reduced the cost to $500,000. It was only after these initial proposals had been rejected by Mitchell that Liddy submitted his "bare-bones" $250,000 plan, in this instance to Mitchell, Magruder, and Frederick LaRue. This time the plan, still stupid but less so than the previous ones, was approved.

Could it be that I, a longtime patsy, and John Mitchell, a hardened and canny politician, might both have been so easily maneuvered into bad deals by the same compliance tactic—I by a Boy Scout selling candy and he by a man selling political disaster?

If we examine the testimony of Jeb Magruder, considered by most Watergate investigators to provide the most faithful account of the crucial meeting at which Liddy's plan was finally accepted, there are some instructive clues. First, Magruder (1974) reports that "no one was particularly overwhelmed with the project"; but "after starting at the grandiose sum of $1 million, we thought that probably $250,000 would be an acceptable figure. . . . We were reluctant to send him away with nothing." Mitchell, caught up in the "feeling that we should leave Liddy a little something . . . signed off on it in the sense of saying, 'Ok, let's give him a quarter of a million dollars and let's see what he can come up with.' " In the context of Liddy's initial extreme requests, it seems that "a quarter of a million dollars" had come to be "a little something" to be left as a return concession. With the clarity afforded by hindsight, Magruder has recalled Liddy's approach in as succinct an illustration of the rejection-then-retreat technique as I have ever heard. "If he had come to us at the outset and said, 'I have a plan to burglarize and wiretap Larry O'Brien's office,' we might have rejected the idea out of hand. Instead he came to us with his elaborate call-girl/kidnapping/mugging/sabotage/wiretapping scheme. . . . He had asked for the whole loaf when he was quite content to settle for half or even a quarter."

It is also instructive that, although he finally deferred to his boss's decision, only one member of the group, Frederick LaRue, expressed any direct opposition to the proposal. Saying with obvious common sense, "I don't think it's worth the risk," he must have wondered why his colleagues, Mitchell and Magruder, did not share his perspective. Of course, there could be many differences between LaRue and the other two men that may have accounted for their differing opinions regarding the advisability of Liddy's plan. But one stands out: Of the three, only LaRue had not been present at the prior two meetings, where Liddy had outlined his much more ambitious programs. Perhaps, then, only LaRue was able to see the third proposal for the clunker that it was and to react to it objectively, uninfluenced by the reciprocity and perceptual contrast forces acting upon the others.

Damned If You Do, Damned If You Don't

A bit earlier we said that the rejection-then-retreat technique had, in addition to the reciprocity rule, a pair of other factors working in its favor. We have already discussed the first of those factors, the perceptual contrast principle. The additional advantage of the technique is not really a psychological principle, as in the case of the other two factors. Rather, it is more of a purely structural feature of the request sequence. Let's once again say that I wish to borrow $5 from you. By beginning with a request for $10, I really can't lose. If you agree to it, I will have received from you twice the amount I would have settled for. If, on the other hand, you turn down my initial request, I can retreat to the $5 favor that I desired from the outset and, through the action of the reciprocity and contrast principles, greatly enhance my likelihood of success. Either way, I benefit; it's a case of heads I win, tails you lose.

The clearest utilization of this aspect of the large-then-small-request sequence occurs in the retail store sales practice of "talking the top of the line." Here the prospect is invariably shown the deluxe model first. If the customer buys, there is frosting on the store's cake. However, if the customer declines, the salesperson effectively counteroffers with a more reasonably priced model. Some proof of the effectiveness of this procedure comes from a report in *Sales Management* magazine, reprinted without comment in *Consumer Reports:*

> *If you were a billiard-table dealer, which would you advertise—the $329 model or the $3,000 model? The chances are you would promote the low-priced item and hope to trade the customer up when he comes to buy. But G. Warren Kelley, new business promotion manager at Brunswick, says you would be wrong. . . . To prove his point, Kelley has actual sales figures from a representative store. . . . During the first week customers . . . were shown the low end of the line . . . and then encouraged to consider more expensive models—the traditional trading-up approach. . . . The average table sale that week was $550. . . . However, during the second week, customers . . . were led instantly to a $3,000 table, regardless of what they wanted to see . . . and then allowed to shop the rest of the line, in declining order of price and quality. The result of selling down was an average sale of over $1,000. ("Quote," 1975, p. 62)*

Given the remarkable effectiveness of the rejection-then-retreat technique, one might think that there could be a substantial disadvantage as well. The victims of the strategy might resent having been cornered into compliance. The resentment could show itself in a couple of ways. First, the victim might decide not to live up to the verbal agreement made with the requester. Second, the victim might come to distrust the manipulative requester, deciding never to deal with that person again. If either or both of these events occurred with any frequency, a requester would want to give serious second thought to the use of the rejection-then-retreat procedure. Research indicates, however, that these victim reactions do not occur with increased frequency when the rejection-then-retreat technique is used. Somewhat astonishingly, it appears that they actually occur *less* frequently! Before trying to understand why this should be, let's first look at the evidence.

Here's My Blood, and Do Call Again

A study published in Canada (Miller, Seligman, Clark, & Bush, 1976) throws light on the question of whether a victim of the rejection-then-retreat tactic will follow through with the agreement to perform a requester's second favor. In addition to recording whether target persons said yes or no to the desired request (to work for two hours a day without pay in a community mental health agency), this experiment also recorded whether they showed up to perform their duties as promised. As usual, the procedure of starting with a larger request (to volunteer for two hours of work per week in the agency for at least two years) produced more verbal agreement to the smaller, retreat request (76 percent), than did the procedure of asking for the smaller request alone (29 percent). The important result, though, concerned the show-up rate *of those who volunteered;* and, again, the rejection-then-retreat procedure was the more effective one (85 versus 50 percent).

A different experiment examined whether the rejection-then-retreat sequence caused victims to feel so manipulated that they would refuse any further requests. In this study (Cialdini & Ascani, 1976), the targets were college students who were each asked to give a pint of blood as part of the annual campus blood drive. Targets in one group were first asked to give a pint of blood every six weeks for a minimum of three years. The other targets were asked only to give a single pint of blood. Those of both groups who agreed and later appeared at the blood center were then asked if they would be willing to give their phone numbers so they could be called upon to donate again in the future. Nearly all the students who were about to give a pint of blood as a result of the rejection-then-retreat technique agreed to donate again (84 percent), while less than half of the other students who appeared at the blood center did so (43 percent). Even for future favors, the rejection-then-retreat strategy proved superior.

The Sweet, Secret Side Effects

Strangely enough, then, it seems that the rejection-then-retreat tactic not only spurs people to agree to a desired request but actually to carry out the request and, finally, to volunteer to perform further requests. What could there be about the technique that makes people who have been duped into compliance so likely to continue to comply? For an answer, we might look at a requester's act of concession, which is the heart of the procedure. We have already seen that, as long as it is not viewed as an obvious trick, the concession will likely stimulate a return concession. What we have not yet examined, however, is a little-known pair of positive by-products of the act of concession: feelings of greater responsibility for and satisfaction with the arrangement. It is this set of sweet side effects that enables the technique to move its victims to fulfill their agreements and to engage in further such agreements.

The desirable side effects of making concessions during an interaction with other people are nicely shown in studies of the way people bargain with each other. One experiment, conducted by social psychologists at UCLA, offers an especially apt demonstration (Benton, Kelley, & Liebling, 1972). A subject in that study faced a "negotiation opponent" and was told to bargain with the opponent concerning how to divide between themselves a certain amount of money provided by the experimenters. The subject was also informed that if no mutual agreement could be reached after a certain period of bargaining, no one would get any money. Unknown to the subject, the opponent was really an experimental assistant who had been previously instructed to bargain with the subject in one of three ways. With some of the subjects, the opponent made an extreme first demand, assigning virtually all of the money to himself and stubbornly persisted in that demand throughout the negotiations. With another group of subjects, the opponent began with a demand that was moderately favorable to himself; he, too, steadfastly refused to move from that position during the negotiations. With a third group, the opponent began with the extreme demand and then gradually retreated to the more moderate one during the course of the bargaining.

There were three important findings that help us to understand why the rejection-then-retreat technique is so effective. First, compared to the two other approaches, the strategy of starting with an extreme demand and then retreating to the more moderate one produced the most money for the person using it. This result is not very surprising in light of the previous evidence we have seen for the power of larger-then-smaller-request tactics to bring about profitable agreements. It is the pair of additional findings of the study that are more striking.

Responsibility

The requester's concession within the rejection-then-retreat technique not only caused targets to say yes more often, it also caused them to feel more responsible for having "dictated" the final agreement. Thus the uncanny ability of the rejection-then-retreat technique to make its targets meet their commitments becomes understandable: A person who feels responsible for the terms of a contract will be more likely to live up to that contract.

Satisfaction

Even though, on the average, they gave the most money to the opponent who used the concessions strategy, the subjects who were the targets of this strategy were the most satisfied with the final arrangement. It appears that an agreement that has been forged through the concessions of one's opponents is quite satisfying. With this in mind, we can begin to explain the second previously puzzling feature of the rejection-then-retreat tactic—the ability to prompt its victims to agree to further requests. Since the tactic uses a concession to bring about compliance, the victim is likely to feel more satisfied with the arrangement as a result. It stands to reason that people who are satisfied with a given arrangement are more likely to be willing to agree to similar arrangements. As one study of retail sales showed, feeling responsible for getting a better deal led to more satisfaction with the process and more repurchases of the product (Schindler, 1998).

DEFENSE

Against a requester who employs the rule for reciprocation, you and I face a formidable foe. By presenting us with either an initial favor or an initial concession, the requester will have enlisted a powerful ally in the campaign for our compliance. At first glance, our fortunes in such a situation would appear dismal. We could comply with the requester's wish and, in so doing, succumb to the reciprocity rule. Or, we could refuse to comply and thereby suffer the brunt of the rule's force upon our deeply conditioned feelings of fairness and obligation. Surrender or suffer heavy casualties. Cheerless prospects indeed.

Fortunately, these are not our only choices. With the proper understanding of the nature of our opponent, we can come away from the compliance battlefield unhurt and sometimes even better off than before. It is essential to recognize that the requester who invokes the reciprocation rule (or any other weapon of influence) to gain our compliance is not the real opponent. Such a requester has chosen to become a jujitsu warrior who aligns himself or herself with the sweeping power of reciprocation and then merely releases that power by providing a first favor or concession. The real opponent is the rule. If we are not to be abused by it, we must take steps to defuse its energy.

Rejecting the Rule

How does one go about neutralizing the effect of a social rule like the one for reciprocation? It seems too widespread to escape and too strong to overpower once it is activated. Perhaps the answer, then, is to prevent its activation. Perhaps we can avoid a confrontation with the rule by refusing to allow a requester to commission its force against us in the first place. Perhaps by rejecting a requester's initial favor or concessions to us, we can evade the problem. Perhaps; but then, perhaps not. Invariably declining a requester's initial offer of a favor or sacrifice works better in theory than in practice. The major problem is that when it is first presented, it is difficult to know whether such an offer is honest or whether it is the initial step in an exploitation attempt. If we always assume the worst, it would not be possible to receive the benefits of any legitimate favors or concessions offered by individuals who had no intention of exploiting the reciprocity rule.

I have a colleague who remembers with anger how his 10-year-old daughter's feelings were terribly hurt by a man whose method of avoiding the jaws of the reciprocity rule was to refuse her kindness. The children of her class were hosting an open house at school for their grandparents, and her job was to give a flower to each visitor entering the school grounds. The first man she approached with a flower growled at her, "Keep it." Not knowing what to do, she extended it toward him again, only to have him demand to know what he had to give in return. When she replied weakly, "Nothing. It's a gift," he fixed her with a disbelieving glare, insisting that he recognized "her game," and brushed on past. The girl was so stung by the experience that she could not approach anyone else and had to be removed from her assignment—one she had anticipated fondly. It is hard to know whom to blame more, the insensitive man or the exploiters who had abused his tendency to reciprocate a gift until his response had soured to a refusal. No matter whom you find more blameworthy, the lesson is clear. We will always encounter authentically generous individuals as well as many people who try to play fairly by the reciprocity rule rather than to exploit it. They will doubtless become insulted by someone who consistently rejects their efforts; social friction and isolation could well result. A policy of blanket rejection, then, seems ill advised.

Another solution holds more promise. It advises us to accept the offers of others but to accept those offers only for what they fundamentally are, not for what they are represented to be. If a person offers us a nice favor, let's say, we might well accept, recognizing that we have obligated ourselves to a return favor sometime in the future. To engage in this sort of arrangement with another is not to be exploited by that person through the rule for reciprocation. Quite the contrary; it is to participate fairly in the "honored network of obligation" that has served us so well, both individually and societally, from the dawn of humanity. However, if the initial favor turns out to be a device, a trick, an artifice designed specifically to stimulate our compliance with a larger return favor, that is a different story. Our partner is not a benefactor but a profiteer; and it is here that we should respond to the action on precisely those terms. Once we have determined that the initial offer was not a favor but a compliance tactic, we need only react to it accordingly to be free of its influence. As long as we perceive and define the action as a compliance device instead of a favor, the giver no longer has the reciprocation rule as an ally: The rule says that favors are to be met with favors; it does not require that tricks be met with favors.

Smoking Out the Enemy

A practical example may make things more concrete. Let's suppose that a woman phoned one day and introduced herself as a member of the Home Fire Safety Association in your town. Suppose she then asked if you would be interested in learning about home fire safety, having your house checked for fire hazards, and receiving a home fire extinguisher—all free of charge. Let's suppose further that you were interested in these things and made an evening appointment to have one of the association's inspectors come over to provide them. When the inspector arrived, he gave you a small hand extinguisher and began examining the possible fire hazards of your home. Afterward he gave you some interesting, though frightening, information about general fire dangers, along with an assessment of your home's vulnerability. Finally he suggested that you obtain a home fire warning system for your house and left.

Such a set of events is not implausible. Various cities and towns have nonprofit associations, usually made up of fire department personnel working on their own time, that provide free home fire-safety inspections of this sort. Were these events to occur, you would clearly have received a favor from the inspector. In accordance with the reciprocation rule, you should stand more ready to provide a return favor if you were to see him in need of aid at some point in the future. An exchange of favors of this kind would be in the best tradition of the reciprocity rule.

A similar set of events with, however, a different ending is also possible. Rather than leaving after recommending a fire-alarm system, the inspector launches into a sales presentation intended to persuade you to buy an expensive, heat-triggered alarm system manufactured by the company he represents. Door-to-door home fire-alarm companies will frequently use this approach. Typically, their product, while effective enough, will be overpriced. Trusting that you will not be familiar with the retail costs of such a system and that, if you decide to buy one, you will feel obligated to the company that provided you with a free extinguisher and home inspection, these companies will pressure you for an immediate sale. Using this free-information-and-inspection gambit, fire-protection sales organizations have flourished around the country.[4]

If you were to find yourself in such a situation with the realization that the primary motive of the inspector's visit was to sell you a costly alarm system, your most effective next action would be a simple, private maneuver. It would involve the mental act of redefinition. Merely define whatever you have received from the inspector—extinguisher, safety information, hazard inspection—not as gifts but as sales devices, and you will be free to decline (or accept) the purchase offer without even a tug from

---

[4]A variety of other business operations use the no-cost information offer extensively. Pest exterminator companies, for instance, have found that most people who agree to a free home examination give the extermination job to the examining company, provided they are convinced that it is needed. They apparently feel an obligation to give their business to the firm that rendered the initial, complimentary service. Knowing that such customers are unlikely to comparison shop for this reason, unscrupulous pest control operations will take advantage of the situation by citing higher-than-competitive prices for work commissioned in this way.

the reciprocity rule: A favor rightly follows a favor—not a piece of sales strategy. If the inspector subsequently responds to your refusal by proposing that you, at least, provide the names of some friends he might call on, use your mental maneuver again. Define this retreat to a smaller request as what you recognize it to be—a compliance tactic. Once this is done, there would be no pressure to offer the names as a return concession, since the reduced request would not be viewed as a real concession. At this point, unhampered by an inappropriately triggered sense of obligation, you may once again be as compliant or noncompliant as you wish.

Provided you are so inclined, you might even turn the inspector's own weapon of influence against him. Recall that the rule for reciprocation entitles a person who has acted in a certain way to a dose of the same thing. If you have determined that the "fire inspector's" gifts were used, not as genuine gifts, but to make a profit from you, then you might want to use them to make a profit of your own. Simply take whatever the inspector is willing to provide—safety information, home extinguisher—thank him politely, and show him out the door. After all, the reciprocity rule asserts that if justice is to be done, exploitation attempts should be exploited.

READER'S REPORT 2.2

From a Former Television and Stereo Salesperson

For quite a while, I worked for a major retailer in their television and stereo department. Continued employment was based on the ability to sell service contracts which are warranty extensions offered by the retailer. Once this fact was explained to me I devised the following plan that used the rejection-then-retreat technique, although I didn't know its name at the time.

A customer had the opportunity to buy from one to three years' worth of service contract coverage at the time of the sale, although the credit I got was the same regardless of the length of coverage. Realizing that most people would not be willing to buy three years' worth of coverage, initially, I would advocate to the customer the longest and most expensive plan. This gave me an excellent opportunity later, after being rejected in my sincere attempt to sell the three-year plan, to retreat to the one-year extension and its relatively small price, which I was thrilled to get. This technique proved highly effective, as I sold sales contracts to an average of 70 percent of my customers, who seemed very satisfied in the process, while others in my department clustered around 40 percent. I never told anyone how I did it until now.

Author's note: Notice how, as is usually the case, use of the rejection-then-retreat tactic also engages the action of the contrast principle. Not only did the initial higher request make the lower one seem like a retreat, it made that second request seem smaller, too.

SUMMARY

- According to sociologists and anthropologists, one of the most widespread and basic norms of human culture is embodied in the rule for reciprocation. The rule requires that one person try to repay, in kind, what another person has provided. By obligating the recipient of an act to repayment in the future, the rule for reciprocation allows one individual to give something to another with confidence that it is not being lost. This sense of future obligation within the rule makes possible the development of various kinds of continuing relationships, transactions, and exchanges that are beneficial to the society. Consequently, all members of the society are trained from childhood to abide by the rule or suffer serious social disapproval.

- The decision to comply with another's request is frequently influenced by the reciprocity rule. One favorite and profitable tactic of certain compliance professionals is to give something before asking for a return favor. The exploitability of this tactic is due to three characteristics of the rule for reciprocation. First, the rule is extremely powerful, often overwhelming the influence of other factors that normally determine compliance with a request. Second, the rule applies even to uninvited first favors, thereby reducing our ability to decide whom we wish to owe and putting the choice in the hands of others. Finally, the rule can spur unequal exchanges; to be rid of the uncomfortable feeling of indebtedness, an individual will often agree to a request for a substantially larger favor than the one he or she received.

- Another way that the rule for reciprocity can increase compliance involves a simple variation on the basic theme: Instead of providing a first favor that stimulates a return favor, an individual can make an initial concession that stimulates a return concession. One compliance procedure, called the rejection-then-retreat technique, or door-in-the-face technique, relies heavily on the pressure to reciprocate concessions. By starting with an extreme request that is sure to be rejected, a requester can then profitably retreat to a smaller request (the one that was desired all along), which is likely to be accepted because it appears to be a concession. Research indicates that, aside from increasing the likelihood that a person will say yes to a request, the rejection-then-retreat technique also increases the likelihood that the person will carry out the request and will agree to such requests in the future.

- Our best defense against the use of reciprocity pressures to gain our compliance is not systematic rejection of the initial offers of others. Rather, we should accept initial favors or concessions in good faith, but be ready to redefine them as tricks should they later be proved as such. Once they are redefined in this way, we will no longer feel a need to respond with a favor or concession of our own.

STUDY QUESTIONS

Content Mastery

1. What is the rule for reciprocity? Why is it so powerful in our society?

2. Which are the three features of the reciprocity rule that make it so exploitable by compliance professionals?

3. Describe how the Regan study illustrates each of the three exploitable features of the rule.

4. How does the rejection-then-retreat technique use the pressure for reciprocation to increase compliance?

5. Why should the rejection-then-retreat technique increase a compliant person's willingness to (a) carry out an agreement and (b) volunteer to do future favors?

Critical Thinking

1. Suppose you wanted a professor to spend an hour helping you with a topic for a term paper. Write a script showing how you might use the rejection-then-retreat tactic to increase the chance of compliance to your request. What should you be careful to avoid when making your first request?

2. One study (Berry & Kanouse, 1987) found that, by paying physicians first, they were much more likely to complete and return a long questionnaire they had received in the mail. If a $20 check accompanied the questionnaire, 78 percent of the physicians filled out the questionnaire and sent it back as requested. But if they learned that the $20 check was to be sent to them after they completed it, only 66 percent did so.

   Another interesting finding concerned the physicians who got the check up front but didn't comply with the questionnaire request: only 26 percent cashed the check (as compared to 95 percent of those who had complied). Explain how the rule for reciprocity can explain both findings.

3. Explain what is meant by the term *noblesse oblige* and how the concept of reciprocity might play a role in it. Hint: John F. Kennedy once said, "For those to whom much is given, much is required."

4. How does the ad that opens this chapter reflect the topic of the chapter?

3 | *Commitment and Consistency*

Hobgoblins of the Mind

SATURN SURVEY

Your name JENNIFER MILLER

Occupation AVICULTURIST   Age 28

Where is your Saturn retailer located?

SATURN OF KEARNY MESA

If you had to share one story or experience about your Saturn, what would it be?

I'M A BIG BELIEVER IN RECYCLING. I FOUND OUT THAT YOU RECLAIM 85% OF THE TOTAL WASTE YOU GENERATE BUILDING SATURNS, MORE THAN 95% OF THE PARTS YOU USE ARRIVE IN REUSABLE CONTAINERS, AND THAT LAST YEAR YOU RECYCLED OVER 50,000 TONS OF WASTE MATERIAL. NEEDLESS TO SAY, I BOUGHT THE GREEN ONE.

Which Saturn do you drive? SW2   Color GREEN

It is easier to resist at the beginning than at the end.

—LEONARDO DA VINCI

A study done by a pair of Canadian psychologists (Knox & Inkster, 1968) uncovered something fascinating about people at the racetrack: just after placing bets they are much more confident of their horses' chances of winning than they are immediately before laying down the bets. Of course, nothing about the horse's chances actually shifts; it's the same horse, on the same track, in the same field; but in the minds of those bettors, its prospects improve significantly once that ticket is purchased. Although a bit puzzling at first glance, the reason for the dramatic change has to do with a common weapon of social influence. Like the other weapons of influence, this one lies deep within us, directing our actions with quiet power. It is, quite simply, our desire to be (and to appear) consistent with what we have already done. *Once we make a choice or take a stand, we will encounter personal and interpersonal pressures to behave consistently with that commitment.* Those pressures will cause us to respond in ways that justify our earlier decision. We simply convince ourselves that we have made the right choice and, no doubt, feel better about our decision (Fazio, Blascovich, & Driscoll, 1992).

By way of illustration, let's examine the story of my neighbor Sara and her live-in boyfriend, Tim. After they met, they dated for a while, even after Tim lost his job, and eventually moved in together. Things were never perfect for Sara: She wanted Tim to marry her and to stop his heavy drinking; Tim resisted both ideas. After an especially difficult period of conflict, Sara broke off the relationship and Tim moved out. At the same time, an old boyfriend of Sara's called her. They started seeing each other socially and quickly became engaged and made wedding plans. They had gone so far as to set a date and issue invitations when Tim called. He had repented and wanted to move back in. When Sara told him her marriage plans, he begged her to change her mind; he wanted to be together with her as before. Sara refused, saying she didn't want to live like that again. Tim even offered to marry her, but she still said she preferred the other boyfriend. Finally, Tim volunteered to quit drinking if she would only relent. Feeling that under those conditions Tim had the edge, Sara decided to break her engagement, cancel the wedding, retract the invitations, and let Tim move back in with her.

Within a month, Tim informed Sara that he didn't think he needed to stop drinking after all. A month later, he decided that they should "wait and see" before getting married. Two years have since passed; Tim and Sara continue to live together exactly as before. Tim still drinks, and there are still no marriage plans, yet Sara is more devoted to him than she ever was. She says that being forced to choose taught her that Tim really is number one in her heart. So, after choosing Tim over her other boyfriend, Sara became happier, even though the conditions under which she had made her choice have never been fulfilled. Obviously, horse-race bettors are not alone in their willingness to believe in the correctness of a difficult choice once made. Indeed, we all fool ourselves from time to time in order to keep our thoughts and beliefs consistent with what we have already done or decided (Conway & Ross, 1984; Goethals & Reckman, 1973; Rosenfeld, Kennedy, & Giacalone, 1986). For instance, immediately after casting a ballot, voters believe more strongly that their candidate will win (Regan & Kilduff, 1988).

WHIRRING ALONG

Psychologists have long understood the power of the consistency principle to direct human action. Prominent early theorists such as Leon Festinger (1957), Fritz Heider (1946), and Theodore Newcomb (1953) viewed the desire for consistency as a central motivator of behavior. Is this tendency to be consistent really strong enough to compel us to do what we ordinarily would not want to do? There is no question about it. The drive to be (and look) consistent constitutes a highly potent weapon of social influence, often causing us to act in ways that are clearly contrary to our own best interest.

Consider what happened when researchers staged thefts on a New York City beach to see if onlookers would risk personal harm to halt the crime. In the study, an accomplice of the researchers would put a beach blanket down five feet from the blanket of a randomly chosen individual—the experimental subject. After several minutes of relaxing on the blanket and listening to music from a portable radio, the accomplice would stand up and leave the blanket to stroll down the beach. Soon thereafter, a researcher, pretending to be a thief, would approach, grab the radio, and try to hurry away with it. As you might guess, under normal conditions, subjects were very reluctant to put themselves in harm's way by challenging the thief—only four people did so in the 20 times that the theft was staged. But when the same procedure was tried another 20 times with a slight twist, the results were drastically different. In these incidents, before leaving the blanket, the accomplice would simply ask the subject to please "watch my things," something everyone agreed to do. Now, propelled by the rule for consistency, 19 of the 20 subjects became virtual vigilantes, running after and stopping the thief, demanding an explanation, often restraining the thief physically or snatching the radio away (Moriarty, 1975).

To understand why consistency is so powerful a motive, we should recognize that, in most circumstances, consistency is valued and adaptive. Inconsistency is commonly thought to be an undesirable personality trait (Allgeier, Byrne, Brooks, & Revnes, 1979; Asch, 1946). The person whose beliefs, words, and deeds don't match is seen as confused, two-faced, even mentally ill. On the other side, a high degree of consistency is normally associated with personal and intellectual strength. It is the heart of logic, rationality, stability, and honesty. A quote attributed to the great British chemist, Michael Faraday, suggests the extent to which being consistent is approved—sometimes more than being right. When asked after a lecture if he meant to imply that a hated academic rival was always wrong, Faraday glowered at the questioner and replied, "He's not that consistent."

Certainly, then, good personal consistency is highly valued in our culture—and well it should be. Most of the time we will be better off if our approach to things is well laced with consistency. Without it our lives would be difficult, erratic, and disjointed (Sheldon, Ryan, Rawsthorne, & Ilardi, 1997).

The Quick Fix

Since it is so typically in our best interests to be consistent, we fall into the habit of being automatically consistent even in situations where it is not the sensible way to be. When it occurs unthinkingly, consistency can be disastrous. Nonetheless, even blind consistency has its attractions.

First, like most other forms of automatic responding, it offers a shortcut through the complexities of modern life. Once we have made up our minds about issues, stubborn consistency allows us a very appealing luxury: We don't have to think hard about the issues anymore. We don't really have to sift through the blizzard of information we encounter every day to identify relevant facts; we don't have to expend the mental energy to weigh the pros and cons; we don't have to make any further tough decisions. Instead, all we have to do when confronted with the issues is *click* on our consistency tape, *whirr*, and we know just what to believe, say, or do. We need only believe, say, or do whatever is consistent with our earlier decision.

The allure of such a luxury is not to be minimized. It allows us a convenient, relatively effortless, and efficient method for dealing with the complexities of daily life that make severe demands on our mental energies and capacities. It is not hard to understand, then, why automatic consistency is a difficult reaction to curb. It offers us a way to evade the rigors of continuing thought. With our consistency tapes operating, we can go about our business happily excused from having to think too much. As Sir Joshua Reynolds noted, "There is no expedient to which a man will not resort to avoid the real labor of thinking."

The Foolish Fortress

There is a second, more perverse attraction of mechanical consistency as well. Sometimes it is not the effort of hard, cognitive work that makes us shirk thoughtful activity but the harsh consequences of that activity. Sometimes it is the cursedly clear and unwelcome set of answers provided by straight thinking that makes us mental slackers. There are certain disturbing things we simply would rather not realize. Because it is a preprogrammed and mindless method of responding, automatic consistency can supply a safe hiding place from troubling realizations. Sealed within the fortress walls of rigid consistency, we can be impervious to the sieges of reason.

One night at an introductory lecture given by the Transcendental Meditation program, I witnessed an illustration of the way people will hide inside the walls of consistency to protect themselves from the troublesome consequences of thought. The lecture itself was presided over by two earnest young men and was designed to recruit new members into the program. The men claimed that the program offered a unique brand of meditation (TM) which would allow us to achieve all manner of desirable things, ranging from simple inner peace to more spectacular abilities— to fly and pass through walls—at the program's advanced (and more expensive) stages.

I had decided to attend the meeting to observe the kind of compliance tactics used in recruitment lectures of this sort and had brought along an interested friend, a university professor whose areas of specialization were statistics and symbolic logic. As the meeting progressed and the lecturers explained the theory behind TM, I noticed my logician friend becoming increasingly restless. Looking more and more pained and shifting about constantly in his seat, he was finally unable to resist. When

FIGURE 3.1 Higher Consciousness
Ads like this one will probably have to be discontinued now that a man has won a court judgment against the TM program by claiming that, contrary to what was promised, he was not taught to fly, only to hop a bit higher (*Kropinski v. Maharishi International University and TM World Plan Executive Council*).

the leaders called for questions at the end of the lecture, he raised his hand and gently but surely demolished the presentation we had just heard. In less than two minutes, he pointed out precisely where and why the lecturers' complex argument was contradictory, illogical, and unsupportable. The effect on the discussion leaders was devastating. After a confused silence, each attempted a weak reply only to halt midway to confer with his partner and finally to admit that my colleague's points were good ones "requiring further study."

More interesting to me, though, was the effect upon the rest of the audience. At the end of the question period, the two recruiters were faced with a crowd of audience members submitting their $75 down payments for admission to the TM program. Nudging, shrugging, and chuckling to one another as they took in the payments, the recruiters betrayed signs of giddy bewilderment. After what appeared to have been an embarrassingly clear collapse of their presentation, the meeting had somehow turned into a great success, generating mystifyingly high levels of compliance from the audience. Although more than a bit puzzled, I chalked up the audience response to a failure to understand the logic of my colleague's arguments. As it turned out, however, just the *reverse* was the case.

Outside the lecture room after the meeting, we were approached by three members of the audience, each of whom had given a down payment immediately after the lecture. They wanted to know why we had come to the session. We explained, and we asked the same question of them. One was an aspiring actor who wanted desperately to succeed at his craft and had come to the meeting to learn if TM would allow him to achieve the necessary self-control to master the art; the recruiters had assured him that it would. The second described herself as a severe insomniac who hoped that TM would provide her with a way to relax and fall asleep easily at night. The third served as unofficial spokesman. He was failing his college courses, because there didn't seem to be enough time to study. He had come to the meeting to find out if TM could help by training him to need fewer hours of sleep each night; the additional time could then be used for study. It is interesting to note that the recruiters informed him as well as the insomniac that Transcendental Meditation techniques could solve their respective, though opposite, problems.

Still thinking that the three must have signed up because they hadn't understood the points made by my logician friend, I began to question them about aspects of his argument. To my surprise, I found that they had understood his comments quite well; in fact, all too well. It was precisely the cogency of his argument that drove them to sign up for the program on the spot. The spokesman put it best: "Well, I wasn't going to put down any money tonight because I'm really quite broke right now; I was going to wait until the next meeting. But when your buddy started talking, I knew I'd better give them my money now, or I'd go home and start thinking about what he said and *never* sign up."

All at once, things began to make sense. These were people with real problems, and they were desperately searching for a way to solve those problems. They were seekers who, if our discussion leaders were to be believed, had found a potential solution in TM. Driven by their needs, they very much wanted to believe that TM was their answer.

Now, in the form of my colleague, intrudes the voice of reason, showing the theory underlying their newfound solution to be unsound. Panic! Something must be done at once before logic takes its toll and leaves them without hope once again. Quickly, quickly, walls against reason are needed; and it doesn't matter that the fortress to be erected is a foolish one. "Quick, a hiding place from thought! Here, take this money. Whew, safe in the nick of time. No need to think about the issues any longer." The decision has been made, and from now on the consistency tape can be played whenever necessary: "TM? Certainly I think it will help me; certainly I expect to continue; certainly I believe in TM. I already put my money down for it, didn't I?" Ah, the comforts of mindless consistency. "I'll just rest right here for a while. It's so much nicer than the worry and strain of that hard, hard search."

Seek and Hide

If, as it appears, automatic consistency functions as a shield against thought, it should not be surprising that such consistency can also be exploited by those who would prefer that we respond to their requests without thinking. For the profiteers, whose interest will be served by an unthinking, mechanical reaction to their requests, our tendency for automatic consistency is a gold mine. So clever are they at arranging to have us play our consistency tapes when it profits them that we seldom realize that we have been taken. In fine jujitsu fashion, they structure their interactions with us so that our own need to be consistent leads directly to their benefit.

Certain large toy manufacturers use just such an approach to reduce a problem created by seasonal buying patterns. Of course, the boom time for toy companies occurs before and during the Christmas holiday season. Their problem is that toy sales then go into a terrible slump for the next couple of months. Their customers have already spent the amount in their toy budgets and are stiffly resistant to their children's pleas for more.

So the toy manufacturers are faced with a dilemma: how to keep sales high during the peak season and, at the same time, retain a healthy demand for toys in the immediately following months. Their difficulty certainly doesn't lie in motivating kids to want more toys after Christmas. The problem lies in motivating postholiday spent-out parents to buy another plaything for their already toy-glutted children. What could the toy companies possibly do to produce that unlikely behavior? Some have tried greatly increased advertising campaigns, others have reduced prices during the slack period, but neither of those standard sales devices has proved successful. Both tactics are costly, and have been ineffective in increasing sales to desired levels. Parents are simply not in a toy-buying mood, and the influences of advertising or reduced expense are not enough to shake that stony resistance.

Certain large toy manufacturers, however, think they have found a solution. It's an ingenious one, involving no more than a normal advertising expense and an understanding of the powerful pull of the need for consistency. My first hint of the way the toy companies' strategy worked came after I fell for it and then, in true patsy form, fell for it again.

It was January, and I was in the town's largest toy store. After purchasing all too many gifts there for my son a month before, I had sworn not to enter that store or any like it for a long, long time. Yet there I was, not only in the diabolic place but also in the process of buying my son another expensive toy—a big, electric road-race set. In front of the road-race display I happened to meet a former neighbor who was buying his son the same toy. The odd thing was that we almost never saw each other anymore. In fact, the last time had been a year earlier in the same store when we were both buying our sons an expensive post-Christmas gift—that time a robot that walked, talked, and laid waste. We laughed about our strange pattern of seeing each other only once a year at the same time, in the same place, while doing the same thing. Later that day, I mentioned the coincidence to a friend who, it turned out, had once worked in the toy business.

"No coincidence," he said knowingly.

"What do you mean, 'No coincidence'?"

"Look," he said, "let me ask you a couple of questions about the road-race set you bought this year. First, did you promise your son that he'd get one for Christmas?"

"Well, yes I did. Christopher had seen a bunch of ads for them on the Saturday morning cartoon shows and said that was what he wanted for Christmas. I saw a couple of ads myself and it looked like fun; so I said OK."

"Strike one," he announced. "Now for my second question. When you went to buy one, did you find all the stores sold out?"

"That's right, I did! The stores said they'd ordered some but didn't know when they'd get any more in. So I had to buy Christopher some other toys to make up for the road-race set. But how did you know?"

"Strike two," he said. "Just let me ask one more question. Didn't this same sort of thing happen the year before with the robot toy?"

"Wait a minute . . . you're right. That's just what happened. This is incredible. How did you know?"

"No psychic powers; I just happen to know how several of the big toy companies jack up their January and February sales. They start prior to Christmas with attractive TV ads for certain special toys. The kids, naturally, want what they see and extract Christmas promises for these items from their parents. Now here's where the genius of the companies' plan comes in: They *undersupply* the stores with the toys they've gotten the parents to promise. Most parents find those toys sold out and are forced to substitute other toys of equal value. The toy manufacturers, of course, make a point of supplying the stores with plenty of these substitutes. Then, after Christmas, the companies start running the ads again for the other, special toys. That juices up the kids to want those toys more than ever. They go running to their parents whining, 'You promised, you promised,' and the adults go trudging off to the store to live up dutifully to their words."

Sorry,
Out of Stock

How the Furby Flies
It seems that every holiday season, parents find at least one highly prized
toy sold out after they have promised it to their children. If the parents
can't secure a toy in time for the holidays, that promise spurs them to purchase one later.

"Where," I said, beginning to seethe now, "they meet other parents they haven't
seen for a year, falling for the same trick, right?"

"Right. Uh, where are you going?"

"I'm going to take the road-race set right back to the store." I was so angry I was
nearly shouting.

"Wait. Think for a minute first. Why did you buy it this morning?"

"Because I didn't want to let Christopher down and because I wanted to teach
him that promises are to be lived up to."

"Well, has any of that changed? Look, if you take his toy away now, he won't
understand why. He'll just know that his father broke a promise to him. Is that what
you want?"

"No," I said, sighing, "I guess not. So, you're telling me that the toy companies doubled their profits on me for the past two years, and I never even knew it; and now that I do, I'm still trapped—by my own words. So, what you're really telling me is, 'Strike three.' " He nodded, "And you're out."

In the years since, I have observed a variety of parental toy-buying sprees similar to the one I experienced during that particular holiday season—for Beanie Babies, Tickle Me Elmo dolls, Furbies, etc. But, historically, the one that best fits the pattern is that of the Cabbage Patch Kids, $25 dolls that were promoted heavily during mid-1980s Christmas seasons but were woefully undersupplied to stores. Some of the consequences were a government false advertising charge against the Kids' maker for continuing to advertise dolls that were not available; frenzied groups of adults battling at toy outlets or paying up to $700 apiece at auction for dolls they had *promised* their children; and an annual $150 million in sales that extended well beyond the Christmas months. During the 1998 holiday season, the least available toy that everyone wanted was the Furby, created by a division of toy giant Hasbro. When asked what frustrated, Furby-less parents should tell their kids, a Hasbro spokeswoman advised the kind of promise that has profited toy manufacturers for decades, "I'll try, but if I can't get it for you now, I'll get it for you later" (Tooher, 1998).

COMMITMENT IS THE KEY

Once we realize that the power of consistency is formidable in directing human action, an important practical question immediately arises: How is that force engaged? What produces the *click* that activates the *whirr* of the powerful consistency tape? Social psychologists think they know the answer: commitment. If I can get you to make a commitment (that is, to take a stand, to go on record), I will have set the stage for your automatic and ill-considered consistency with that earlier commitment. Once a stand is taken, there is a natural tendency to behave in ways that are stubbornly consistent with the stand.

As we've already seen, social psychologists are not the only ones who understand the connection between commitment and consistency. Commitment strategies are aimed at us by compliance professionals of nearly every sort. Each of the strategies is intended to get us to take some action or make some statement that will trap us into later compliance through consistency pressures. Procedures designed to create commitment take various forms. Some are bluntly straightforward; others are among the most subtle compliance tactics we will encounter. On the blunt side, consider the approach of Jack Stanko, used-car sales manager for an Albuquerque auto dealership. While leading a session called "Used Car Merchandising" at a National Auto Dealers Association convention in San Francisco, he advised 100 sales-hungry dealers as follows: "Put 'em on paper. Get the customer's OK on paper. Get the money up front. Control 'em. Control the deal. Ask 'em if they would buy the car right now if the price is right. Pin 'em down" (Rubinstein, 1985). Obviously, Mr. Stanko—an expert in these matters—believes that the way to customer compliance is through their commitments, thereby to "control 'em" for profit.

Commitment practices involving substantially more finesse can be just as effective. For instance, suppose you wanted to increase the number of people in your area who would agree to go door-to-door collecting donations for your favorite charity. You would be wise to study the approach taken by social psychologist Steven J. Sherman. He simply called a sample of Bloomington, Indiana, residents as part of a survey he was taking and asked them to predict what they would say if asked to spend three hours collecting money for the American Cancer Society. Of course, not wanting to seem uncharitable to the survey-taker or to themselves, many of these people said that they would volunteer. The consequence of this subtle committment procedure was a 700 percent increase in volunteers when, a few days later, a representative of the American Cancer Society did call and ask for neighborhood canvassers (Sherman, 1980). Using the same strategy, but this time asking citizens to predict whether they would vote on election day, other researchers have been able to increase significantly the turnout at the polls among those called (Greenwald, Carnot, Beach, & Young, 1987; Spangenberg & Greenwald, in press). Courtroom combatants appear to have adopted this practice of extracting a lofty initial commitment that is designed to spur future consistent behavior. When screening potential jurors before a trial, Jo-Ellen Demitrius, the woman currently reputed to be the best consultant in the business of jury selection asks an artful question: "If you were the only person who believed in my client's innocence, could you withstand the pressure of the rest of the jury to change your mind?" How could any self-respecting prospective juror say no? And, having made the promise, how could any self-respecting selected juror repudiate it later?

Perhaps an even more crafty commitment technique has been developed by telephone solicitors for charity. Have you noticed that callers asking you to contribute to some cause or another these days seem to begin things by inquiring about your current health and well-being? "Hello, Mr./Ms. Targetperson," they say. "How are you feeling this evening?," or "How are you doing today?" The caller's intent with this sort of introduction is not merely to seem friendly and caring. It is to get you to respond—as you normally do to such polite, superficial inquiries—with a polite, superficial comment of your own: "Just fine" or "Real good" or "I'm doing great, thanks." Once you have publicly stated that all is well, it becomes much easier for the solicitor to corner you into aiding those for whom all is not well: "I'm glad to hear that, because I'm calling to ask if you'd be willing to make a donation to help out the unfortunate victims of . . . "

The theory behind this tactic is that people who have just asserted that they are doing/feeling fine—even as a routine part of a sociable exchange—will consequently find it awkward to appear stingy in the context of their own admittedly favored circumstances. If all this sounds a bit far-fetched, consider the findings of consumer researcher Daniel Howard (1990), who put the theory to test. Residents of Dallas, Texas, were called on the phone and asked if they would agree to allow a representative of the Hunger Relief Committee to come to their homes to sell them cookies, the proceeds from which would be used to supply meals for the needy. When tried alone, that request (labeled the standard solicitation approach) produced only 18 percent agreement. However, if the caller initially asked, "How are you feeling this evening?" and waited for a reply before proceeding with the standard approach, several noteworthy things happened. First, of the 120 individuals called, most (108) gave the customary favorable reply ("Good," "Fine," "Real well," etc.). Second, 32 percent of the people who got the How-are-you-feeling-tonight question agreed to receive the cookie seller at their homes, nearly twice the success rate of the standard solicitation approach. Third, true to the consistency principle, almost everyone (89 percent) who agreed to such a visit did in fact make a cookie purchase when contacted at home.

The question of what makes a commitment effective has numerous answers. A variety of factors affects the ability of a commitment to constrain our future behavior. One large-scale program designed to produce compliance illustrates how several of the factors work. The remarkable thing about this program is that it was systematically employing these factors decades ago, well before scientific research had identified them.

During the Korean War, many captured American soldiers found themselves in prisoner-of-war camps run by the Chinese Communists. It became clear early in the conflict that the Chinese treated captives quite differently than did their allies, the North Koreans, who favored harsh punishment to gain compliance. Specifically avoiding the appearance of brutality, the Red Chinese engaged in what they termed their "lenient policy," which was, in reality, a concerted and sophisticated psychological assault on their captives. After the war, American psychologists questioned the returning prisoners intensively to determine what had occurred, in part because of the unsettling success of some aspects of the Chinese program. For example, the Chinese were very effective in getting Americans to inform on one another, in striking contrast to the behavior of American POWs in World War II. For this reason, among others, escape plans were quickly uncovered and the escapes themselves almost always unsuccessful. "When an escape did occur," wrote psychologist Edgar Schein (1956), a principal American investigator of the Chinese indoctrination program in Korea, "the Chinese usually recovered the man easily by offering a bag of rice to anyone turning him in." In fact, nearly all American prisoners in the Chinese camps are said to have collaborated with the enemy in one way or another.[1]

An examination of the prison-camp program shows that the Chinese relied heavily on commitment and consistency pressures to gain the desired compliance from their captives. Of course, the first problem facing the Chinese was to find a way to

---

[1] It is important to note that the collaboration was not always intentional. The American investigators defined collaboration as "any kind of behavior which helped the enemy," and it thus included such diverse activities as signing peace petitions, running errands, making radio appeals, accepting special favors, making false confessions, informing on fellow prisoners, divulging military information, etc.

get any collaboration at all from the Americans. These prisoners had been trained to provide nothing but name, rank, and serial number. Short of physical brutalization, how could the captors hope to get such men to give military information, turn in fellow prisoners, or publicly denounce their country? The Chinese answer was elementary: Start small and build.

For instance, prisoners were frequently asked to make statements that were so mildly anti-American or pro-Communist that they seemed inconsequential ("The United States is not perfect." "In a Communist country, unemployment is not a problem."). Once these minor requests had been complied with, however, the men found themselves pushed to submit to related, yet more substantive, requests. A man who had just agreed with his Chinese interrogator that the United States was not perfect might then be asked to indicate some of the ways in which he thought this was the case. Once he had so explained, he might be asked to make a list of these "problems with America" and to sign his name to it. Later he might be asked to read his list in a discussion group with other prisoners. "After all, it's what you really believe, isn't it?" Still later, he might be asked to write an essay expanding on his list and discussing these problems in greater detail.

The Chinese might then use his name and his essay in an anti-American radio broadcast beamed not only to the entire camp but to other POW camps in North Korea as well as to American forces in South Korea. Suddenly he would find himself a "collaborator," having given aid and comfort to the enemy. Aware that he had written the essay without any strong threats or coercion, many times a man would change his self-image to be consistent with the deed and with the new "collaborator" label, often resulting in even more extensive acts of collaboration. Thus, while "only a few men were able to avoid collaboration altogether," according to Schein, "the majority collaborated at one time or another by doing things which seemed to them trivial but which the Chinese were able to turn to their own advantage. . . . This was particularly effective in eliciting confessions, self-criticism, and information during interrogation" (1956).

U.S. Acres

Start Small and Build
Permission of Paws, Inc.

Other groups of people interested in compliance are also aware of the usefulness and power of this approach. Charitable organizations, for instance, will often use progressively escalating commitments to induce individuals to perform major favors. Research has shown that such trivial first commitments as agreeing to be interviewed can begin a "momentum of compliance" that induces such later behaviors as organ or bone marrow donations (Carducci, Deuser, Bauer, Large, & Ramaekers, 1989; Schwartz, 1970).

Many business organizations employ this approach regularly as well. For the salesperson, the strategy is to obtain a large purchase by starting with a small one. Almost any small sale will do because the purpose of that small transaction is not profit, it is commitment. Further purchases, even much larger ones, are expected to flow naturally from the commitment. An article in the trade magazine *American Salesman* put it succinctly:

> *The general idea is to pave the way for full-line distribution by starting with a small order. . . . Look at it this way—when a person has signed an order for your merchandise, even though the profit is so small it hardly compensates for the time and effort of making the call, he is no longer a prospect— he is a customer (Green, 1965, p. 14).*

The tactic of starting with a little request in order to gain eventual compliance with related larger requests has a name: the foot-in-the-door technique. Social scientists first became aware of its effectiveness in 1966 when psychologists Jonathan Freedman and Scott Fraser published an astonishing set of data. They reported the results of an experiment in which a researcher, posing as a volunteer worker, had gone door to door in a residential California neighborhood making a preposterous request of homeowners. The homeowners were asked to allow a public-service billboard to be installed on their front lawns. To get an idea of the way the sign would look, they were shown a photograph depicting an attractive house, the view of which was almost completely obscured by a very large, poorly lettered sign reading DRIVE CAREFULLY. Although the request was normally and understandably refused by the great majority of the residents in the area (only 17 percent complied), one particular group of people reacted quite favorably. A full 76 percent of them offered the use of their front yards.

The prime reason for their startling compliance has to do with something that had happened to them about two weeks earlier: They had made a small commitment to driver safety. A different "volunteer worker" had come to their doors and asked them to accept and display a little three-inch-square sign that read BE A SAFE DRIVER. It was such a trifling request that nearly all of them had agreed to it, but the effects of that request were enormous. Because they had innocently complied with a trivial safe-driving request a couple of weeks before, these homeowners became remarkably willing to comply with another such request that was massive in size.

Freedman and Fraser didn't stop there. They tried a slightly different procedure on another sample of homeowners. These people first received a request to sign a petition that favored "keeping California beautiful." Of course, nearly everyone signed since state beauty, like efficiency in government or sound prenatal care, is one of those issues no one opposes. After waiting about two weeks, Freedman and Fraser sent a new "volunteer worker" to these same homes to ask the residents to allow the big DRIVE CAREFULLY sign to be erected on their lawns. In some ways, the response of these homeowners was the most astounding of any in the study. Approximately half of these people consented to the installation of the DRIVE CAREFULLY billboard, even though the small commitment they had made weeks earlier was not to driver safety but to an entirely different public-service topic, state beautification.

At first, even Freedman and Fraser were bewildered by their findings. Why should the little act of signing a petition supporting state beautification cause people to be so willing to perform a different and much larger favor? After considering and discarding other explanations, Freedman and Fraser came upon one that offered a solution to the puzzle: Signing the beautification petition changed the view these people had

Just Sign on the Plotted Line
Have you ever wondered what the groups that ask you to sign their petitions do with all the signatures they obtain? Often they don't do anything with them, as the principal purpose of the petition may simply be to get the signers committed to the group's position and, consequently, more willing to take future steps that are consistent with it.

of themselves. They saw themselves as public-spirited citizens who acted on their civic principles. When, two weeks later, they were asked to perform another public service by displaying the DRIVE CAREFULLY sign, they complied in order to be consistent with their newly formed self-images. According to Freedman and Fraser:

> *What may occur is a change in the person's feelings about getting involved or taking action. Once he has agreed to a request, his attitude may change, he may become, in his own eyes, the kind of person who does this sort of thing, who agrees to requests made by strangers, who takes action on things he believes in, who cooperates with good causes. (p. 201)*

What the Freedman and Fraser findings tell us, then, is to be very careful about agreeing to trivial requests. Such an agreement can not only increase our compliance with very similar, much larger requests, it can also make us more willing to perform a variety of larger favors that are only remotely connected to the little one we did earlier. It's this second, general kind of influence concealed within small commitments that scares me.

It scares me enough that I am rarely willing to sign a petition anymore, even for a position I support. Such an action has the potential to influence not only my future behavior but also my self-image in ways I may not want. Further, once a person's self-image is altered, all sorts of subtle advantages become available to someone who wants to exploit that new image.

Who among Freedman and Fraser's homeowners would have thought that the "volunteer worker" who asked them to sign a state beautification petition was really interested in having them display a safe-driving billboard two weeks later? Who among them could have suspected that their decision to display the billboard was largely a result of signing the petition? No one, I'd guess. If there were any regrets after the billboard went up, who could they conceivably hold responsible but *themselves* and their own damnably strong civic spirits? They probably never even considered the guy with the "keeping California beautiful" petition and all that knowledge of social jujitsu.

Hearts and Minds

Notice that all of the foot-in-the-door experts seem to be excited about the same thing: You can use small commitments to manipulate a person's self-image; you can use them to turn citizens into "public servants," prospects into "customers," prisoners into "collaborators." Once you've got a person's self-image where you want it, that person should comply *naturally* with a whole range of requests that are consistent with this new self-view.

Not all commitments affect self-image, however. There are certain conditions that should be present for a commitment to be effective in this way: they should be active, public, effortful, and freely chosen. The major intent of the Chinese was not simply to extract information from their prisoners. It was to indoctrinate them, to change their attitudes and perceptions of themselves, of their political system, of their country's role in the war, and of communism. Dr. Henry Segal, chief of the neuro-psychiatric evaluation team that examined returning POWs at the end of the Korean War, reported that war-related beliefs had been substantially shifted. Significant in-roads had been made in the political attitudes of the men:

> *Many expressed antipathy toward the Chinese Communists but at the same time praised them for "the fine job they had done in China." Others stated that "although communism won't work in America, I think it's a good thing for Asia." (Segal, 1954, p. 360)*

It appears that the real goal of the Chinese was to modify, at least for a time, the hearts and minds of their captives. If we measure their achievement in terms of "de-fection, disloyalty, changed attitudes and beliefs, poor discipline, poor morale, poor *esprit,* and doubts as to America's role," Segal concluded, "their efforts were highly successful." Let's examine more closely how they managed it.

The Magic Act

Our best evidence of people's true feelings and beliefs comes less from their words than from their deeds. Observers trying to decide what people are like look closely at their actions. Researchers have discovered that people themselves use this same evidence—their own behavior—to decide what they are like; it is a primary source of information about one's own beliefs, values, and attitudes (Bem, 1972; Vallacher & Wegner, 1985).

The rippling impact of behavior on one's self-concept and future behavior can be seen in research investigating the effect of active versus passive commitments (Al-lison & Messick, 1988; Fazio, Sherman, & Herr, 1982). For instance, in one study, college students volunteered for an AIDS education project in the local schools. The researchers arranged for half to volunteer actively by filling out a form stating that they wanted to participate. The other half volunteered passively by *failing* to fill out a form stating that they *didn't* want to participate. Three to four days later, when asked to begin their volunteer activity, the great majority (74 percent) who actually appeared for duty came from the ranks of those who had actively agreed to partici-pate. What's more, those who volunteered actively were more likely to explain their decisions by implicating their personal values, preferences, and traits (Cioffi & Gar-ner, 1996). In all, it seems that active commitments give us the kind of information we use to shape self-image, which then shapes future actions, which solidify the new self-image.

Understanding fully this route to altered self-perception, the Chinese set about arranging the prison-camp experience so that their captives would consistently *act* in desired ways. Before long, the Chinese knew, these actions would begin to take their toll, causing the prisoners to change their views of themselves to align with what they had done.

Writing was one sort of committing action that the Chinese urged incessantly upon the captives. It was never enough for prisoners to listen quietly or even to agree verbally with the Chinese line; they were always pushed to write it down as well. Schein (1956) describes a standard indoctrination session tactic of the Chinese:

> *A further technique was to have the man write out the question and then the [pro-Communist] answer. If he refused to write it voluntarily, he was asked to copy it from the notebooks, which must have seemed like a harmless enough concession. (p. 161)*

Oh, those "harmless" concessions. We've already seen how apparently trifling commitments can lead to further consistent behavior. As a commitment device, a written declaration has some great advantages. First, it provides physical evidence that an act has occurred. Once a prisoner wrote what the Chinese wanted, it was very difficult for him to believe that he had not done so. The opportunities to forget or to deny to himself what he had done were not available, as they were for purely verbal statements. No; there it was in his own handwriting, an irrevocably documented act driving him to make his beliefs and his self-image consistent with what he had undeniably done. Second, a written testament can be shown to other people. Of course, that means it can be used to persuade those people. It can persuade them to change their own attitudes in the direction of the statement. More importantly for the purpose of commitment, it can persuade them that the author genuinely believes what was written.

People have a natural tendency to think that a statement reflects the true attitude of the person who made it. What is surprising is that they continue to think so even when they know that the person did not freely choose to make the statement. Some scientific evidence that this is the case comes from a study by psychologists Edward Jones and James Harris (1967), who showed people an essay that was favorable to Fidel Castro and asked them to guess the true feelings of its author. Jones and Harris told some of these people that the author had chosen to write a pro-Castro essay; they told other people that the author had been required to write in favor of Castro. The strange thing was that even those people who knew that the author had been assigned to do a pro-Castro essay guessed that the writer liked Castro. It seems that a statement of belief produces a *click, whirr* response in those who view it. Unless there is strong evidence to the contrary, observers automatically assume that someone who makes such a statement means it (Allison, Mackie, Muller, & Worth, 1993).

Think of the double-barreled effects on the self-image of a prisoner who wrote a pro-Chinese or anti-American statement. Not only was it a lasting personal reminder of his action, it was also likely to persuade those around him that it reflected his actual beliefs. As we will see in Chapter 4, what those around us think is true of us is enormously important in determining what we ourselves think is true. For example, one study found that one week after hearing that they were considered charitable people, homemakers in New Haven, Connecticut, gave much more money to a canvasser from the Multiple Sclerosis Association (Kraut, 1973). Apparently the mere knowledge that someone viewed them as charitable caused these people to make their actions consistent with that view.

Savvy politicians have long used the committing character of labels to great advantage. One of the best at it was former president of Egypt, Anwar Sadat. Before international negotiations began, Sadat would assure his bargaining opponents that they and the citizens of their country were widely known for their cooperativeness and fairness. With this kind of flattery, he not only created positive feelings, he also connected his opponent's identities to a course of action that served his goals. According to master-negotiator, Henry Kissinger (1982), Sadat was successful because he got others to act in his interests by giving them a reputation to uphold.

Once an active commitment is made, then, self-image is squeezed from both sides by consistency pressures. From the inside, there is a pressure to bring self-image into line with action. From the outside, there is a sneakier pressure—a tendency to adjust this image according to the way others perceive us (Schlenker, Dlugolecki, & Doherty, 1994). Because others see us as believing what we have written (even when we've had little choice in the matter), we once again experience a pull to bring self-image into line with the written statement.

In Korea, several subtle devices were used to get prisoners to write, without direct coercion, what the Chinese wanted. For example, the Chinese knew that many prisoners were anxious to let their families know that they were alive. At the same time, the men knew that their captors were censoring the mail and that only some letters were being allowed out of camp. To ensure that their own letters should be released, some prisoners began including in their messages peace appeals, claims of kind treatment, and statements sympathetic to communism. The hope was that the Chinese would want such letters to surface and would, therefore, allow their delivery. Of course, the Chinese were happy to cooperate because those letters served their interests marvelously. First, their worldwide propaganda effort benefited greatly from the appearance of pro-Communist statements by American servicemen. Second, in the service of prisoner indoctrination, the Chinese had, without raising a finger of physical force, gotten many men to go on record supporting the Communist cause.

A similar technique involved political essay contests that were regularly held in camp. The prizes for winning were invariably small—a few cigarettes or a bit of fruit—but were sufficiently scarce that they generated a lot of interest from the men. Usually the winning essay was one that took a solidly pro-Communist stand . . . but not always. The Chinese were wise enough to realize that most of the prisoners would not enter a contest that they thought they could win only by writing a Communist tract. Moreover, the Chinese were clever enough to know how to plant in the captives small commitments to communism that could be nurtured into later bloom. So, occasionally, the winning essay was one that generally supported the United States but that bowed once or twice to the Chinese view. The effects of this strategy were exactly what the Chinese wanted. The men continued to participate voluntarily in the contests because they saw that they could win with essays highly favorable to their own country. Perhaps without realizing it, however, they began to shade their essays a bit toward communism in order to have a better chance of winning. The Chinese were ready to pounce on any concession to Communist dogma and to bring consistency pressures to bear upon it. In the case of a written declaration within a voluntary essay, they had a perfect commitment from which to build toward collaboration and conversion.

Other compliance professionals also know about the committing power of written statements. The enormously successful Amway Corporation, for instance, has a way to spur their sales personnel to greater and greater accomplishments. Members of the staff are asked to set individual sales goals and commit themselves to those goals by personally recording them on paper:

> *One final tip before you get started: Set a goal and* write it down. *Whatever the goal, the important thing is that you set it, so you've got something for which to aim—and that you write it down. There is something magical about writing things down. So set a goal and write it down. When you reach that goal, set another and write that down. You'll be off and running.*

If the Amway people have found "something magical about writing things down," so have other business organizations. Some door-to-door sales companies use the magic of written commitments to battle the "cooling-off" laws that exist in many states. The laws are designed to allow customers a few days after agreeing to purchase an item to cancel the sale and receive a full refund. At first this legislation hurt the hard-sell companies deeply. Because they emphasize high-pressure tactics, their customers often buy, not because they want the products but because they are duped or intimidated into the sale. When the laws went into effect, these customers began canceling in droves.

The companies have since learned a beautifully simple trick that cuts the number of such cancellations drastically. They merely have the customer, rather than the salesperson, fill out the sales agreement. According to the sales-training program of a prominent encyclopedia company, that personal commitment alone has proved to be "a very important psychological aid in preventing customers from backing out of their contracts." Like the Amway Corporation, these organizations have found that something special happens when people put their commitments on paper: They live up to what they have written down.

Another common way for businesses to cash in on the "magic" of written declarations occurs through the use of an innocent-looking promotional device. Before I began to study weapons of social influence, I used to wonder why big companies such as Procter & Gamble and General Foods are always running those "25-, 50-, or 100-words or less" testimonial contests. They all seem to be alike. A contestant is to compose a short personal statement that begins with the words, "I like the product because . . ." and goes on to laud the features of whatever cake mix or floor wax happens to be at issue. The company judges the entries and awards prizes to the winners. What puzzled me was what the companies got out of the deal. Often the contest requires no purchase; anyone submitting an entry is eligible. Yet, the companies appear to be willing to incur the costs of contest after contest.

I am no longer puzzled. The purpose behind the testimonial contest—to get as many people as possible to endorse a product—is the same as the purpose behind the political essay contests: to get endorsements for Chinese communism. In both instances the process is the same. Participants voluntarily write essays for attractive prizes that they have only a small chance to win. They know that for an essay to have any chance of winning at all, however, it must include praise for the product. So they search to find praiseworthy features of the product, and they describe them in their essays. The result is hundreds of POWs in Korea or hundreds of thousands of people in America who testify in writing to the products' appeal and who, consequently, experience that magical pull to believe what they have written.

The Public Eye

One reason that written testaments are effective in bringing about genuine personal change is that they can so easily be made public. The prisoner experience in Korea showed the Chinese to be quite aware of an important psychological principle: Public commitments tend to be lasting commitments. The Chinese constantly arranged to have the pro-Communist statements of their captives seen by others. They were posted around camp, read by the author to a prisoner discussion group, or even read on the camp radio broadcast. As far as the Chinese were concerned, the more public the better. Why?

Whenever one takes a stand that is visible to others, there arises a drive to maintain that stand in order to *look* like a consistent person (Tedeschi, Schlenker, & Bonoma, 1971; Schlenker et al., 1994). Remember that earlier in this chapter I described how desirable good personal consistency is as a trait; how someone without it may be judged as fickle, uncertain, pliant, scatterbrained, or unstable; how someone with it is viewed as rational, assured, trustworthy, and sound. Given this context, it is hardly surprising that people try to avoid the look of inconsistency. For appearances' sake, then, the more public a stand, the more reluctant we will be to change it.

An illustration of the way public commitments can lead to consistent further action was provided in a famous experiment performed by two prominent social psychologists, Morton Deutsch and Harold Gerard (1955). The basic procedure was to have college students first estimate in their minds the length of lines they were shown. At this point, one sample of the students had to commit themselves publicly to their initial judgments by writing their estimates down, signing their names to them, and turning them in to the experimenter. A second sample of students also committed themselves to their first estimates, but they did so privately by writing them down on a Magic Writing Pad and then erasing them by lifting the Magic Pad's plastic cover before anyone could see what they had written. A third set of students did not commit themselves to their initial estimates at all; they just kept the estimates in mind privately.

In these ways, Deutsch and Gerard had cleverly arranged for some students to commit themselves publicly, some privately, and some not at all, to their initial decisions. What Deutsch and Gerard wanted to find out was which of the three types of students would be most inclined to stick with their first judgments after receiving information that those judgments were incorrect. Therefore, all the students were given new evidence suggesting that their initial estimates were wrong, and they were then given the chance to change their estimates.

The results were quite clear. The students who had never written down their first choices were the least loyal to those choices. When new evidence was presented that questioned the wisdom of decisions that had never left their heads, these students were the most influenced by the new information to change what they had viewed as the "correct" decision. Compared to these uncommitted students, those who had merely written their decisions for a moment on a Magic Pad were significantly less willing to change their minds when given the chance. Even though they had committed themselves under anonymous circumstances, the act of writing down their first judgments caused them to resist the influence of contradictory new data and to remain consistent with their preliminary choices. However, Deutsch and Gerard found that, by far, it was the students who had publicly recorded their initial positions who most resolutely refused to shift from those positions later. Public commitments had hardened them into the most stubborn of all.

This sort of stubbornness can occur even in situations in which accuracy should be more important than consistency. In one study, when 6- or 12-person experimental juries were deciding a close case, hung juries were significantly more frequent if the jurors had to express their opinions with a visible show of hands rather than by secret ballot. Once jurors had stated their initial views publicly, they were reluctant to allow themselves to change publicly. Should you ever find yourself as the foreperson of a jury under these conditions, you could reduce the risk of a hung jury by choosing a secret rather than public balloting technique (Kerr & MacCoun, 1985).

The Deutsch and Gerard finding that we are truest to our decisions if we have bound ourselves to them publicly can be put to good use. Consider the organizations dedicated to helping people rid themselves of bad habits. Many weight-reduction clinics, for instance, understand that often a person's private decision to lose weight will be too weak to withstand the blandishments of bakery windows, wafting cooking scents, and late-night Sara Lee commercials. So they see to it that the decision is buttressed by the pillars of public commitment. They require their clients to write down an immediate weight-loss goal and *show* that goal to as many friends, relatives, and neighbors as possible. Clinic operators report that frequently this simple technique works where all else has failed.

Of course, there's no need to pay a special clinic in order to engage a visible commitment as any ally. One San Diego woman described to me how she employed a public promise to help herself finally stop smoking:

I remember it was after I heard about another scientific study showing that smoking causes cancer. Every time one of those things came out, I used to get determined to quit, but I never could. This time, though, I decided I had to do something. I'm a proud person. It matters to me if other people see me in a bad light. So I thought, "Maybe I can use that pride to help me dump this damn habit." So I made a list of all the people who I really wanted to respect me. Then I went out and got some blank business cards and I wrote on the back of each card, "I promise you that I will never smoke another cigarette."

Within a week, I had given or sent a signed card to everybody on my list—my dad, my brother back East, my boss, my best girlfriend, my ex-husband, everybody but one—the guy I was dating then. I was just crazy about him, and I really wanted him to value me as a person. Believe me, I thought twice about giving him a card because I knew that if I couldn't keep my promise to him I'd die. But one day at the office—he worked in the same building as I did—I just walked up to him, handed him the card, and walked away without saying anything.

Quitting "cold turkey" was the hardest thing I've ever done. There must have been a thousand times when I thought I had to have a smoke. But whenever that happened, I'd just picture how all the people on my list would think less of me if I couldn't stick to my guns. And that's all it took, I've never taken another puff.[2]

READER'S REPORT 3.1

From a Canadian University Professor

I just read a newspaper article on how a restaurant owner used public commitments to solve a big problem of customers who didn't show-up for their table reservations. I don't know if he read your book or not first, but he did something that fits perfectly with the commitment/consistency principle you talk about. He told his receptionists to stop saying, "Please call us if you change your plans," and to start asking, "Will you please call us if you change your plans?" and to wait for a response. His no-show rate immediately dropped from 30 percent to 10 percent.

Author's note: What was it about this subtle shift that led to such a dramatic difference? For me, it was the receptionist's request for (and pause for) the caller's promise. By spurring patrons to make a public commitment, this approach increased the chance that they would follow through on it. By the way, the canny proprietor was Gordon Sinclair of Gordon's restaurant in Chicago.

---

[2]This public commitment tactic may work especially well for individuals with high levels of pride or public self-consciousness (Feingstein, Scheier, & Buss, 1975). For example, it worked successfully for Charles DeGaulle, whose remarkable achievements for France were said to be matched only by his ego. When asked to explain why announcing to everyone that he would stop his heavy smoking obliged him to quit forever, he is reported to have replied gravely, "DeGaulle cannot go back on his word" (Quoted in D. Cook, 1984).

The Effort Extra

The evidence is clear that the more effort that goes into a commitment, the greater is its ability to influence the attitudes of the person who made it. We can find that evidence quite nearby or as far away as the back regions of the primitive world.

Let's begin close to home with the entertainment section of tomorrow's newspaper, where an important piece of information is missing from ads for popular music concerts—the price. Why should it be that concert promoters are increasingly hiding the cost of admission from fans? Perhaps they're afraid that their ever-higher prices will scare ticket buyers away. But, interested fans will find out the price of a seat as soon as they call or visit a ticket outlet, right? True, but promoters have recognized that potential concertgoers are more likely to buy tickets *after* that call or visit than before. Even phoning to inquire about ticket prices constitutes an initial commitment to the concert. Combine that with the time and effort expended waiting interminably on hold after speed-redialing through jammed phone lines, and the promoters have fans precisely where they want them once the cost is revealed—at the end of an active, public, effortful commitment to the event.

More far-flung illustrations of the power of effortful commitments exist, as well. There is a tribe in southern Africa, the Thonga, that requires each of its boys to go through an elaborate initiation ceremony before he can be counted a man of the tribe. As with boys in many other primitive tribes, a Thonga boy endures a great deal before he is admitted to adult membership in the group. Anthropologists Whiting, Kluckhohn, and Anthony (1958) have described this three-month ordeal in brief but vivid terms:

> *When a boy is somewhere between 10 and 16 years of age, he is sent by his parents to "circumcision school," which is held every 4 or 5 years. Here in company with his age-mates he undergoes severe hazing by the adult males of the society. The initiation begins when each boy runs the gauntlet between two rows of men who beat him with clubs. At the end of this experience he is stripped of his clothes and his hair is cut. He is next met by a man covered with lion manes and is seated upon a stone facing this "lion man." Someone then strikes him from behind and when he turns his head to see who has struck him, his foreskin is seized and in two movements cut off by the "lion man." Afterward he is secluded for three months in the "yard of mysteries," where he can be seen only by the initiated.*
>
> *During the course of his initiation, the boy undergoes six major trials: beatings, exposure to cold, thirst, eating of unsavory foods, punishment, and the threat of death. On the slightest pretext, he may be beaten by one of the newly initiated men, who is assigned to the task by the older men of the tribe. He sleeps without covering and suffers bitterly from the winter cold. He is forbidden to drink a drop of water during the whole three months. Meals are often made nauseating by the half-digested grass from the stomach of an antelope, which is poured over his food. If he is caught*

breaking any important rule governing the ceremony, he is severely pun-
ished. For example, in one of these punishments, sticks are placed between
the fingers of the offender, then a strong man closes his hand around that
of the novice, practically crushing his fingers. He is frightened into sub-
mission by being told that in former times boys who had tried to escape or
who had revealed the secrets to women or to the uninitiated were hanged
and their bodies burned to ashes. (p. 360)

On the face of it, these rites seem extraordinary and bizarre. Yet, at the same time, they are remarkably similar in principle and even in detail to the common initiation ceremonies of school fraternities. During the traditional "Hell Week" held yearly on college campuses, fraternity pledges must persevere through a variety of activities designed by the older members to test the limits of physical exertion, psychological strain, and social embarrassment. At week's end, the boys who have persisted through the ordeal are accepted for full group membership. Mostly their tribulations have left them no more than greatly tired and a bit shaky, although sometimes the negative effects are more serious.

What is interesting is how closely the particular features of Hell Week tasks match those of tribal initiation rites. Recall that anthropologists identified six major trials to be endured by a Thonga initiate during his stay in the "yard of mysteries." A scan of newspaper reports shows that each trial also has its place in the hazing rituals of Greek-letter societies:

- *Beatings.* Fourteen-year-old Michael Kalogris spent three weeks in a Long Island hospital recovering from internal injuries suffered during a Hell Night initiation ceremony of his high-school fraternity, Omega Gamma Delta. He had been administered the "atomic bomb" by his prospective brothers, who told him to hold his hands over his head and keep them there while they gathered around to slam fists into his stomach and back simultaneously and repeatedly.
- *Exposure to cold.* On a winter night, Frederick Bronner, a California junior college student, was taken 3,000 feet up and 10 miles into the hills of a national forest by his prospective fraternity brothers. Left to find his way home wearing only a thin sweat shirt and slacks, Fat Freddy, as he was called, shivered in a frigid wind until he tumbled down a steep ravine, fracturing bones and hurting his head. Prevented by his injuries from going on, he huddled there against the cold until he died of exposure.
- *Thirst.* Two Ohio State University freshmen found themselves in the "dungeon" of their prospective fraternity house after breaking the rule requiring all pledges to crawl into the dining area prior to Hell Week meals. Once locked in the house storage closet, they were given only salty foods to eat for nearly two days. Nothing was provided for drinking purposes except a pair of plastic cups in which they could catch their own urine.

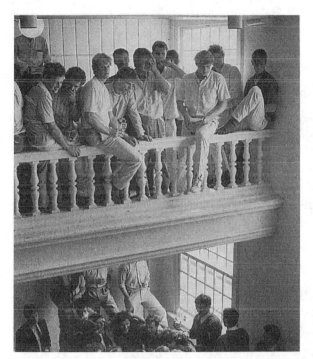

Hazy Daze

Initiation ceremonies are common to all manner of exclusive groups, although the type of initiation experience can vary widely. A Dutch debating society (left) hazes its initiates by requiring public songs and chants, while an East Los Angeles female street gang (below) pummels a new member.

- *Eating of unsavory foods.* At Kappa Sigma house on the campus of the University of Southern California, the eyes of eleven pledges bulged when they saw the sickening task before them. Eleven quarter-pound slabs of raw liver lay on a tray. Thick cut and soaked in oil, each was to be swallowed whole, one to a boy. Gagging and choking repeatedly, young Richard Swanson failed three times to down his piece. Determined to succeed, he finally got the oil-soaked meat into his throat where it lodged and, despite all efforts to remove it, killed him.
- *Punishment.* In Wisconsin, a pledge who forgot one section of a ritual incantation to be memorized by all initiates was punished for his error. He was required to keep his feet under the rear legs of a folding chair while the heaviest of his fraternity brothers sat down and drank a beer. Although the pledge did not cry out during the punishment, a bone in each of his feet was broken.
- *Threats of death.* A pledge of Zeta Beta Tau fraternity was taken to a beach area of New Jersey and told to dig his "own grave." Seconds after he complied with orders to lie flat in the finished hole, the sides collapsed, suffocating him before his prospective fraternity brothers could dig him out.

There is another striking similarity between the initiation rites of tribal and fraternal societies: They simply will not die. Resisting all attempts to eliminate or suppress them, such hazing practices have been phenomenally resilient. Authorities, in the form of colonial governments or university administrations, have tried threats, social pressures, legal actions, banishments, bribes, and bans to persuade groups to remove the hazards and humiliations from their initiation ceremonies. None has been successful. Oh, there may be a change while the authority is watching closely, but this is usually more apparent than real—the harsher trials occurring under more secret circumstances until the pressure is off when they can surface again.

On some college campuses, officials have tried to eliminate dangerous hazing practices by substituting a "Help Week" of civic service or by taking direct control of the initiation rituals. When such attempts are not slyly circumvented by fraternities, they are met with outright physical resistance. For example, in the aftermath of Richard Swanson's choking death at USC, the university president issued new rules requiring that all pledging activities be reviewed by school authorities before going into effect and that adult advisers be present during initiation ceremonies. According to one national magazine, "the new 'code' set off a riot so violent that city police and fire detachments were afraid to enter campus."

Resigning themselves to the inevitable, other college representatives have given up on the possibility of abolishing the degradations of Hell Week. "If hazing is a universal human activity, and every bit of evidence points to this conclusion, you most likely won't be able to ban it effectively. Refuse to allow it openly and it will go underground. You can't ban sex, you can't prohibit alcohol, and you probably can't eliminate hazing!" (Gordon & Gordon, 1963).

What is it about hazing practices that make them so precious to these societies? What could make the groups want to evade, undermine, or contest any effort to ban the degrading and perilous features of their initiation rights? Some have argued that the groups themselves are composed of psychological or social miscreants whose twisted needs demand that others be harmed and humiliated. The evidence, however, does not support such a view. Studies done on the personality traits of fraternity members, for instance, show them to be, if anything, slightly healthier than other college students in their psychological adjustment (for a review, see C. S. Johnson, 1972). Similarly, fraternities are known for their willingness to engage in beneficial community projects for the general social good. What they are not willing to do, however, is substitute these projects for their initiation ceremonies. One survey at the University of Washington (Walker, 1967) found that, of the fraternity chapters examined, most had a type of Help Week tradition but that this community service was *in addition* to Hell Week. In only one case was such service directly related to initiation procedures.

The picture that emerges of the perpetrators of hazing practices is of normal individuals who tend to be psychologically stable and socially concerned but who become aberrantly harsh as a group at only one time—immediately before the admission of new members to the society. The evidence, then, points to the ceremony as the culprit. There must be something about its rigors that is vital to the group. There must be some function to its harshness that the society will fight relentlessly to maintain. What?

My own view is that the answer appeared in 1959 in the results of a study little known outside of social psychology. A pair of young researchers, Elliot Aronson and Judson Mills, decided to test their observation that "persons who go through a great deal of trouble or pain to attain something tend to value it more highly than persons who attain the same thing with a minimum of effort." The real stroke of inspiration came in their choice of the initiation ceremony as the best place to examine this possibility. They found that college women who had to endure a severely embarrassing initiation ceremony in order to gain access to a sex discussion group convinced themselves that their new group and its discussions were extremely valuable, even though Aronson and Mills had rehearsed the other group members to be as "worthless and uninteresting" as possible. Different coeds who went through a much milder initiation ceremony or went through no initiation at all, were decidedly less positive about the "worthless" new group they had joined. Additional research showed the same results when coeds were required to endure pain rather than embarrassment to get into a group (Gerard & Mathewson, 1966). The more electric shock a woman received as part of the initiation ceremony, the more she later persuaded herself that her new group and its activities were interesting, intelligent, and desirable.

Now the harassments, the exertions, even the beatings of initiation rituals begin to make sense. The Thonga tribesman with tears in his eyes, watching his 10-year-old son tremble through a night on the cold ground of the "yard of mysteries," the college sophomore punctuating his Hell Night paddling of his fraternity "little brother" with bursts of nervous laughter, these are not acts of sadism. They are acts of group survival. They function, oddly enough, to spur future society members to find the group more attractive and worthwhile. As long as it is the case that people like and believe in what they have struggled to get, these groups will continue to arrange effortful and troublesome initiation rites. The loyalty and dedication of those who emerge will increase to a great degree the chances of group cohesiveness and survival. Indeed, one study of 54 tribal cultures found that those with the most dramatic and stringent initiation ceremonies were those with the greatest group solidarity (Young, 1965). Given Aronson and Mills' demonstration that the severity of an initiation ceremony significantly heightens the newcomer's *commitment* to the group, it is hardly surprising that groups will oppose all attempts to eliminate this crucial link to their future strength.

Military groups and organizations are by no means exempt from these same processes. The agonies of "boot camp" initiations to the armed services are legendary and effective. The novelist William Styron testified to this effectiveness after recounting the misery of his own U.S. Marine concentration-camp-like "training nightmare:"

> *There is no ex-Marine of my acquaintance . . . who does not view the training as a crucible out of which he emerged in some way more resilient, simply braver and better for the wear (Styron, 1977, p. 3).*

Although the rigors of basic training are widely approved by military brass, a policy of "zero tolerance" is said to exist for incidents of aberrantly harsh hazing like those contained in two videotapes uncovered by TV news sources in 1997. The tapes depicted the practice of "blood pinning," in which marine paratroopers who have completed 10 training jumps receive their golden wing pins. The pins, each with a pair of half-inch points protruding from the back, are affixed to an initiate's shirt and then ground, punched, slammed, and slapped into his chest while he writhes and screams (Gleick, 1997). Despite claims of outrage and disgust from military leaders in the aftermath, only one of the 30 marines caught perpetrating the pain was recommended for discharge. A few were assigned to receive counseling, while the participation of most (20) was simply ignored. Official pronouncements of "zero tolerance" notwithstanding, I find it instructive that the slaps delivered to the initiates were thunderous and to the heart. But, to the initiators, they were light and to the wrist. Once again, it appears that, for groups concerned about fostering a lasting sense of solidarity and distinction, the hardship of demanding initiation activities will not be easily undermined.

The Inner Choice

Examination of such diverse activities as the indoctrination practices of the Chinese Communists and the initiation rituals of college fraternities provides some valuable information about commitment. It appears that the commitments most effective in changing a person's self-image and future behavior are those that are active, public, and effortful. However, there is another property of effective commitment more important than the other three combined. To understand what it is, we first need to solve a pair of puzzles in the actions of Communist interrogators and college fraternity brothers.

The first puzzle comes from the refusal of fraternity chapters to allow public-service activities to be part of their initiation ceremonies. Recall Walker's survey (1967), which reported that community projects, though frequent, were nearly always separated from the membership-induction program. Why? If an effortful commitment is what fraternities are after in their initiation rites, surely they could structure enough distasteful and strenuous civic activities for their pledges; there is plenty of exertion and unpleasantness to be found in the world of old-age-home repairs, mental-health-center yard work, and hospital bedpan duty. Besides, community-spirited endeavors of this sort would do much to improve the highly unfavorable public and media image of fraternity Hell Week rites; a survey (Phalen, 1951) showed that for every positive newspaper story concerning Hell Week, there were five negative stories. If only for public-relations reasons, then, fraternities should want to incorporate community-service efforts into their initiation practices. But they don't.

To examine the second puzzle, we need to return to the Chinese prison camps of Korea and the political essay contests held for American captives. The Chinese wanted as many Americans as possible to enter these contests so that, in the process, they might write comments favorable to the Communist view. If, however, the idea was to attract large numbers of entrants, why were the prizes so small? A few extra cigarettes or a little fresh fruit were often all that a contest winner could expect. In the setting, even these prizes were valuable, but, still, there were much larger rewards—warm clothing, special mail privileges, increased freedom of movement in camp—that the Chinese could have used to increase the number of essay writers. Yet they specifically chose to employ the smaller rather than the larger, more motivating rewards.

Although the settings are quite different, the surveyed fraternities refused to allow civic activities into their initiation ceremonies for the same reason that the Chinese withheld large prizes in favor of less powerful inducements: They wanted the participants to *own* what they had done. No excuses, no ways out were allowed. A pledge who suffered through an arduous hazing could not be given the chance to believe he did so for charitable purposes. A prisoner who salted his political essay with anti-American comments could not be permitted to shrug it off as motivated by a big reward. No, the fraternity chapters and Chinese Communists were playing for keeps. It was not enough to wring commitments out of their men; those men had to be made to take inner responsibility for their actions.

Given the Chinese Communist government's affinity for the political essay contest as a commitment device, it should come as no surprise that a wave of such contests appeared in the aftermath of the 1989 massacre in Tiannanmen Square, where pro-democracy protesters were gunned down by government soldiers. In Beijing alone, nine state-run newspapers and television stations sponsored essay competitions on the "quelling of the counterrevolutionary rebellion." Still acting in accord with its long-standing and insightful de-emphasis of rewards for public commitments, the Beijing government left the contest prizes unspecified.

Social scientists have determined that *we accept inner responsibility for a behavior when we think we have chosen to perform it in the absence of strong outside pressure.* A large reward is one such external pressure. It may get us to perform certain actions, but it won't get us to accept inner responsibility for the acts.[3] Consequently, we won't feel committed to them. The same is true of a strong threat; it may motivate immediate compliance, but it is unlikely to produce long-term commitment.

All this has important implications for rearing children. It suggests that we should never heavily bribe or threaten our children to do the things we want them truly to believe in. Such pressures will probably produce temporary compliance with our wishes. However, if we want more than just that, if we want our children to believe in the correctness of what they have done, if we want them to continue to perform the desired behavior when we are not present to apply those outside pressures, then we must somehow arrange for them to accept inner responsibility for the actions we want them to take. An experiment by Jonathan Freedman (1965) gives us some hints about what to do and what not to do in this regard.

Freedman wanted to see if he could prevent second-to-fourth-grade boys from playing with a fascinating toy, just because he had said that it was wrong to do so some six weeks earlier. Anyone familiar with seven- to nine-year-old boys must realize the enormity of the task, but Freedman had a plan. If he could first get the boys to convince themselves that it was wrong to play with the forbidden toy, perhaps that belief would keep them from playing with it thereafter. The difficulty was making the boys believe that it was wrong to amuse themselves with the toy—an extremely expensive, battery-controlled robot.

Freedman knew it would be easy enough to have a boy obey temporarily. All he had to do was threaten the boy with severe consequences should he be caught playing with the toy. As long as he was nearby to deal out stiff punishment, Freedman figured that few boys would risk operating the robot. He was right. After showing a boy an array of five toys and warning him, "It is wrong to play with the robot. If you play with the robot, I'll be very angry and will have to do something about it," Freedman left the room for a few minutes. During that time, the boy was observed secretly through a one-way mirror. Freedman tried this threat procedure on 22 different boys, and 21 of them never touched the robot while he was gone.

So a strong threat was successful while the boys thought they might be caught and punished. Of course, Freedman had already guessed that. He was really interested in the effectiveness of the threat in guiding the boys' behavior later on, when he was no longer around. To find out what would happen then, he sent a young

---

[3]In fact, large material rewards may even reduce or "undermine" our inner responsibility for an act, causing a subsequent reluctance to perform it when the reward is no longer present (Deci & Ryan, 1985; Higgins, Lee, Kwon, & Trope, 1995; Lepper & Greene, 1978).

woman back to the boys' school about six weeks after he had been there. She took the boys out of the class one at a time to participate in an experiment. Without ever mentioning any connection with Freedman, she escorted each boy back to the room containing the five toys and gave him a drawing test. While she was scoring the test, she told the boy that he was free to play with any toy in the room. Of course, almost all of the boys played with a toy. The interesting result was that, of the boys who played with a toy, 77 percent chose to play with the robot that had been forbidden to them earlier. Freedman's severe threat, which had been so successful six weeks before, was almost totally unsuccessful when he was no longer able to back it up with punishment.

However, Freedman wasn't finished yet. He changed his procedure slightly with a second sample of boys. These boys, too, were initially shown the array of five toys by Freedman and warned not to play with the robot while he was briefly out of the room because "It is wrong to play with the robot." This time, Freedman provided no strong threat to frighten a boy into obedience. He simply left the room and observed through the one-way mirror to see if his instruction against playing with the forbidden toy was enough. It was. Just as with the other sample, only 1 of the 22 boys touched the robot during the short time Freedman was gone.

The real difference between the two samples of boys came six weeks later, when they had a chance to play with the toys while Freedman was no longer around. An astonishing thing happened with the boys who earlier had been given no strong threat against playing with the robot: When given the freedom to play with any toy they wished, most avoided the robot, even though it was by far the most attractive of the five toys available (the others were a cheap plastic submarine, a child's baseball glove without a ball, an unloaded toy rifle, and a toy tractor). When these boys played with one of the five toys, only 33 percent chose the robot.

Something dramatic had happened to both groups of boys. For the first group, it was the severe threat they heard from Freedman to back up his statement that playing with the robot was "wrong." It had been quite effective, while Freedman could catch them violating his rule. Later, though, when he was no longer present to observe the boys' behavior, his threat was impotent and his rule was, consequently, ignored. It seems clear that the threat had not taught the boys that operating the robot was wrong, only that it was unwise to do so when the possibility of punishment existed.

For the other boys, the dramatic event had come from inside, not outside. Freedman had instructed them, too, that playing with the robot was wrong, but he had added no threat of punishment should they disobey him. There were two important results. First, Freedman's instruction alone was enough to prevent the boys from operating the robot while he was briefly out of the room. Second, the boys took personal responsibility for their choices to stay away from the robot during that time. They decided that they hadn't played with it because *they* didn't want to. After all, there were no strong punishments associated with the toy to explain their behavior otherwise. Thus, weeks later, when Freedman was nowhere around, they still ignored the robot because they had been changed inside to believe that they did not want to play with it.

Adults facing the child-rearing experience can take a cue from the Freedman study. Suppose a couple wants to impress upon their daughter that lying is wrong. A strong, clear threat ("It's bad to lie, honey, so if I catch you at it, I'll cut your tongue out") might well be effective when the parents are present or when the girl thinks she can be discovered. However, it will not achieve the larger goal of convincing her that she does not want to lie because *she* thinks it's wrong. To do that, a much subtler approach is required. A reason must be given that is just strong enough to get her to be truthful most of the time but is not so strong that she sees it as the obvious reason for her truthfulness. It's a tricky business because this barely sufficient reason changes from child to child. For one child, a simple appeal may be enough ("It's bad to lie, honey, so I hope you won't do it"); for another, it may be necessary to add a somewhat stronger reason (" . . . because if you do, I'll be disappointed in you"); for a third child, a mild form of warning may be required as well (" . . . and I'll probably have to do something I don't want to do"). Wise parents will know which kind of reason will work on their own children. The important thing is to use a reason that will initially produce the desired behavior and will, at the same time, allow a child to take personal responsibility for that behavior. Thus, the less detectable outside pressure such a reason contains, the better. Selecting just the right reason is not an easy task for parents, but the effort should pay off. It is likely to mean the difference between short-lived compliance and long-term commitment. As Samuel Butler wrote more than 300 years ago, "He who agrees against his will / Is of the same opinion still."

Growing Legs to Stand On

For a pair of reasons we have already talked about, compliance professionals love commitments that produce inner change. First, that change is not just specific to the situation where it first occurred; it covers a whole range of related situations, too. Second, the effects of the change are lasting. So, once people have been induced to take actions that shift their self-images to that of, let's say, public-spirited citizens, they are likely to be public-spirited in a variety of other circumstances where their compliance may also be desired. And they are likely to continue their public-spirited behavior for as long as their new self-images hold.

There is yet another attraction in commitments that lead to inner change—they "grow their own legs." There is no need for the compliance professional to undertake a costly and continuing effort to reinforce the change; the pressure for consistency will take care of all that. After people come to view themselves as public-spirited citizens, they will automatically begin to see things differently. They will convince themselves that it is the correct way to be and will begin to pay attention to facts they hadn't noticed before about the value of community service. They will make themselves available to hear arguments they hadn't heard before favoring civic action and will find such arguments more persuasive than before. In general, because of the need to be consistent within their system of beliefs, they will assure themselves that their choice to take public-spirited action was right. What is important about this process of generating additional reasons to justify the commitment is that the reasons are *new*. Thus, even if the original reason for the civic-minded behavior were taken away, these newly discovered reasons alone might be enough to support their perceptions that they had behaved correctly.

The advantage to an unscrupulous compliance professional is tremendous. Because we build new struts to undergird choices we have committed ourselves to, an exploitative individual can offer us an inducement for making such a choice. After the decision has been made, the individual can remove that inducement, knowing that our decision will probably stand on its own newly created legs. Car dealers frequently try to benefit from this process through a trick they call "throwing a low-ball." I first encountered the tactic while posing as a sales trainee at a local Chevrolet dealership. After a week of basic instruction, I was allowed to watch the regular salespeople perform. One practice that caught my attention right away was the low-ball.

For certain customers, a very good price, perhaps as much as $400 below competitors' prices, is offered on a car. The good deal, however, is not genuine; the dealer never intends it to go through. Its only purpose is to cause prospects to *decide* to buy one of the dealership's cars. Once the decision is made, a number of activities develop the customer's sense of personal commitment to the car—a fistful of purchase forms are filled out, extensive financing terms are arranged, sometimes the customer is encouraged to drive the car for a day before signing the contract, "so you can get the feel of it and show it around the neighborhood and at work." During this time, the dealer knows, customers typically develop a range of new reasons to support their choice and to justify the investments they have now made (Brockner & Rubin, 1985; Teger, 1980).

Then something happens. Occasionally an "error" in the calculations is discovered— maybe the salesperson forgot to add the cost of the air conditioner, and if the buyer still requires air-conditioning, $400 must be added to the price. To throw suspicion off themselves, some dealers let the bank handling the financing find the mistake. At other times, the deal is disallowed at the last moment; the salesperson checks with his or her boss, who cancels it because "the dealership would be losing money." For only another $400 the car can be had, which, in the context of a multithousand-dollar deal, doesn't seem too steep since, as the salesperson emphasizes, the cost is equal to competitors' and "This is the car you chose, right?"

Another, even more insidious form of low-balling occurs when the salesperson makes an inflated trade-in offer on the prospect's old car as part of the buy/trade package. The customer recognizes the offer as overly generous and jumps at the deal. Later, before the contract is signed, the used-car manager says that the salesperson's estimate was $400 too high and reduces the trade-in allowance to its actual, blue-book level. The customer, realizing that the reduced offer is the fair one, accepts it as appropriate and sometimes feels guilty about trying to take advantage of the sales-person's high estimate. I once witnessed a woman provide an embarrassed apology to a salesman who had used the last version of low-balling on her—this while she was signing a new-car contract giving him a huge commission. He looked hurt but man-aged a forgiving smile.

No matter which variety of low-balling is used, the sequence is the same: An advantage is offered that induces a favorable purchase decision. Then, sometime after the decision has been made, but before the bargain is sealed, the original purchase advantage is deftly removed. It seems almost incredible that a customer would buy a car under these circumstances. Yet it works—not on everybody, of course, but it is effective enough to be a staple compliance procedure in many car showrooms. Au-tomobile dealers have come to understand the ability of a personal commitment to build its own support system, a support system of new justifications for the commit-ment. Often these justifications provide so many strong legs for the decision to stand on that when the dealer pulls away only one leg, the original one, there is no col-lapse. The loss can be shrugged off by the customer who is consoled, even made happy, by the array of other good reasons favoring the choice. It never occurs to the buyer that those additional reasons might never have existed had the choice not been made in the first place.

After watching the low-ball technique work so impressively in the car show-room, I decided to test its effectiveness in another setting where I could see if the basic idea worked with a bit of a twist. That is, the car salespeople I observed threw the low-ball by proposing sweet deals, getting favorable decisions as a result, and then taking away the sweet part of the offers. If my thinking about the essence of the low-ball procedure was correct, I recognized that I should be able to get the tactic to work in a somewhat different way: I could offer a good deal, which would produce the crucial decisional commitment, and then I could *add* an *un*pleasant feature to the arrangement. Because the effect of the low-ball technique was to get an individual to stick with a deal, even after circumstances had changed to make it a poor one, the tactic should work whether a positive aspect of the deal was removed or a negative aspect was added.

So, to test this latter possibility, my colleagues John Cacioppo, Rod Bassett, John Miller, and I ran an experiment designed to get Introductory Psychology students at Ohio State University to agree to perform an unpleasant activity: to wake up very early to participate in a 7:00 A.M. study "on thinking processes." When calling one sample of students, we immediately informed them of the 7:00 A.M. starting time. Only 24 percent were willing to participate. However, when calling a second sam-ple of students, we threw a low-ball: We first asked if they wanted to participate in a study of thinking processes, and after they responded—56 percent of them posi-tively—we mentioned the 7:00 A.M. start time and gave them the chance to change their minds. *None* of them did. What's more, in keeping with their commitment to participate, 95 percent of the low-balled students did come to the Psychology Building at 7:00 A.M. as promised. I know this to be the case because I recruited two research assistants to be on site at that time to conduct the thinking processes experiment and to take the names of the students who appeared.[4]

The impressive thing about the low-ball tactic is its ability to make a person feel pleased with a poor choice. Those who have only poor choices to offer us are especially fond of the technique. We can find them throwing low-balls in business, social, and personal situations. For instance, there's my neighbor Tim, a true low-ball aficionado. Recall that he's the one who, by promising to change his ways, got his girlfriend, Sara, to cancel her impending marriage to another and take him back. Since her decision to choose Tim, Sara has become more devoted to him than ever, even though he has not fulfilled his promises. She explains this by saying that she has allowed herself to see all sorts of positive qualities in Tim she had never recognized before.

I know full well that Sara is a low-ball victim. Just as I had watched buyers fall for the give-it-and-take-it-away-later strategy in the car showroom, I watched her fall for the same trick with Tim. For his part, Tim remains the guy he has always been. Because the new attractions Sara has discovered (or created) in him are quite real for her, she now seems satisfied with the same arrangement that was unacceptable before her enormous commitment. The decision to choose Tim, poor as it may have been objectively, has grown its own supports and appears to have made Sara genuinely happy. I have never mentioned to Sara what I know about lowballing. The reason for my silence is not that I think her better off in the dark on the issue. As a general guiding principle, more information is always better than less information. It's just that, if I said a word, I am confident she would hate me for it.

Standing Up for the Public Good

Depending on the motives of the person wishing to use them, any of the compliance techniques discussed in this book can be employed for good or for ill. It should not be surprising, then, that the low-ball tactic can be used for more socially beneficial purposes than selling new cars or reestablishing relationships with former lovers. One research project done in Iowa (Pallak, Cook, & Sullivan, 1980), for example,

---

[4]There is no foundation to the rumor that, in recruiting my research assistants for this task, I first asked if they wanted to administer a study on thinking processes and, after they agreed, informed them of the 7:00 A.M. starting time.

In addition to the just-described study, several other experiments have attested to the effectiveness of the low-ball procedure in a variety of circumstances (see Brownstein & Katzev, 1985; Burger & Petty, 1981; Joule, 1987; see Cialdini, Cacioppo, Bassett, & Miller, 1978, for full details).

shows how the low-ball procedure can influence homeowners to conserve energy. The project began at the start of the Iowa winter when residents who heated their homes with natural gas were contacted by an interviewer. The interviewer gave them some energy-conservation tips and asked them to try to save fuel in the future. Although they all agreed to try, when the researchers examined the utility records of these families after a month and again at winter's end, it was clear that no real savings had occurred. The residents who had promised to make a conservation attempt used just as much natural gas as did a random sample of their neighbors who had not been contacted by an interviewer. Good intentions coupled with information about saving fuel, then, were not enough to change habits.

Even before the project began, Pallak and his research team had recognized that something more would be needed to shift long-standing energy-use patterns. So they tried a slightly different procedure on a comparable sample of Iowa natural-gas users. These people, too, were contacted by an interviewer, who provided energy-saving hints and asked them to conserve, but for these families, the interviewer offered something else: Those residents agreeing to save energy would have their names publicized in newspaper articles as public-spirited, fuel-conserving citizens. The effect was immediate. One month later, when the utility companies checked their meters, the homeowners in this sample had saved an average of 422 cubic feet of natural gas apiece. The chance to have their names in the paper had motivated these residents to substantial conservation efforts for a period of a month.

Then the rug was pulled out. The researchers extracted the reason that had initially caused the people to save fuel. Each family that had been promised publicity received a letter saying it would not be possible to publicize its name after all.

At the end of the winter, the research team examined the effect the letter had on the natural-gas usage of the families. Did they return to their old, wasteful habits when the chance to be in the newspaper was removed? Hardly. For each of the remaining winter months, these families actually conserved *more* fuel than they had during the time they thought they would be publicly celebrated for it! In terms of percentage of energy savings, they had managed a 12.2 percent gas savings during the first month because they expected to see themselves lauded in the paper. However, after the letter arrived informing them to the contrary, they did not return to their previous energy-use levels; instead, they increased their savings to a 15.5 percent level for the rest of the winter.

Although we can never be completely sure of such things, one explanation for their persistent behavior presents itself immediately. These people had been low-balled into a conservation commitment through a promise of newspaper publicity. Once made, that commitment started generating its own support: The homeowners began acquiring new energy habits, began feeling good about their public-spirited efforts, began convincing themselves of the vital need to reduce American dependence on foreign fuel, began appreciating the monetary savings in their utility bills, began feeling proud of their capacity for self-denial, and most important, began viewing themselves as conservation-minded. With all these new reasons present to justify the commitment

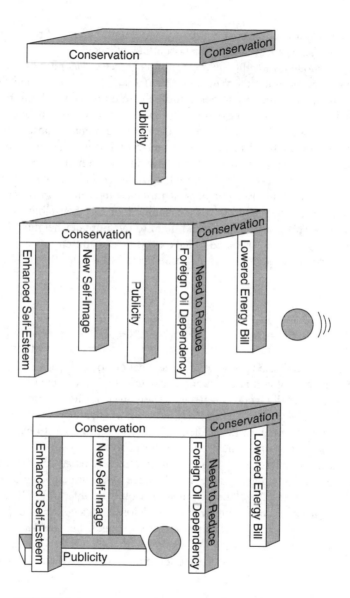

FIGURE 3.2   The Low-Ball for the Long-Term
In this illustration of the Iowa energy research, we can see how
the original conservation effort rested on the promise of publicity
(*top*). Before long, however, this energy commitment led to the
sprouting of new, self-generated supports, allowing the research
team to throw its low-ball (*middle*). The consequence was a per-
sisting level of conservation that stood firmly on its own legs
after the initial publicity prop had been knocked down (*bottom*).

to use less energy, it is no wonder that the commitment remained firm even after the original reason, newspaper publicity, had been kicked away.

Strangely enough, though, when the publicity factor was no longer a possibility, these families did not merely maintain their fuel-saving effort, they heightened it. Any of a number of interpretations could be offered for that still stronger effort, but I have a favorite. In a way, the opportunity to receive newspaper publicity had prevented the homeowners from fully owning their commitment to conservation. Of all the reasons supporting the decision to try to save fuel, it was the only one that had come from the outside; it was the only one preventing the homeowners from thinking that they were conserving gas because they believed in it. So when the letter arrived canceling the publicity agreement, it removed the only impediment to these residents' images of themselves as fully concerned, energy-conscious citizens. This unqualified, new self-image then pushed them to even greater heights of conservation. Much like Sara, they appeared to have become committed to a choice through an initial inducement and were still more dedicated to it after the inducement had been removed.[5]

DEFENSE

The only effective defense I know against the weapons of influence embodied in the combined principles of commitment and consistency is an awareness that, although consistency is generally good, even vital, there is a foolish, rigid variety to be shunned. We must be wary of the tendency to be automatically and unthinkingly consistent, for it lays us open to the maneuvers of those who want to exploit the mechanical commitment–consistency sequence for profit.

Since automatic consistency is so useful in allowing us an economical and appropriate way of behaving most of the time, however, we can't decide merely to eliminate it from our lives altogether. The results would be disastrous. If, rather than whirring along in accordance with our prior decisions and deeds, we stopped to think through the merits of each new action before performing it, we would never have time to accomplish anything significant. We need even that dangerous, mechanical brand of consistency. The only way out of the dilemma is to know when such consistency

---

[5]Fortunately, it is not necessary to use so deceptive an approach as the low-ball technique to employ the power of the commitment/consistency principle in public-service campaigns. An impressive series of studies by Richard Katzev and his students at Reed College has demonstrated the effectiveness of commitment tactics like written pledges and foot-in-the-door procedures in increasing such energy conservation behaviors as recycling, electricity usage, and bus ridership (Bachman & Katzev, 1982; Katzev & Johnson, 1983, 1984; Katzev & Pardini, 1988; Pardini & Katzev, 1983–84).

is likely to lead to a poor choice. There are certain signals—two separate kinds of signals—to tip us off. We register each type in a different part of our bodies.

Stomach Signs

The first signal is easy to recognize. It occurs right in the pit of our stomachs when we realize we are trapped into complying with a request we *know* we don't want to perform. It has happened to me a hundred times. An especially memorable instance, though, took place on a summer evening well before I began to study compliance tactics. I answered my doorbell to find a stunning young woman dressed in shorts and a revealing halter top. I noticed, nonetheless, that she was carrying a clipboard and was asking me to participate in a survey. Wanting to make a favorable impression, I agreed and, I do admit, stretched the truth in my interview answers in order to present myself in the most positive light. Our conversation went as follows:

Stunning Young Woman: Hello! I'm doing a survey on the entertainment habits of city residents, and I wonder if you could answer a few questions for me.

Cialdini: Do come in.

SYW: Thank you. I'll just sit right here and begin. How many times per week would you say you go out to dinner?

C: Oh, probably three, maybe four times a week. Whenever I can, really; I love fine restaurants.

SYW: How nice. And do you usually order wine with your dinner?

C: Only if it's imported.

SYW: I see. What about movies? Do you go to the movies much?

C: The cinema? I can't get enough of good films. I especially like the sophisticated kind with the words on the bottom of the screen. How about you? Do you like to see films?

SYW: Uh . . . yes, I do. But let's get back to the interview. Do you go to many concerts?

C: Definitely. The symphonic stuff mostly, of course. But I do enjoy a quality pop group as well.

SYW: (writing rapidly). Great! just one more question. What about touring performances by theatrical or ballet companies? Do you see them when they're in town?

C: Ah, the ballet—the movement, the grace, the form—I love it. Mark me down as *loving* the ballet. See it every chance I get.

SYW: Fine. Just let me recheck my figures here for a moment, Mr. Cialdini.

C: Actually, it's Dr. Cialdini. But that sounds so formal. Why don't you call me Bob?

SYW: All right, *Bob.* From the information you've already given me, I'm pleased to say you could save up to $1,200 a year by joining *Clubamerica!* A small membership fee entitles you to discounts on most of the activities you've mentioned. Surely someone as socially vigorous as yourself would want to take advantage of the tremendous savings our company can offer on all the things you've already told me you do.

C: (trapped like a rat). Well . . . uh . . . I . . . uh . . . I guess so.

I remember quite well feeling my stomach tighten as I stammered my agreement. It was a clear call to my brain, "Hey, you're being taken here!" But I couldn't see a way out. I had been cornered by my own words. To decline her offer at that point would have meant facing a pair of distasteful alternatives: If I tried to back out by protesting that I was not actually the man-about-town I had claimed to be during the interview, I would come off a liar; trying to refuse without that protest would make me come off a fool for not wanting to save $1,200. I bought the entertainment package, even though I knew I had been set up. The need to be consistent with what I had already said snared me.

No more, though. I listen to my stomach these days, and I have discovered a way to handle people who try to use the consistency principle on me. I just tell them exactly what they are doing. This tactic has become the perfect counterattack for me. Whenever my stomach tells me I would be a sucker to comply with a request merely because doing so would be consistent with some prior commitment I was tricked into, I relay that message to the requester. I don't try to deny the importance of consistency; I just point out the absurdity of foolish consistency. Whether, in response, the requester shrinks away guiltily or retreats in bewilderment, I am content. I have won; an exploiter has lost.

I sometimes think about the way it would be if that stunning young woman of years ago were to try to sell me an entertainment-club membership now. I have it all worked out. The entire interaction would be the same, except for the end:

SYW: . . . Surely someone as socially vigorous as yourself would want to take advantage of the tremendous savings our company can offer on all the things you've already told me you do.

C: (with great self-assurance). Quite wrong. You see, I recognize what has gone on here. I know that your story about doing a survey was just a pretext for getting people to tell you how often they go out and that, under those circumstances, there is a natural tendency to exaggerate. And I refuse to allow myself to be locked into a mechanical sequence of commitment and consistency when I know it's wrong-headed. No *click, whirr* for me.

SYW: Huh?

C: Okay, let me put it this way: (1) It would be stupid of me to spend money on something I don't want. (2) I have it on excellent authority, direct from my stomach, that I don't want your entertainment plan. (3) Therefore, if you still believe that I will buy it, you probably also still believe in the Tooth Fairy. Surely, someone as intelligent as yourself would be able to understand that.

SYW: (trapped like a stunning young rat) Well . . . uh . . . I . . . uh . . . I guess so.

Heart-of-Hearts Signs

Stomachs are not especially perceptive or subtle organs. Only when it is *obvious* that we are about to be conned are they likely to register and transmit that message. At other times, when it is not clear that we are being taken, our stomachs may never catch on. Under those circumstances we have to look elsewhere for a clue. The situation of my neighbor Sara provides a good illustration. She made an important commitment to Tim by canceling her prior marriage plans. The commitment has grown its own supports, so that even though the original reasons for the commitment are gone, she remains in harmony with it. She has convinced herself with newly formed reasons that she did the right thing, so she stays with Tim. It is not difficult to see why there would be no tightening in Sara's stomach as a result. Stomachs tell us when we are doing something we think is wrong for us. Sara *thinks* no such thing. To her mind, she has chosen correctly and is behaving consistently with that choice.

Yet, unless I badly miss my guess, there is a part of Sara that recognizes her choice as a mistake and her current living arrangement as a brand of foolish consistency. Where, exactly, that part of Sara is located we can't be sure, but our language does give it a name: heart of hearts. It is, by definition, the one place where we cannot fool ourselves. It is the place where none of our justifications, none of our rationalizations penetrate. Sara has the truth there, although right now she can't hear its signal clearly through the noise and static of the new support apparatus she has erected.

If Sara has erred in her choice of Tim, how long can she go without clearly recognizing it, without having a massive heart-of-hearts attack? There is no telling. One thing is certain, however: As time passes, the various alternatives to Tim are disappearing. She had better determine soon whether she is making a mistake.

Easier said than done, of course. She must answer an extremely intricate question: "Knowing what I now know, if I could go back in time, would I make the same choice?" The problem lies in the "knowing what I now know" part of the question. just what does she now know, accurately, about Tim? How much of what she thinks of him is the result of a desperate attempt to justify the commitment she made? She claims that, since her decision to take him back, he cares for her more, is trying hard to stop his excessive drinking, has learned to make a wonderful omelet, etc. Having tasted a couple of his omelets, I have my doubts. The important issue, though, is whether *she* believes these things, not just intellectually—but in her heart of hearts.

There may be a little device Sara can use to find out how much of her current satisfaction with Tim is real and how much is foolish consistency. Psychological evidence indicates that we experience our feelings toward something a split second before we can intellectualize about it (Murphy & Zajonc, 1993). My suspicion is that the message sent by the heart of hearts is a pure, basic feeling. Therefore, if we train ourselves to be attentive, we should register the feeling ever so slightly before our cognitive apparatus engages. According to this approach, were Sara to ask herself the crucial "would I make the same choice again?" question, she would be well advised to look for and trust the first flash of feeling she experienced in response. It would likely be the signal from her heart of hearts, slipping through undistorted just before the means by which she could kid herself flooded in.[6]

I have begun using the same device myself whenever I even suspect I might be acting in a foolishly consistent manner. One time, for instance, I had stopped at the self-service pump of a filling station advertising a price per gallon a couple of cents below the rate of other stations in the area; but with pump nozzle in hand, I noticed that the price listed on the pump was two cents higher than the display sign price. When I mentioned the difference to a passing attendant, who I later learned was the owner, he mumbled unconvincingly that the rates had changed a few days ago, but there hadn't been time to correct the display. I tried to decide what to do. Some reasons for staying came to mind—"I really do need gasoline badly." "This pump is available, and I am in sort of a hurry." "I think I remember that my car runs better on this brand of gas."

I needed to determine whether those reasons were genuine or mere justifications for my decision to stop there. So I asked myself the crucial question, "Knowing what I know about the real price of this gasoline, if I could go back in time, would I make the same choice again?" Concentrating on the first burst of impression I sensed, I received a clear and unqualified answer. I would have driven right past. I wouldn't even have slowed down. I knew then that, without the price advantage, those other reasons would not have brought me there. They hadn't created the decision; the decision had created them.

That settled, there was another decision to be faced. Since I was already there holding the hose, wouldn't it be better to use it than to suffer the inconvenience of going elsewhere to pay the same price? Fortunately, the station attendant–owner came over and helped me make up my mind. He asked why I wasn't pumping any gas. I told him I didn't like the price discrepancy and he said with a snarl, "Listen, nobody's gonna tell me how to run my business. If you think I'm cheating you, just put that hose down *right now* and get off my property as fast as you can do it, bud." Already certain he was a cheat, I was happy to act consistently with my belief and his wishes. I dropped the hose on the spot . . . and drove over it on my way to the closest exit. Sometimes consistency can be a marvelously rewarding thing.

---

[6]This is not to say that what we feel about an issue is always different from or always to be trusted more than what we think about it. However, the data are clear that our emotions and beliefs often do not point in the same direction. Therefore, in situations involving a commitment likely to have generated supporting rationalizations, feelings may well provide the truer counsel. This would be especially so when, as in the question of Sara's happiness, the issue at hand concerns an emotion (Wilson et al., 1989).

READER'S REPORT 3.2

From a Woman Living in Portland, Oregon

I was walking through downtown Portland on my way to a lunch appointment when a young, attractive man stopped me with a friendly smile and a powerful line. "Excuse me," he said, "I'm involved in a contest and I need a good-looking woman like your-self to help me win." I was truly skeptical since I know there are many women more attractive than myself running around; however, I was caught off guard and was curi-ous to find out what he wanted. He explained that he would receive points for a con-test by getting total strangers to give him a kiss. Now, I consider myself to be a fairly level-headed person who shouldn't have believed his line, but he was quite persistent, and since I was almost late for my lunch appointment, I thought, "What the heck, I'll give the guy a kiss and get out of here." So I did something totally against my common sense and pecked this total stranger on the cheek in the middle of downtown Portland!

I thought that would be the end of it, but I soon learned that it was just the be-ginning. Much to my distress, he followed the kiss with the line, "You are a great kisser, but the real contest I am involved in is to sell magazine subscriptions. You must be an active person. Would any of these magazines interest you?" At this point I should have slugged the guy and walked away, but somehow, because I had complied with his initial request, I felt a need to be consistent and I complied with his second re-quest. Yes, much to my own disbelief, I actually subscribed to *SKI* magazine (which I occasionally enjoy reading, but had no intention to subscribing to), gave him a $5 ini-tial subscription fee and left as quickly as possible, feeling quite frustrated with what I had just done and not understanding why I had done it.

Although it still pains me to think about it, in reflecting on the incident after read-ing your book I've now figured out what happened. The reason this tactic worked so effectively is because once small commitments have been made (in this case, giving a kiss), people tend to add justifications to support the commitment, and then are will-ing to commit themselves further. In this situation, I justified complying with the sec-ond request because it was consistent with my initial action. If I had only listened to my "stomach signs," I could have saved myself a lot of humiliation.

Authors' note: By extracting a kiss, the salesman exploited the consistency principle in two ways. First, by the time he asked for her aid in the magazine contest, his prospect had already gone on record—with that kiss—as agreeing to help him win a contest. Second, it seems only natural (i.e., congruent) that if a woman feels positively enough toward a man to kiss him, she should feel positively toward helping him out.

SUMMARY

- Psychologists have long recognized a desire in most people to be and look con-sistent within their words, beliefs, attitudes, and deeds. This tendency for con-sistency is fed from three sources. First, good personal consistency is highly valued by society. Second, aside from its effect on public image, generally consistent conduct provides a beneficial approach to daily life. Third, a consistent orientation affords a valuable shortcut through the complexity of modern existence. By being consistent with earlier decisions, one reduces the need to process all the relevant information in future similar situations; instead, one merely needs to recall the earlier decision and to respond consistently with it.

- Within the realm of compliance, securing an initial commitment is the key. After making a commitment (that is, taking a stand or position), people are more willing to agree to requests that are in keeping with the prior commitment. Thus, many compliance professionals try to induce people to take an initial position that is consistent with a behavior they will later request from these people. Not all commitments are equally effective, however, in producing consistent future action. Commitments are most effective when they are active, public, effortful, and viewed as internally motivated (uncoerced).

- Commitment decisions, even erroneous ones, have a tendency to be self-perpetuating because they can "grow their own legs." That is, people often add new reasons and justifications to support the wisdom of commitments they have already made. As a consequence, some commitments remain in effect long after the conditions that spurred them have changed. This phenomenon explains the effectiveness of certain deceptive compliance practices such as "throwing the low-ball."

- To recognize and resist the undue influence of consistency pressures on our compliance decisions, we should listen for signals coming from two places within us: our stomachs and our heart of hearts. Stomach signs appear when we realize that we are being pushed by commitment and consistency pressures to agree to requests we know we don't want to perform. Under these circumstances, it is best to explain to the requester that such compliance would constitute a brand of foolish consistency in which we prefer not to engage. Heart-of-heart signs are different. They are best employed when it is not clear to us that an initial commitment was wrongheaded. Here, we should ask ourselves a crucial question, "Knowing what I know, if I could go back in time, would I make the same commitment?" One informative answer may come as the first flash of feeling registered.

STUDY QUESTIONS

Content Mastery

1. Why do we want to look and be consistent in most situations?

2. Why do we find even rigid, stubborn consistency desirable in many situations?

3. Which four factors cause a commitment to affect a person's self-image and consequent future action?

4. What makes written commitments so effective?

5. What is the relationship between the compliance tactic of low-balling and the term "growing its own legs"?

Critical Thinking

1. Suppose you were advising American soldiers on a way to avoid consistency pressures like those used to gain collaboration from the POWs during the Korean War. What would you tell them?

2. In referring to the fierce loyalty of Harley-Davidson motorcycle owners, one commentator has said, "if you can persuade your customers to tattoo your name on their chests, you'll probably never have to worry about them shifting brands." Explain why this would be true. In your answer, make reference to each of the four factors that maximize the power of a commitment on future action.

3. Imagine that you are having trouble motivating yourself to study for an important exam that is less than a week away. Drawing upon your knowledge of the commitment process, describe what you would do to get yourself to put in the necessary study time. Be sure to explain why your chosen actions ought to work.

4. Think about the traditional large wedding ceremony that is characteristic of most cultures. Which features of that kind of event can be seen as commitment-enhancing devices for the couple and their families?

5. How does the ad that opens this chapter reflect the topic of the chapter?

4

Social Proof

Truths Are Us

Toyota Camry is the #1 selling car in America for the second year in a row.* Looks like we all share more in common than we think.

TOYOTA | *everyday*

©1999 Toyota Motor Sales, U.S.A., Inc. Buckle Up! Do it for those who love you. *Based on R.L. Polk 1997, 1998 calendar years total car registrations. 1-800-GO-TOYOTA ◆ www.toyota.com

I don't know anyone who likes canned laughter. In fact, when I surveyed the people who came into my office one day—several students, two telephone repairmen, a number of university professors, and the janitor—the reaction was invariably critical. Television, with its incessant system of laugh tracks and technically augmented mirth, received the most heat. The people I questioned hated canned laughter. They called it stupid, phony, and obvious. Although my sample was small, I would bet that it closely reflects the negative feelings of most of the American public toward laugh tracks.

Why, then, is canned laughter so popular with television executives? They have won their exalted positions and splendid salaries by knowing how to give the public what it wants. Yet they religiously employ the laugh tracks that their audiences find distasteful, and they do so over the objections of many of their most talented artists. It is not uncommon for acclaimed directors, writers, or actors to demand the elimination of canned responses from the television projects they undertake. These demands are only sometimes successful, and when they are, it is not without a battle, as has been the case with ABC's critically acclaimed situation-comedy *Sports Night*. Although the show's producers pressed from the start for laugh-track-free airings, network officials have relented in only one instance—when an episode explored the sensitive issue of sexual assault (Collins, 1998).

What can it be about canned laughter that is so attractive to television executives? Why are these shrewd and tested people championing a practice that their potential watchers find disagreeable and their most creative talents find personally insulting? The answer is both simple and intriguing: They know what the research says. Experiments have found that the use of canned merriment causes an audience to laugh longer and more often when humorous material is presented and to rate the material as funnier (Fuller & Sheehy-Skeffington, 1974; Smyth & Fuller, 1972). In addition, some evidence indicates that canned laughter is most effective for poor jokes (Nosanchuk & Lightstone, 1974).

In light of these data, the actions of television executives make perfect sense. The introduction of laugh tracks into their comic programming increases the humorous and appreciative responses of an audience, even—and especially—when the material is of poor quality. Is it any surprise, then, that television, glutted as it is with artless situation-comedies, is saturated with canned laughter? Those executives know precisely what they are doing.

With the mystery of the widespread use of laugh tracks solved, we are left with a more perplexing question: Why does canned laughter work on us the way it does? It is no longer the television executives who appear peculiar; they are acting logically and in their own interests. Instead, it is the behavior of the audience that seems strange. Why should we laugh more at comedy material afloat in a sea of mechanically fabricated merriment? And why should we think that comic flotsam funnier? The executives aren't really fooling us. Anyone can recognize dubbed laughter. It is so blatant, so clearly counterfeit, that there can be no confusing it with the real thing. We know full well that the hilarity we hear is irrelevant to the humorous quality of the joke it follows, is created not spontaneously by a genuine audience but artificially by a technician at a control board. Yet, transparent forgery that it is, it works on us!

THE PRINCIPLE OF SOCIAL PROOF

To discover why canned laughter is so effective, we first need to understand the nature of yet another potent weapon of influence: the principle of social proof. This principle states that we determine what is correct by finding out what other people think is correct. The principle applies especially to the way we decide what constitutes correct behavior. *We view a behavior as correct in a given situation to the degree that we see others performing it.* Whether the question is what to do with an empty popcorn box in a movie theater, how fast to drive on a certain stretch of highway, or how to eat the chicken at a dinner party, the actions of those around us will be important guides in defining the answer.

The tendency to see an action as appropriate when others are doing it works quite well normally. As a rule, we will make fewer mistakes by acting in accord with social evidence than by acting contrary to it. Usually, when a lot of people are doing something, it is the right thing to do. This feature of the principle of social proof is simultaneously its major strength and its major weakness. Like the other weapons of influence, it provides a convenient shortcut for determining the way to behave but, at the same time, makes one who uses the shortcut vulnerable to the attacks of profiteers who lie in wait along its path.

In the case of canned laughter, the problem comes when we begin responding to social proof in such a mindless and reflexive fashion that we can be fooled by partial or fake evidence. Our folly is not that we use others' laughter to help decide what is humorous; that is in keeping with the well-founded principle of social proof. The folly is that we do so in response to patently fraudulent laughter. Somehow, one disembodied feature of humor—a sound—works like the essence of humor. The example from Chapter 1 of the turkey and the polecat is instructive. Because the peculiar cheep-cheep of turkey chicks is normally associated with newborn turkeys, their mothers will display or withhold maternal care solely on the basis of that sound. Remember how, consequently, it was possible to fool a mother turkey with a stuffed polecat as long as the replica played the recorded cheep-cheep of a baby turkey. The simulated chick sound was enough to start the mother turkey's maternal tape whirring.

The lesson of the turkey and the polecat illustrates uncomfortably well the relationship between the average viewer and the laugh-track-playing television executive. We have become so accustomed to taking the humorous reactions of others as evidence of what deserves laughter that we too can be made to respond to the sound, and not the substance, of the real thing. Much as a cheep-cheep noise removed from the reality of a chick can stimulate a female turkey to mother, so can a recorded ha-ha removed from the reality of a genuine audience stimulate us to laugh. The television executives are exploiting our preference for shortcuts, our tendency to react automatically on the basis of partial evidence. They know that their tapes will cue our tapes. *Click, whirr*

People Power

Television executives are hardly alone in their use of social evidence for profit. Our tendency to assume that an action is more correct if others are doing it is exploited in a variety of settings. Bartenders often salt their tip jars with a few dollar bills at the beginning of an evening to simulate tips left by prior customers and thereby to give the impression that tipping with folding money is proper barroom behavior. Church ushers sometimes salt collection baskets for the same reason and with the same positive effect on proceeds. Evangelical preachers are known to seed their audience with ringers, who are rehearsed to come forward at a specified time to give witness and donations. For example, a research team at Arizona State University infiltrated the Billy Graham organization and reported on such advance preparations prior to one of his Crusade visits: "By the time Graham arrives in town and makes his altar call, an army of six thousand wait with instructions on when to come forth at varying intervals to create the impression of a spontaneous mass outpouring" (Altheide & Johnson, 1977).

Advertisers love to inform us when a product is the "fastest-growing" or "largest-selling" because they don't have to convince us directly that the product is good; they need only say that many others think so, which seems proof enough. The producers of charity telethons devote inordinate amounts of time to the incessant listing of viewers who have already pledged contributions. The message being communicated to the holdouts is clear: "Look at all the people who have decided to give. It *must* be the correct thing to do." Certain nightclub owners manufacture a brand of visible social proof for their clubs' quality by creating long waiting lines outside when there is plenty of room inside. Salespeople are taught to spice their pitches with numerous accounts of individuals who have purchased the product. Sales and motivation consultant Cavett Robert captures the principle nicely in his advice to sales trainees: "Since 95 percent of the people are imitators and only 5 percent initiators, people are persuaded more by the actions of others than by any proof we can offer."

Researchers, too, have employed procedures based on the principle of social proof—sometimes with astounding results.[1] One psychologist in particular, Albert Bandura, has led the way in developing such procedures to eliminate undesirable

---

[1] A program of investigation conducted by Kenneth Craig and his associates demonstrates how the experience of pain can be affected by the principle of social proof. In one study (Craig & Prkachin, 1978), subjects who received a series of electric shocks felt less pain (as indicated by self-reports, psychophysical measures of sensory sensitivity, and such physiological responses as heart rate and skin conductivity) when they were in the presence of another subject who was tolerating the shocks as if they were not painful.

Fifty Million Americans Can't Be Wrong

behavior. Bandura and his colleagues have shown how people suffering from pho-
bias can be rid of these extreme fears in an amazingly simple fashion. For instance,
in an early study (Bandura, Grusec, & Menlove, 1967), nursery-school-age children,
chosen because they were terrified of dogs, merely watched a little boy playing happily with a dog for 20 minutes a day. This exhibition produced such marked changed

in the reactions of the fearful children that, after only four days, 67 percent of them were willing to climb into a playpen with a dog and remain confined there petting and scratching the dog while everyone else left the room. Moreover, when the researchers tested the children's fear levels again, one month later, they found that the improvement had not diminished during that time; in fact, the children were more willing than ever to interact with dogs. An important practical discovery was made in a second study of children who were exceptionally afraid of dogs (Bandura & Menlove, 1968): To reduce these children's fears, it was not necessary to provide live demonstrations of another child playing with a dog; film clips had the same impact. The most effective clips were those depicting a variety of other children interacting with their dogs. Apparently, the principle of social proof works best when the proof is provided by the actions of many other people.[2]

The powerful influence of filmed examples in changing the behavior of children can be used as therapy for various other problems. Some striking evidence is available in the research of psychologist Robert O'Connor (1972) on socially withdrawn preschool children. We have all seen children of this sort: terribly shy, standing alone at the fringes of the games and groupings of their peers. O'Connor worried that this early behavior was the beginning of what could become a long-term pattern of isolation, which in turn could create persistent difficulties in social comfort and adjustment throughout adulthood. In an attempt to reverse the pattern, O'Connor made a film containing 11 different scenes in a nursery-school setting. Each scene began by showing a different solitary child watching some social activity and then actively participating, to everyone's enjoyment. O'Connor selected a group of the most severely withdrawn children from four preschools and showed them this film. The impact was impressive. After watching the film, the isolates immediately began to interact with their peers at a level equal to that of the normal children in the schools. Even more astonishing was what O'Connor found when he returned to the schools six weeks later to observe. While the withdrawn children who had not seen O'Connor's film remained as isolated as ever, those who *had* viewed it were now leading their schools in amount of social activity. It seems that this 23-minute movie, viewed

---

[2]Any reader who doubts that the seeming appropriateness of an action is importantly influenced by the number of others performing it might try a small experiment. Stand on a busy sidewalk, pick an empty spot in the sky or on a tall building, and stare at it for a full minute. Very little will happen around you during that time—most people will walk past without glancing up, and virtually no one will stop to stare with you. Now, on the next day, go to the same place and bring along four friends to look upward too. Within 60 seconds, a crowd of passersby will have stopped to crane their necks skyward with the group. For those pedestrians who do not join you, the pressure to look up at least briefly will be nearly irresistable; if the results of your experiment are like those of one performed by three social psychologists in New York, you and your friends will cause 80 percent of all passersby to lift their gaze to your empty spot (Milgram, Bickman, & Berkowitz, 1969).

Looking for Higher (and Higher) Meaning
The draw of the crowd is devilishly strong.
© Punch/Rothco

just once, was enough to reverse a potential pattern of lifelong maladaptive behavior. Such is the potency of the principle of social proof.[3]

After the Deluge

When it comes to illustrating the strength of social proof, there is one illustration that is far and away my favorite. Several features account for its appeal: It offers a su-

---

[3]Other research besides O'Connor's suggests that there are two sides to the filmed-social-proof coin, however. The dramatic effect of filmed depictions on what children find appropriate has been a source of great distress for those concerned with frequent depictions of violence and aggression on television (Eron & Huesmann, 1985). Although the consequences of televised violence on the aggressive actions of children are far from simple (Freedman, 1984), the data from a well-controlled experiment by psychologists Robert Liebert and Robert Baron (1972) have an ominous look. Some children were shown excerpts from a television program in which people intentionally harmed each other. Afterward, these children acted in a significantly more harmful way toward other children than did those who had watched a nonviolent television program (a horse race). The finding that children act more aggressively toward one another after seeing aggression on television held true for the two age groups tested (5- to 6- and 8- to 9-year-olds) and for both girls and boys.

perb example of the much underused method of participant observation, in which a scientist studies a process by becoming immersed in its natural occurrence; it provides information of interest to such diverse groups as historians, psychologists, and theologians; and, most important, it shows how social evidence can be used on us—not by others, but by ourselves—to assure us that what we prefer to be true will seem to be true.

The story is an old one, requiring an examination of ancient data, for the past is dotted with millennial religious movements. Various sects and cults have prophesied that on a particular date there would arrive a period of redemption and great happiness for those who believed in the group's teachings. In each instance it has been predicted that the beginning of a time of salvation would be marked by an important and undeniable event, usually the cataclysmic end of the world. Of course, these predictions have invariably proved false, to the acute dismay of the members of such groups.

However, immediately following the obvious failure of the prophecy, history records an enigmatic pattern. Rather than disbanding in disillusion, the cultists often become strengthened in their convictions. Risking the ridicule of the populace, they take to the streets, publicly asserting their dogma and seeking converts with a fervor that is intensified, not diminished, by the clear disconfirmation of a central belief. So it was with the Montanists of second-century Turkey, with the Anabaptists of sixteenth-century Holland, with the Sabbataists of seventeenth-century Izmir, and with the Millerites of nineteenth-century America. And, thought a trio of interested social scientists, so it might be with a doomsday cult based in modern-day Chicago. The scientists—Leon Festinger, Henry Riecken, and Stanley Schachter—who were then colleagues at the University of Minnesota, heard about the Chicago group and felt it worthy of close study. Their decision to investigate by joining the group, incognito, as new believers and by placing additional paid observers among its ranks resulted in a remarkably rich firsthand account of the goings-on before and after the day of predicted catastrophe (Festinger, Riecken, & Schachter, 1964).

The cult of believers was small, never numbering more than 30 members. Its leaders were a middle-aged man and woman, whom for purposes of publication, the researchers renamed Dr. Thomas Armstrong and Mrs. Marian Keech. Dr. Armstrong, a physician on the staff of a college student-health service, had a long-held interest in mysticism, the occult, and flying saucers; as such, he served as a respected authority on these subjects for the group. Mrs. Keech, though, was the center of attention and activity. Earlier in the year she had begun to receive messages from spiritual beings, whom she called the Guardians, located on other planets. It was these messages, flowing through Marian Keech's hand via the device of "automatic writing," that formed the bulk of the cult's religious belief system. The teachings of the Guardians were loosely linked to traditional Christian thought.

The transmissions from the Guardians, always the subject of much discussion and interpretation among the group, gained new significance when they began to foretell of a great impending disaster—a flood that would begin in the Western Hemisphere and eventually engulf the world. Although the cultists were understandably alarmed at first, further messages assured them that they and all those who believed in the lessons sent through Mrs. Keech would survive. Before the calamity, space-men were to arrive and carry off the believers in flying saucers to a place of safety, presumably on another planet. Very little detail was provided about the rescue except that the believers were to make themselves ready for pickup by rehearsing certain passwords to be exchanged ("I left my hat at home." "What is your question?" "I am my own porter.") and by removing all metal from their clothes—because the wearing or carrying of metal made saucer travel "extremely dangerous."

As Festinger, Riecken, and Schachter observed the preparations during the weeks prior to the flood date, they noted with special interest two significant aspects of the members' behavior. First, the level of commitment to the cult's belief system was very high. In anticipation of their departure from doomed Earth, irrevocable steps were taken by the group members. Most incurred the opposition of family and friends to their beliefs but persisted, nonetheless, in their convictions, often when it meant losing the affections of these others. In fact, several of the members were threatened by neighbors or family with legal actions designed to have them declared insane. Dr. Armstrong's sister filed a motion to have his two younger children removed from his custody. Many believers quit their jobs or neglected their studies to devote full time to the movement. Some even gave or threw away their personal belongings, expecting them shortly to be of no use. These were people whose certainty that they had the truth allowed them to withstand enormous social, economic, and legal pressures and whose commitment to their dogma grew as they resisted each pressure.

The second significant aspect of the believers' preflood actions was a curious form of inaction. For individuals so clearly convinced of the validity of their creed, they did surprisingly little to spread the word. Although they initially publicized the news of the coming disaster, they made no attempt to seek converts, to proselyte actively. They were willing to sound the alarm and to counsel those who voluntarily responded to it, but that was all.

The group's distaste for recruitment efforts was evident in various ways besides the lack of personal persuasion attempts. Secrecy was maintained in many matters—extra copies of the lessons were burned, passwords and secret signs were instituted, the contents of certain private tape recordings were not to be discussed with outsiders (so secret were the tapes that even longtime believers were prohibited from taking notes of them). Publicity was avoided. As the day of disaster approached, increasing numbers of newspaper, television, and radio reporters converged on the group's headquarters in the Keech house. For the most part, these people were turned away or ignored. The most frequent answer to their questions was, "No comment." Although discouraged for a time, the media representatives returned with a vengeance when Dr. Armstrong's religious activities caused him to be fired from his post on the college health service staff; one especially persistent newsman had to be threatened with a lawsuit. A similar siege was repelled on the eve of the flood when a swarm of reporters pushed and pestered the believers for information. Afterward, the researchers summarized the group's preflood stance on public exposure and recruitment in respectful tones: "Exposed to a tremendous burst of publicity, they had made every attempt to dodge fame; given dozens of opportunities to proselyte, they had remained evasive and secretive and behaved with an almost superior indifference" (Festinger et al., 1964).

Eventually, when all the reporters and would-be converts had been cleared from the house, the believers began making their final preparations for the arrival of the spaceship scheduled for midnight that night. The scene as viewed by Festinger, Riecken, and Schachter must have seemed like absurdist theater. Otherwise ordinary people—housewives, college students, a high-school boy, a publisher, a physician, a hardware-store clerk and his mother—were participating earnestly in tragic comedy. They took direction from a pair of members who were periodically in touch with the Guardians; Marian Keech's written messages were being supplemented that evening by "the Bertha," a former beautician through whose tongue the "Creator" gave instruction. They rehearsed their lines diligently, calling out in chorus the responses to be made before entering the rescue saucer: "I am my own porter." "I am my own pointer." They discussed seriously whether the message from a caller identifying himself as Captain Video—a TV space character of the time—was properly interpreted as a prank or a coded communication from their rescuers.

In keeping with the admonition to carry nothing metallic aboard the saucer, the believers wore clothing from which all metal pieces had been torn out. The metal eyelets in their shoes had been ripped away. The women were braless or wore brassieres whose metal stays had been removed. The men had yanked the zippers out of their pants, which were supported by lengths of rope in place of belts.

The group's fanaticism concerning the removal of all metal was vividly experienced by one of the researchers who remarked, 25 minutes before midnight, that he had forgotten to extract the zipper from his trousers. As the observers tell it, "this knowledge produced a near panic reaction. He was rushed into the bedroom where Dr. Armstrong, his hands trembling and his eyes darting to the clock every few seconds, slashed out the zipper with a razor blade and wrenched its clasps free with wirecutters." The hurried operation finished, the researcher was returned to the living room—a slightly less metallic but, one supposes, much paler man.

As the time appointed for their departure grew very close, the believers settled into a lull of soundless anticipation. Luckily, the trained scientists gave a detailed account of the events that transpired during this momentous period.

The last ten minutes were tense ones for the group in the living room. They had nothing to do but sit and wait, their coats in their laps. In the tense silence two clocks ticked loudly, one about ten minutes faster than the other. When the faster of the two pointed to twelve-five, one of the observers remarked aloud on the fact. A chorus of people replied that midnight had not yet come. Bob Eastman affirmed that the slower clock was correct; he had set it himself only that afternoon. It showed only four min-utes before midnight.

These four minutes passed in complete silence except for a single ut-terance. When the [slower] clock on the mantel showed only one minute re-maining before the guide to the saucer was due, Marian exclaimed in a strained, high-pitched voice: "And not a plan has gone astray!" The clock chimed twelve, each stroke painfully clear in the expectant hush. The be-lievers sat motionless.

One might have expected some visible reaction. Midnight had passed and nothing had happened. The cataclysm itself was less than seven hours away. But there was little to see in the reactions of the people in the room. There was no talking, no sound. People sat stock-still, their faces seemingly frozen and expressionless. Mark Post was the only person who even moved. He lay down on the sofa and closed his eyes but did not sleep. Later, when spoken to, he answered monosyllabically but otherwise lay immobile. The others showed nothing on the surface, although it became clear later that they had been hit hard. . . .

Gradually, painfully, an atmosphere of despair and confusion settled over the group. They reexamined the prediction and the accompanying messages. Dr. Armstrong and Mrs. Keech reiterated their faith. The be-lievers mulled over their predicament and discarded explanation after ex-planation as unsatisfactory. At one point, toward 4 A.M., Mrs. Keech broke down and cried bitterly. She knew, she sobbed, that there were some who were beginning to doubt but that the group must beam light to those who needed it most and that the group must hold together. The rest of the be-lievers were losing their composure, too. They were all visibly shaken and many were close to tears. It was now almost 4:30 A.M. and still no way of handling the disconfirmation had been found. By now, too, most of the group were talking openly about the failure of the escort to come at midnight. The group seemed near dissolution. (Festinger et al., 1964, pp. 162–163, 168)

In the midst of gathering doubt, as cracks crawled through the believers' con-fidence, the researchers witnessed a pair of remarkable incidents, one after another. The first occurred at about 4:45 A.M. when Marian Keech's hand suddenly began transcribing through "automatic writing" the text of a holy message from above. When read aloud, the communication proved to be an elegant explanation for the events of that night. "The little group, sitting alone all night long, had spread so much light that God had saved the world from destruction." Although neat and ef-ficient, this explanation was not wholly satisfying by itself; for example, after hear-ing it, one member simply rose, put on his hat and coat, and left, never to return. Something additional was needed to restore the believers to their previous levels of faith.

It was at this point that the second notable incident occurred to supply that need. Once again, the words of those who were present offer a vivid description:

The atmosphere in the group changed abruptly and so did their behavior. Within minutes after she had read the message explaining the disconfirmation, Mrs. Keech received another message instructing her to publicize the explanation. She reached for the telephone and began dialing the number of a newspaper. While she was waiting to be connected, someone asked: "Marian, is this the first time you have called the newspaper yourself?" Her reply was immediate: "Oh yes, this is the first time I have ever called them. I have never had anything to tell them before, but now I feel it is urgent." The whole group could have echoed her feelings, for they all felt a sense of urgency. As soon as Marian had finished her call, the other members took turns telephoning newspapers, wire service, radio stations, and national magazines to spread the explanation of the failure of the flood. In their desire to spread the word quickly and resoundingly, the believers now opened for public attention matters that had been thus far utterly secret. Where only hours earlier they had shunned newspaper reporters and felt that the attention they were getting in the press was painful, they now became avid seekers for publicity. (Festinger et al., 1964, p. 170)

Not only had the long-standing policies concerning secrecy and publicity done an about-face, so too had the group's attitude toward potential converts. Whereas likely recruits who previously visited the house had been mostly ignored, turned away, or treated with casual attention, the day following the disconfirmation saw a different story. All callers were admitted, all questions were answered, attempts were made to proselyte all such visitors. The members' unprecedented willingness to accommodate new recruits was perhaps best demonstrated when nine high-school students arrived on the following night to speak with Mrs. Keech.

They found her at the telephone deep in a discussion of flying saucers with a caller whom, it later turned out, she believed to be a spaceman. Eager to continue talking to him and at the same time anxious to keep her new guests, Marian simply included them in the conversation and, for more than an hour, chatted alternately with her guests in the living room and the "spaceman" on the other end of the telephone. So intent was she on proselyting that she seemed unable to let any opportunity go by. (Festinger et al., 1964, p. 178)

To what can we attribute the believers' radical turnabout? Within a few hours, they had moved from clannish and taciturn hoarders of the Word to expansive and eager disseminators of it. What could have possessed them to choose such an ill-timed instant—when the failure of the flood was likely to cause nonbelievers to view the group and its dogma as laughable?

The crucial event occurred sometime during "the night of the flood" when it became increasingly clear that the prophecy would not be fulfilled. Oddly, it was not their prior certainty that drove the members to propagate the faith, it was an encroaching sense of uncertainty. It was the dawning realization that if the spaceship and flood predictions were wrong, so might be the entire belief system on which they rested. For those huddled in the Keech living room, that growing possibility must have seemed hideous.

The group members had gone too far, given up too much for their beliefs to see them destroyed; the shame, the economic cost, the mockery would be too great to bear. The overarching need of the cultists to cling to those beliefs seeps poignantly from their own words. From a young woman with a 3-year-old child:

> *I have to believe the flood is coming on the twenty-first because I've spent all my money. I quit my job, I quit computer school. . . . I have to believe. (p. 168)*

From Dr. Armstrong to one of the researchers four hours after the failure of the saucermen to arrive:

> *I've had to go a long way. I've given up just about everything. I've cut every tie. I've burned every bridge. I've turned my back on the world. I can't afford to doubt. I have to believe. And there isn't any other truth. (p. 168)*

Imagine the corner in which Dr. Armstrong and his followers found themselves as morning approached. So massive was the commitment to their beliefs that no other truth was tolerable. Yet that set of beliefs had just taken a merciless pounding from physical reality: No saucer had landed, no spacemen had knocked, no flood had come, nothing had happened as prophesied. Since the only acceptable form of truth had been undercut by physical proof, there was but one way out of the corner for the group. It had to establish another type of proof for the validity of its beliefs: social proof.

This, then, explains their sudden shift from secretive conspirators to zealous missionaries. It also explains the curious timing of the shift—precisely when a direct disconfirmation of their beliefs had rendered them least convincing to outsiders. It was necessary to risk the scorn and derision of the nonbelievers because publicity and recruitment efforts provided the only remaining hope. If they could spread the Word, if they could inform the uninformed, if they could persuade the skeptics, and if, by so doing, they could win new converts, their threatened but treasured beliefs would become *truer.* The principle of social proof says so: *The greater the number of people who find any idea correct, the more a given individual will perceive the idea to be correct.* The group's assignment was clear; since the physical evidence could not be changed, the social evidence had to be. Convince and ye shall be convinced.[4]

CAUSE OF DEATH: UNCERTAIN(TY)

All the weapons of influence discussed in this book work better under some conditions than under others. If we are to defend ourselves adequately against any such weapon, it is vital that we know its optimal operating conditions in order to recognize when we are most vulnerable to its influence. We have already had a hint of one time when the principle of social proof worked best with the Chicago believers. It was a sense of shaken confidence that triggered their craving for converts. In general, when we are unsure of ourselves, when the situation is unclear or ambiguous, when uncertainty reigns, we are most likely to look to and accept the actions of others as correct (Tesser, Campbell, & Mickler, 1983; Wooten & Reed, 1998).

In the process of examining the reactions of other people to resolve our uncertainty, however, we are likely to overlook a subtle, but important fact: Those people are probably examining the social evidence, too. Especially in an ambiguous situation, the tendency for everyone to be looking to see what everyone else is doing can lead to a fascinating phenomenon called *pluralistic ignorance.* A thorough understanding of the pluralistic ignorance phenomenon helps explain a regular occurrence in our country that has been termed both a riddle and a national disgrace: the failure of entire groups of bystanders to aid victims in agonizing need of help.

The classic example of such bystander inaction and the one that has produced the most debate in journalistic, political, and scientific circles began as an ordinary homicide case in New York City's borough of Queens. A woman in her late twenties,

---

[4]Perhaps because of the quality of ragged desperation with which they approached their task, the believers were wholly unsuccessful at enlarging their number. Not a single convert was gained. At that point, in the face of the dual failures of physical and social proof, the cult quickly disintegrated. Less than three weeks after the date of the predicted flood, group members were scattered and maintained only sporadic communication with one another. In one final—and ironic—disconfirmation of prediction, it was the movement that perished in the flood.

Ruin has not always been the fate of doomsday groups whose predictions proved unsound, however. When such groups have been able to build social proof for their beliefs through effective recruitment efforts, they have grown and prospered. For example, when the Dutch Anabaptists saw their prophesied year of destruction, 1533, pass uneventfully, they became rabid seekers after converts, pouring unprecedented amounts of energy into the cause. One extraordinarily eloquent missionary, Jakob van Kampen, is reported to have baptized 100 persons in a single day. So powerful was the snowballing social evidence in support of the Anabaptist position that it rapidly overwhelmed the disconfirming physical evidence and turned two-thirds of the population of Holland's great cities into adherents.

Catherine Genovese, was killed in a late-night attack on her street as she returned from work. Murder is never an act to be passed off lightly, but in a city the size and tenor of New York, the Genovese incident warranted no more space than a fraction of a column in the *New York Times.* Catherine Genovese's story would have died with her on that day in March 1964 if it hadn't been for a mistake.

The metropolitan editor of the *Times,* A. M. Rosenthal, happened to be having lunch with the city police commissioner a week later. Rosenthal asked the commissioner about a different Queens-based homicide, and the commissioner, thinking he was being questioned about the Genovese case, revealed something staggering that had been uncovered by the police investigation. It was something that left everyone who heard it, the commissioner included, aghast and grasping for explanations. Catherine Genovese had not experienced a quick, muffled death. It had been a long, loud, tortured, *public* event. Her assailant had chased and attacked her in the street three times over a period of 35 minutes before his knife finally silenced her cries for help. Incredibly, 38 of her neighbors watched from the safety of their apartment windows without so much as lifting a finger to call the police.

Rosenthal, a former Pulitzer Prize winning reporter, knew a story when he heard one. On the day of his lunch with the commissioner, he assigned a reporter to investigate the "bystander angle" of the Genovese incident. Within a week, the *Times* published a long, front-page article that was to create a swirl of controversy and speculation. The initial paragraphs of that report provided the tone and focus of the story:

> *For more than half an hour 38 respectable, law-abiding citizens in Queens watched a killer stalk and stab a woman in three separate attacks in Kew Gardens.*
>
> *Twice the sound of their voices and the sudden glow of their bedroom lights interrupted him and frightened him off. Each time he returned, sought her out, and stabbed her again. Not one person telephoned the police during the assault; one witness called after the woman was dead.*
>
> *That was two weeks ago today. But Assistant Chief Inspector Frederick M. Lussen, in charge of the borough's detectives and a veteran of 25 years of homicide investigations, is still shocked.*
>
> *He can give a matter-of-fact recitation of many murders. But the Kew Gardens slaying baffles him—not because it is a murder, but because "good people" failed to call the police. (Ganzberg, 1964, p. 7)*

As with Assistant Chief Inspector Lussen, shock and bafflement were the standard reactions of almost everyone who learned the story's details. The shock struck first, leaving the police, the newspeople, and the reading public stunned. The bafflement followed quickly. How could 38 "good people" fail to act under those circumstances? No one could understand it. Even the murder witnesses themselves were bewildered. "I don't know," they answered one after another. "I just don't know." A few offered weak reasons for their inaction. For example, two or three people explained that they were "afraid" or "did not want to get involved." These reasons, however, do not stand up to close scrutiny: A simple anonymous call to the police could have saved Catherine Genovese without threatening the witnesses' future safety or free time. No, it wasn't the observers' fear or reluctance to complicate their lives that explained their lack of action; something else was going on there that even they could not fathom.

Confusion, though, does not make for good news copy. So the press as well as the other media—several papers, TV stations, and magazines that were pursuing follow-up stories—emphasized the only explanation available at the time: The witnesses, no different from the rest of us, hadn't cared enough to get involved. Americans were becoming a nation of selfish, insensitive people. The rigors of modern life, especially city life, were hardening them. They were becoming "The Cold Society," unfeeling and indifferent to the plight of their fellow citizens.

In support of this interpretation, news stories began appearing regularly in which various kinds of public apathy were detailed. Also supporting such an interpretation were the remarks of a range of armchair social commentators, who, as a breed, seem never to admit to bafflement when speaking to the press. They, too, saw the Genovese case as having large-scale social significance. All used the word *apathy,* which, it is interesting to note, had been in the headline of the *Times's* front-page story, although they accounted for the apathy differently. One attributed it to the effects of TV violence, another to repressed aggressiveness, but most implicated the "depersonalization" of urban life with its "megalopolitan societies" and its "alienation of the individual from the group." Even Rosenthal, the newsman who first broke the story and who ultimately made it the subject of a book, subscribed to the city-caused apathy theory.

> *Nobody can say why the 38 did not lift the phone while Miss Genovese was being attacked, since they cannot say themselves. It can be assumed, however, that their apathy was indeed one of the big-city variety. It is almost a matter of psychological survival, if one is surrounded and pressed by millions of people, to prevent them from constantly impinging on you, and the only way to do this is to ignore them as often as possible. Indifference to one's neighbor and his troubles is a conditioned reflex in life in New York as it is in other big cities. (A. M. Rosenthal, 1964, pp. 82–83)*

As the Genovese story grew—aside from Rosenthal's book, it became the focus of numerous newspaper and magazine pieces, several television news documentaries, and an off-Broadway play—it attracted the professional attention of a pair of New York-based psychology professors, Bibb Latané and John Darley (1968b). They examined the reports of the Genovese incident and, on the basis of their knowledge of social psychology, hit on what had seemed like the most unlikely explanation of all—the fact that 38 witnesses were present. Previous accounts of the story had invariably emphasized that no action was taken, *even though* 38 individuals had looked on. Latané and Darley suggested that no one had helped precisely *because* there were so many observers.

The psychologists speculated that, for at least two reasons, a bystander to an emergency will be unlikely to help when there are a number of other bystanders present. The first reason is fairly straightforward. *With several potential helpers around, the personal responsibility of each individual is reduced:* "Perhaps someone else will give or call for aid, perhaps someone else already has." So with everyone thinking that someone else will help or has helped, no one does. The second reason is the more psychologically intriguing one; it is founded on the principle of social proof and involves the pluralistic ignorance effect. Very often an emergency is not obviously an emergency. Is the man lying in the alley a heart-attack victim or a drunk sleeping one off? Is the commotion next door an assault requiring the police or an especially loud marital spat where intervention would be inappropriate and unwelcome? What is going on? In times of such uncertainty, the natural tendency is to look around at the actions of others for clues. We can learn from the way the other witnesses are reacting whether the event is or is not an emergency.

What is easy to forget, though, is that everybody else observing the event is likely to be looking for social evidence, too. Because we all prefer to appear poised and unflustered among others, we are likely to search for that evidence placidly, with brief, camouflaged glances at those around us. Therefore everyone is likely to see everyone else looking unruffled and failing to act. As a result, and by the principle of social proof, the event will be roundly interpreted as a nonemergency. This, according to Latané and Darley (1968b) is the state of pluralistic ignorance "in which each person decided that since nobody is concerned, nothing is wrong. Meanwhile, the danger may be mounting to the point where a single individual, uninfluenced by the seeming calm of others, *would* react."[5]

---

[5]The potentially tragic consequences of the pluralistic ignorance phenomenon are starkly illustrated in a UPI news release from Chicago:

> *A university coed was beaten and strangled in daylight hours near one of the most popular tourist attractions in the city, police said Saturday.*
>
> *The nude body of Lee Alexis Wilson, 23, was found Friday in dense shrubbery alongside the wall of the Art Institute by a 12-year-old boy playing in the bushes.*
>
> *Police theorized she may have been sitting or standing by a fountain in the Art Institute's south plaza when she was attacked. The assailant apparently then dragged her into the bushes. She apparently was sexually assaulted, police said.*
>
> *Police said thousands of persons must have passed the site and one man told them he heard a scream about 2 P.M. but did not investigate because no one else seemed to be paying attention.*

A Scientific Approach

The fascinating upshot of Latané and Darley's reasoning is that, for an emergency victim, the idea of "safety in numbers" may often be completely wrong. It might be that someone in need of emergency aid would have a better chance of survival if a single bystander, rather than a crowd, were present. To test this unusual thesis, Darley, Latané, their students, and colleagues performed a systematic and impressive program of research that produced a clear set of findings (for a review, see Latané & Nida, 1981). Their basic procedure was to stage emergency events that were observed

Victim?
At times like this one, when the need for emergency aid is unclear, even genuine victims are unlikely to be helped in a crowd. Think how, if you were the second passerby in this picture, you might be influenced by the first passerby to believe that no aid was called for.

by a single individual or by a group of people. They then recorded the number of times the emergency victim received help under those circumstances. In their first experiment (Darley & Latané, 1968), a New York college student who appeared to be having an epileptic seizure received help 85 percent of the time when there was a single bystander present but only 31 percent of time with five bystanders present. With almost all the single bystanders helping, it becomes difficult to argue that ours is "The Cold Society" where no one cares for suffering others. Obviously it was something about the presence of other bystanders that reduced helping to shameful levels.

Other studies have examined the importance of social proof in causing wide-spread witness "apathy." They have done so by planting within a group of witnesses to a possible emergency people who are rehearsed to act as if no emergency were occurring. For instance, in another New York-based experiment (Latané & Darley, 1968a), 75 percent of lone individuals who observed smoke seeping from under a door reported the leak; however, when similar leaks were observed by three-person groups, the smoke was reported only 38 percent of the time. The smallest number of bystanders took action, though, when the three-person groups included two individuals who had been coached to ignore the smoke; under those conditions, the leaks were reported only 10 percent of time. In a similar study conducted in Toronto (A. S. Ross, 1971), single bystanders provided emergency aid 90 percent of the time, whereas such aid occurred in only 16 percent of the cases when a bystander was in the presence of two passive bystanders.

Social scientists now have a good idea of when bystanders will offer emergency aid. First, and contrary to the view that we have become a society of callous, uncaring people, once witnesses are convinced that an emergency situation exists, aid is very likely. Under these conditions, the number of bystanders who either intervene themselves or summon help is quite comforting. For example, in four separate experiments done in Florida (R. D. Clark & Word, 1972, 1974), accident scenes involving a maintenance man were staged. When it was clear that the man was hurt and required assistance, he was helped 100 percent of the time in two of the experiments. In the other two experiments, where helping involved contact with potentially dangerous electric wires, the victim still received bystander aid in 90 percent of the instances. In addition, these extremely high levels of assistance occurred whether the witnesses observed the event singly or in groups.

The situation becomes very different when, as in many cases, bystanders cannot be sure that the event they are witnessing is an emergency. Then a victim is much more likely to be helped by a lone bystander than by a group, especially if the people in the group are strangers to one another (Latané & Rodin, 1969). It seems that the pluralistic ignorance effect is strongest among strangers: Because we like to look graceful and sophisticated in public and because we are unfamiliar with the reactions of those we do not know, we are unlikely to give off or correctly read expressions of concern when in a group of strangers. Therefore, a possible emergency is viewed as a nonemergency and a victim suffers.

A close look at this set of research findings reveals an enlightening pattern. All the conditions that decrease an emergency victim's chances for bystander aid exist normally and innocently in the city, in contrast to rural areas:

1. Cities are more clamorous, distracting, rapidly changing places where it is difficult to be certain of the nature of the events one encounters.
2. Urban environments are more populous; consequently, people are more likely to be with others when witnessing a potential emergency situation.
3. City dwellers know a much smaller percentage of fellow residents than do people who live in small towns; therefore, city dwellers are more likely to find themselves in a group of strangers when observing an emergency.

These three natural characteristics of urban environments—their confusion, their populousness, and their low levels of acquaintanceship—fit in very well with the factors shown by research to decrease bystander aid. Without ever having to resort to such sinister concepts as "urban depersonalization" and "megalopolitan alienation," then, we can explain why so many instances of bystander inaction occur in our cities.

Devictimizing Yourself

Explaining the dangers of modern urban life in less ominous terms does not dispel them. Furthermore, as the world's populations move increasingly to the cities—half of all humanity will be city dwellers within a decade—there will be a growing need to reduce those dangers. Fortunately, our newfound understanding of the bystander "apathy" process offers real hope. Armed with this scientific knowledge, an emergency victim can increase enormously the chances of receiving aid from others. The key is the realization that groups of bystanders fail to help because the bystanders are unsure rather than unkind. They don't help because they are unsure an emergency actually exists and whether they are responsible for taking action. When they are sure of their responsibilities for intervening in a clear emergency, people are exceedingly responsive!

Once it is understood that the enemy is the simple state of uncertainty, it becomes possible for emergency victims to reduce this uncertainty, thereby protecting themselves. Imagine, for example, you are spending a summer afternoon at a music concert in a park. As the concert ends and people begin leaving, you notice a slight numbness in one arm but dismiss it as nothing to be alarmed about. Yet, while moving with the crowd to the distant parking areas, you feel the numbness spreading down to your hand and up one side of your face. Feeling disoriented, you decide to sit against a tree for a moment to rest. Soon you realize that something is drastically wrong. Sitting down has not helped; in fact, the control and coordination of your muscles has worsened, and you are starting to have difficulty moving your mouth and tongue to speak. You try to get up but can't. A terrifying thought rushes to mind: "Oh, God, I'm having a stroke!" Groups of people are passing by and most are paying no attention. The few who notice the odd way you are slumped against the tree or the strange look on your face check the social evidence around them and, seeing that no one else is reacting with concern, walk on convinced that nothing is wrong.

Were you to find yourself in such a predicament, what could you do to overcome the odds against receiving help? Because your physical abilities would be deteriorating, time would be crucial. If, before you could summon aid, you lost your speech or mobility or consciousness, your chances for assistance and for recovery would plunge drastically. It would be essential to try to request help quickly. What would be the most effective form of that request? Moans, groans, or outcries probably would not do. They might bring you some attention, but they would not provide enough information to assure passersby that a true emergency existed.

If mere outcries are unlikely to produce help from the passing crowd, perhaps you should be more specific. Indeed, you need to do more than try to gain attention; you should call out clearly your need for assistance. You must not allow bystanders to define your situation as a nonemergency. Use the word "Help" to show your need for emergency aid, and don't worry about being wrong. Embarrassment is a villain to be crushed. If you think you are having a stroke, you cannot afford to be worried about the possibility of overestimating your problem. The difference is that between a moment of embarrassment and possible death or lifelong paralysis.

Even a resounding call for help is not your most effective tactic. Although it may reduce bystanders' doubts that a real emergency exists, it will not remove several other important uncertainties within each onlooker's mind: What kind of aid is required? Should I be the one to provide the aid, or should someone more qualified do it? Has someone else already gone to get professional help, or is it my responsibility? While the bystanders stand gawking at you and grappling with these questions, time vital to your survival could he slipping away.

Clearly, then, as a victim you must do more than alert bystanders to your need for emergency assistance; you must also remove their uncertainties about how that assistance should be provided and who should provide it. What would be the most efficient and reliable way to do so?

Based on the research findings we have seen, my advice would be to isolate one individual from the crowd: Stare, speak, and point directly at that person and no one else: "You, sir, in the blue jacket, I need help. Call an ambulance." With that one utterance you would dispel all the uncertainties that might prevent or delay help. With that one statement you will have put the man in the blue jacket in the role of "rescuer." He should now understand that emergency aid is needed; he should understand that he, not someone else, is responsible for providing the aid; and, finally, he should understand exactly how to provide it. All the scientific evidence indicates that the result should be quick, effective assistance.

In general, then, your best strategy when in need of emergency help is to reduce the uncertainties of those around you concerning your condition and their responsibilities. Be as precise as possible about your need for aid. Do not allow bystanders to come to their own conclusions because, especially in a crowd, the principle of social proof and the consequent pluralistic ignorance effect might well cause them to view your situation as a nonemergency. Of all the techniques in this book designed to produce compliance with a request, this one is the most important to remember. After all, the failure of your request for emergency aid could mean your life.

READER'S REPORT 4.1

From a Woman Living in Wroclaw, Poland

I was going through a well-lighted road crossing when I thought I saw somebody fall into a ditch left by workers. The ditch was well protected, and I was not sure if I really saw it—maybe it was just imagination. One year ago, I would continue on my way, believing that people who had been closer saw better. But I had read your book. So, I stopped and returned to check if it was true. And it was. A man fell into this hole and was lying there shocked. The ditch was quite deep, so people walking nearby couldn't see anything. When I tried to do something, two guys walking on this street stopped to help me pull the man out.

Today, the newspapers wrote that during the last three weeks of winter, 120 people died in Poland, frozen. This guy could have been 121—that night the temperature was −21C.

He should be grateful to your book that he is alive.

Author's note: Several years ago, I was involved in a rather serious automobile accident that occurred at an intersection. Both I and the other driver were hurt: He was slumped, unconscious, over his steering wheel while I had staggered, bloody, from behind mine. Cars began to roll slowly past us; their drivers gawked but did not stop. Like the Polish woman, I had read the book, too; so, I knew what to do. I pointed directly at the driver of one car: "Call the police." To a second and third driver: "Pull over, we need help." Not only was their aid rapid, it was infectious. More drivers began stopping—spontaneously—to tend to the other victim. The principle of social proof was working for us now. The trick had been to get the ball rolling in the direction of help. Once that was accomplished, social proof's natural momentum did the rest.

MONKEY ME, MONKEY DO

A bit earlier I stated that the principle of social proof, like all other weapons of influence, works better under some conditions than under others. We have already explored one of those conditions: uncertainty. Without question, when people are uncertain, they are more likely to use others' actions to decide how they themselves should act. In addition, there is another important working condition: similarity. The principle of social proof operates most powerfully when we are observing the behavior of people just like us (Festinger, 1954). It is the conduct of such people that gives us the greatest insight into what constitutes correct behavior for ourselves. Therefore, we are more inclined to follow the lead of a similar individual than a dissimilar one (Abrams, Wetherell, Cochrane, Hogg, & Turner, 1990; Burn, 1991; Schultz, 1999).

That is why I believe we are seeing an increasing number of average-person-on-the-street testimonials on TV these days. Advertisers now know that one successful way to sell a product to ordinary viewers (who compose the largest potential market) is to demonstrate that other "ordinary" people like and use it. Whether the product is a brand of soft drink or a pain reliever or a laundry detergent, we hear volleys of praise from John or Mary Everyperson.

More compelling evidence for the importance of similarity in determining whether we will imitate another's behavior comes from scientific research. An especially apt illustration can be found in a study done by psychologists at Columbia University (Hornstein, Fisch, & Holmes, 1968). The researchers placed wallets on the ground in various locations around midtown Manhattan to observe what would happen when they were found. Each wallet contained $2.00 in cash, a $26.30 check, and various information providing the name and address of the wallet's "owner." In addition to these items, the wallet also contained a letter making it evident that the wallet had been lost not once, but twice. The letter was written to the wallet's owner from a man who had found it earlier and whose intention was to return it. The finder indicated in his letter that he was happy to help and that the chance to be of service in this way had made him feel good.

It was evident to anyone who found one of these wallets that this well-intentioned individual had then lost the wallet himself on the way to the mailbox—the wallet was wrapped in an envelope addressed to the owner. The researchers wanted to know how many people finding such a wallet would follow the lead of the first finder and mail it, intact, to the original owner. Before they dropped the wallets, however, the researchers varied one feature of the letter it contained. Some of the letters were written in standard English by someone who seemed to be an average American, while the other letters were written in broken English by the first finder, who identified himself as a recently arrived foreigner. In other words, the person who had initially found the wallet and had tried to return it was depicted by the letter as being either similar or dissimilar to most Americans.

The interesting question was whether the people who found the wallet and letter would be more influenced to mail the wallet if the first person who had tried to do so were similar to them. The answer was plain: Only 33 percent of the wallets were returned when the first finder was seen to be dissimilar, but 70 percent were returned when he was thought to be a similar other. These results suggest an important qualification of the principle of social proof. We will use the actions of others to decide on proper behavior for ourselves, *especially when we view those others to be similar to ourselves.*

This tendency applies not only to adults but to children as well. Health researchers have found, for example, that a school-based antismoking program had lasting effects only when it used same-age peer leaders as teachers (Murray, Leupker, Johnson, & Mittlemark, 1984). Another study found that children who saw a film depicting a child's positive visit to the dentist lowered their own dental anxieties principally when they were the same age as the child in the film (Melamed, Yurcheson, Fleece, Hutcherson, & Hawes, 1978). I wish I had known about this second study when, a few years before it was published, I was trying to reduce a different kind of anxiety in my son, Chris.

I live in Arizona where backyard swimming pools abound. Regrettably, each year, several young children drown after falling into an unattended pool. I was determined, therefore, to teach Chris how to swim at an early age. The problem was not that he was afraid of the water; he loved it, but he would not get into the pool without wearing his inflatable inner tube, no matter how I tried to coax, talk, or shame him out of it. After getting nowhere for two months, I hired a graduate student of mine to help. Despite his background as a lifeguard and swimming instructor, he failed as I had. He couldn't persuade Chris to attempt even a stroke outside of his plastic ring.

About this time, Chris was attending a day camp that provided a number of activities to its group, including the use of a large pool, which he scrupulously avoided. One day, shortly after the graduate student incident, I went to get Chris from camp and, with my mouth agape, watched him run down the diving board and jump into the deepest part of the pool. Panicked, I began pulling off my shoes to jump in to his rescue when I saw him bob to the surface and paddle safely to the side of the pool—where I dashed, shoes in hand, to meet him.

"Chris, you can swim!" I said excitedly. "You can swim!"

"Yes," he responded casually, "I learned how today."

"This is terrific! This is just terrific," I burbled, gesturing expansively to convey my enthusiasm. "But, how come you didn't need your plastic ring today?"

Looking somewhat embarrassed because his father seemed to be raving while inexplicably soaking his socks in a small puddle and waving his shoes around, Chris explained:

"Well, I'm 3 years old, and Tommy is 3 years old. And Tommy can swim without a ring, so that means I can, too."

I could have kicked myself. Of course it would be *to little Tommy*, not to a 6'2" graduate student, that Chris would look for the most relevant information about what he could or should do. Had I been more thoughtful about solving Chris' swimming problem, I could have employed Tommy's good example earlier and, perhaps, saved myself a couple of frustrating months. I could have simply noted at the day camp that Tommy was a swimmer and then arranged with his parents for the boys to spend a weekend afternoon swimming in our pool. My guess is that Chris' plastic ring would have been abandoned by the end of the day.

Monkey Die

Any factor that can spur 70 percent of New Yorkers to return a wallet, with all its contents included, must be considered impressive. Yet the outcome of the lost-wallet study offers just a hint of the immense impact that the conduct of similar others has on human behavior. More powerful examples exist in addition to this one. To my mind, the most telling illustration of this impact starts with a seemingly nonsensical statistic: After a suicide has made front-page news, airplanes—private planes, corporate jets, airliners—begin falling out of the sky at an alarming rate.

For example, it has been shown (Phillips, 1979) that immediately following certain kinds of highly publicized suicide stories, the number of people who die in commercial-airline crashes increases by 1,000 percent! Even more alarming: The increase is not limited to airplane deaths. The number of automobile fatalities shoots up as well (Phillips, 1980). What could possibly be responsible?

One explanation suggests itself immediately: The same social conditions that cause some people to commit suicide cause others to die accidentally. For instance, certain individuals, the suicide-prone, may react to stressful societal events (economic downturns, rising crime rates, international tensions) by ending it all. Others will react differently to these same events; they might become angry, impatient, nervous, or distracted. To the degree that such people operate or maintain the cars and planes of our society, the vehicles will be less safe, and consequently, we will see a sharp increase in the number of automobile and air fatalities.

According to this "social conditions" interpretation, then, some of the same societal factors that cause intentional deaths also cause accidental ones, and that is why we find so strong a connection between suicide stories and fatal crashes. Another fascinating statistic indicates that this is not the correct explanation: Fatal crashes increase dramatically only in those regions where the suicide has been highly publicized. Other places, existing under similar social conditions, whose newspapers have *not* publicized the story, have shown no comparable jump in such fatalities. Furthermore, within those areas where newspaper space has been allotted, the wider the publicity given the suicide, the greater has been the rise in subsequent crashes. Thus, it is not some set of common societal events that stimulates suicides on the one hand and fatal accidents on the other. Instead, it is the publicized suicide story itself that produces the car and plane wrecks.

To explain the strong association between suicide-story publicity and subsequent crashes, a "bereavement" account has been suggested. Because, it has been argued, front-page suicides often involve well-known and respected public figures, perhaps their highly publicized deaths throw many people into states of shocked sadness. Stunned and preoccupied, these individuals become careless around cars and planes. The consequence is the sharp increase in deadly accidents involving such vehicles that we see after front-page suicide stories. Although the bereavement theory can account for the connection between the degree of publicity given a story and subsequent crash fatalities—the more people who learn of the suicide, the larger will be the number of bereaved and careless individuals—it *cannot* explain another startling fact: Newspaper stories reporting suicide victims who died alone produce an increase in the frequency of single-fatality wrecks only, whereas stories reporting suicide-plus-murder incidents produce an increase in multiple-fatality wrecks only. Simple bereavement could not cause such a pattern.

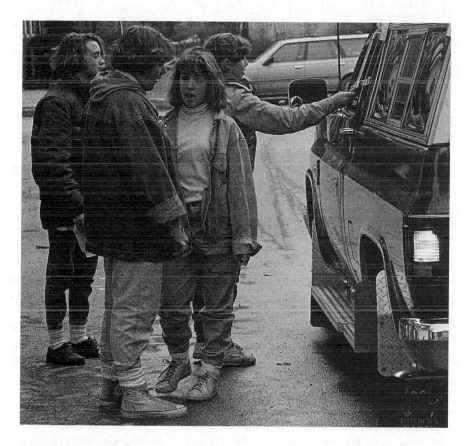

Free-Thinking Youth
We frequently think of teenagers as rebellious and independent-minded. It is important
to recognize, however, that typically that is true only with respect to their parents.
Among similar others, they conform massively to what social proof tells them is
proper.

The influence of suicide stories on car and plane crashes, then, is fantastically
specific. Stories of pure suicides, in which only one person dies, generate wrecks in
which only one person dies; stories of suicide-murder combination, in which there
are multiple deaths, generate wrecks in which there are multiple deaths. If neither
"social conditions" nor "bereavement" can make sense of this bewildering array of
facts, what can? There is a sociologist at the University of California in San Diego
who thinks he has found the answer. His name is David Phillips, and he points a convincing finger at something called the "Werther effect."

The story of the Werther effect is both chilling and intriguing. More than two
centuries ago, the great man of German literature, Johann von Goethe, published a

novel entitled *Die Leiden des jungen Werthers (The Sorrows of Young Werther)*. The book, in which the hero, named Werther, commits suicide, had a remarkable impact. Not only did it provide Goethe with immediate fame, but it also sparked a wave of emulative suicides across Europe. So powerful was this effect that authorities in several countries banned the novel.

Phillips's own work has traced the Werther effect to modern times (Phillips, 1974). His research has demonstrated that, immediately following a front-page suicide story, the suicide rate increases dramatically in those geographical areas where the story has been highly publicized. It is Phillips's argument that certain troubled people who read of another's self-inflicted death kill themselves in imitation. In a morbid illustration of the principle of social proof, these people decide how they should act on the basis of how some other troubled person has acted.

Phillips derived his evidence for the modern-day Werther effect from examining the suicide statistics in the United States between 1947 and 1968. He found that, within two months after every front-page suicide story, an average of 58 more people than usual killed themselves. In a sense, each suicide story killed 58 people who otherwise would have gone on living. Phillips also found that this tendency for suicides to beget suicides occurred principally in those parts of the country where the first suicide was highly publicized. He observed that the wider the publicity given the first suicide, the greater the number of later suicides (see Figure 4.1).

If the facts surrounding the Werther effect seem to you suspiciously like those surrounding the influence of suicide stories on air and traffic fatalities, the similarities have not been lost on Phillips, either. In fact, he contends that all the excess deaths following a front-page suicide incident can be explained as the same thing: copycat suicides. Upon learning of another's suicide, an uncomfortably large number of people decide that suicide is an appropriate action for themselves as well. Some of these individuals then proceed to commit the act in a straightforward, no-bones-about-it fashion, causing the suicide rate to jump.

Others, however, are less direct. For any of several reasons—to protect their reputations, to spare their families the shame and hurt, to allow their dependents to collect on insurance policies—they do not want to appear to have killed themselves. They would rather seem to have died accidentally. So, purposively but furtively, they cause the wreck of a car or a plane they are operating or are simply riding in. This can be accomplished in a variety of all-too-familiar-sounding ways. A commercial airline pilot can dip the nose of the aircraft at a crucial point of takeoff or can inexplicably land on an already occupied runway against the instructions from the control tower; the driver of a car can suddenly swerve into a tree or into oncoming traffic; a passenger in an automobile or corporate jet can incapacitate the operator, causing the deadly crash; the pilot of a private plane can, despite all radio warnings, plow into another aircraft. Thus, the alarming climb in crash fatalities that we find following front-page suicides is, according to Phillips, most likely due to the Werther effect secretly applied.

I consider this insight brilliant. First, it explains all of the data beautifully. If these wrecks really are hidden instances of imitative suicide, it makes sense that we

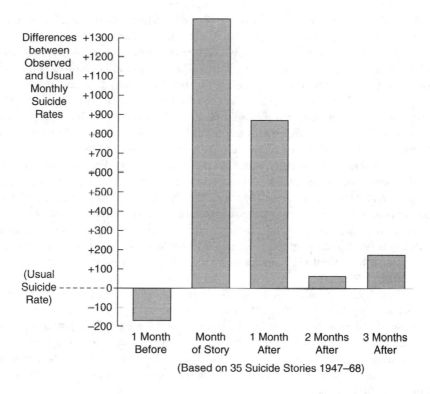

(Based on 35 Suicide Stories 1947–68)

FIGURE 4.1 Fluctuation in Number of Suicides before, during, and after Month of Suicide Story

This evidence raises an important ethical issue. The suicides that follow these stories are *excess* deaths. After the initial spurt, the suicide rates do not drop below traditional levels but only return to those levels. Statistics like these might well give pause to newspaper editors inclined to sensationalize suicide accounts, as those accounts are likely to lead to the deaths of scores of people. More recent data indicate that in addition to newspaper editors, television broadcasters have cause for concern about the effects of the suicide stories they present. Whether they appear as news reports, information features, or fictional movies, these stories create an immediate cluster of self-inflicted deaths, with impressionable, imitation-prone teenagers being the most frequent victims (Bollen & Phillips, 1982; Gould & Shaffer, 1986; Phillips & Cartensen, 1986, 1988; Schmidtke & Hafner, 1988).

should see an increase in the wrecks after suicide stories appear. It makes sense that the greatest rise in wrecks should occur after the suicide stories that have been most widely publicized and have, consequently, reached the most people. It also makes sense that the number of crashes should jump appreciably only in those geographical areas where the suicide stories were publicized. It even makes sense that single-victim suicides should lead only to single-victim crashes, whereas multiple-victim suicide incidents should lead only to multiple-victim crashes. Imitation is the key.

In addition, there is a second valuable feature of Phillips's insight. Not only does it allow us to explain the existing facts, it also allows us to predict new facts that had never been uncovered before. For example, if the abnormally frequent crashes following publicized suicides are genuinely the result of imitative rather than accidental actions, they should be more deadly as a result. That is, people trying to kill themselves will likely arrange (with a foot on the accelerator instead of the brake, with the nose of the plane down instead of up) for the impact to be as lethal as possible. The consequence should be quick and sure death. When Phillips examined the records to check on this prediction, he found that the average number of people killed in a fatal crash of a commercial airliner is more than three times greater if the crash happened one week after a front-page suicide story than if it happened one week before. A similar phenomenon can be found in traffic statistics, where there is evidence for the deadly efficiency of post-suicide-story auto crashes. Victims of fatal car wrecks that follow front-page suicide stories die four times more quickly than normal (Phillips, 1980).

Still another fascinating prediction flows from Phillips's idea. If the increase in wrecks following suicide stories truly represents a set of copycat deaths, then the imitators should be most likely to copy the suicides of people who are similar to them. The principle of social proof states that we use information about the way others have behaved to help us determine proper conduct for ourselves. As the dropped-wallet experiment showed, we are most influenced in this fashion by the actions of people who are like us.

Therefore, Phillips reasoned, if the principle of social proof is behind the phenomenon, there should be some clear similarity between the victim of the highly publicized suicide and those who cause subsequent wrecks. Realizing that the clearest test of this possibility would come from the records of automobile crashes involving a single car and a lone driver, Phillips compared the age of the suicide-story victim with the ages of the lone drivers killed in single-car crashes immediately after the story appeared in print. Once again the predictions were strikingly accurate: When the newspaper detailed the suicide of a young person, it was young drivers who then piled their cars into trees, poles, and embankments with fatal results; but when the news story concerned an older person's suicide, older drivers died in such crashes (Phillips, 1980).

This last statistic is the clincher for me. I am left wholly convinced and, simultaneously, wholly amazed by it. Evidently, the principle of social proof is so wide-ranging and powerful that its domain extends to the fundamental decision for life or death. Phillips's findings illustrate a distressing tendency for suicide publicity to motivate certain people who are similar to the victim to kill themselves—because they now find the idea of suicide more legitimate. Truly frightening are the data indicating that many innocent people die in the bargain (see Figure 4.2).

As if the frightening features of Phillips's suicide data weren't enough, his additional research (Phillips, 1983) brings more cause for alarm: Homicides in this

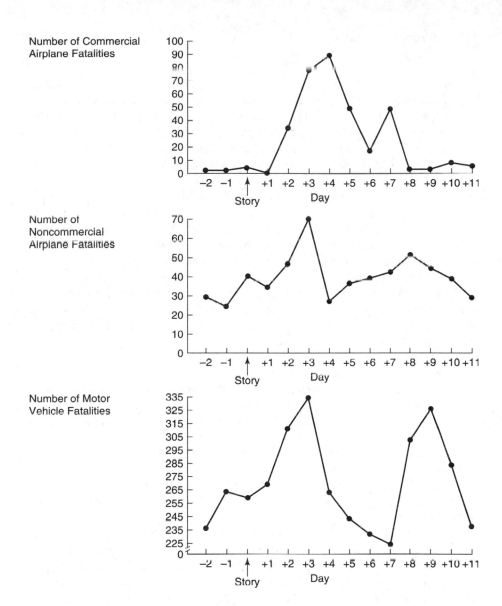

FIGURE 4.2 Daily Fluctuation in Number of Accident Fatalities before, on, and after Suicide Story Date

As is apparent from these graphs, the greatest danger exists three to four days following the news story's publication. After a brief drop-off, there comes another peak approximately one week later. By the eleventh day, there is no hint of an effect. This pattern across various types of data indicates something noteworthy about secret suicides. Those who try to disguise their imitative self-destruction as accidents wait a few days before committing the act—perhaps to build their courage, to plan the incident, or to put their affairs in order. Whatever the reason for the regularity of this pattern, we know that travelers' safety is most severely jeopardized three to four days after a suicide-murder story and then again, but to a lesser degree, a few days later. We would be well advised, then, to take special care in our travels at these times.

country have a simulated, copycat character after highly publicized acts of violence. Heavyweight championship prize fights that receive coverage on network evening news appear to produce measurable increases in the United States homicide rate. This analysis of heavyweight championship fights (between 1973 and 1978) is perhaps most compelling in its demonstration of the remarkably specific nature of the imitative aggression that is generated. When such a match was lost by a black fighter, the homicide rate during the following 10 days rose significantly for young black male victims but not young white males. On the other hand, when a white fighter lost a match, it was young white men, but not young black men, who were killed more frequently in the next 10 days. When these results are combined with the parallel findings in Phillips's suicide data, it is clear that widely publicized aggression has the nasty tendency to spread to similar victims, no matter whether the aggression is inflicted on the self or on another.

Perhaps nowhere are we brought into more dramatic contact with the unsettling side of the principle of social proof than in the realm of copycat crime. Back in the 1970s, our attention was brought to the phenomenon in the form of airplane hijackings, which seemed to spread like airborne viruses. In the 1980s, our focus shifted to product tamperings, such as the famous cases of Tylenol capsules injected with cyanide and Gerber baby food products laced with glass. According to FBI forensic experts, each nationally publicized incident of this sort spawned an average of 30 more incidents (Toufexis, 1993). More recently, we've been jolted by the specter of contagious mass murders, occurring first in workplace settings and then, incredibly, in the schools of our nation. For instance, immediately following the bloody rampage by two Littleton, Colorado, high-school students on April 20, 1999, police responded to scores of similar threats, plots, and attempts by troubled students. Two of those attempts proved "successful": A 14-year-old in Taber, Alberta, and a 15-year-old in Conyers, Georgia, killed or wounded a total of eight classmates within 10 days of the Littleton massacre.

Events of this magnitude demand analysis and explanation. Some common thread needs to be identified to make sense of it all. In the case of the workplace murders, observers noticed how often the killing fields were the backrooms of U.S. post offices. So, the finger of blame was pointed at the "intolerable strains" of the U.S. postal environment. As for the school-based slaughter, commentators remarked on an odd commonality: All the affected schools were located in rural or suburban communities rather than in the ever-simmering cauldrons of inner-city neighborhoods. So, the media instructed us as to the "intolerable strains" of growing up in small town or suburban America. By these accounts, the stressors of U.S. post office environments and of small town American life created the explosive reactions of those who worked and lived there. The explanation is straightforward: Similar social conditions beget similar responses.

But you and I have been down the "similar social conditions" road before in trying to understand anomalous patterns of fatalities. Recall how Phillips (1979) considered the possibility that a set of common social conditions in a particular en-

Malfunctioning Copier

Five minutes before the start of school on May 20, 1999, 15-year-old Thomas ("TJ") Solomon opened fire on his classmates, shooting six of them before he was stopped by a heroic teacher. In struggling to comprehend the underlying causes, we must recognize the effect on him of the publicity surrounding a year-long string of similar incidents—first in Jonesboro, Arkansas, then in Springfield Oregon, then in Littleton, Colorado, and then, just two days earlier, in Taber, Alberta. As one of his friends declared in response to the question of why distraught students were suddenly turning murderous at school, "Kids like TJ are seeing it and hearing it all the time now. It's like the new way out for them" (Cohen, 1999).

vironment might explain a rash of suicides there? It wasn't a satisfactory explanation for the suicides; and I don't think it is a satisfactory account for the murder sprees, either. Let's see if we can locate a better alternative by first trying to regain contact with reality: The "intolerable strains" of working at the post office or of living in rural/suburban America!? Come on. Compared to working in the coal mines or compared to living on the gang-ruled, mean streets of inner cities? Come on. Certainly the environments where the mass slaying occurred have their tensions. But they appear no more severe (and often appear less severe) than many other environments where such incidents have not taken place. No, the similar social conditions theory doesn't offer a plausible account.

Then what does? I'd nod right at the principle of social proof, which asserts that people, especially when they are unsure of themselves, follow the lead of similar others. Who is more similar to a disgruntled postal employee than another disgruntled postal employee? And who is more similar to troubled small town American teenagers than other troubled small town American teenagers? It is a regrettable constant of modern life that many people live their lives in psychological pain. How they deal with the pain depends on numerous factors, one of which is a recognition of how others *just like them* have chosen to deal with it. As we saw in Phillips's data, a highly publicized suicide prompts copycat suicides from similar others—from *copies* of the cat. I believe the same can be said for a highly publicized multiple murder. As is the case for suicide stories, media officials need to think deeply about how and how prominently to present reports of killing sprees. Such reports are not only riveting, sensational, and newsworthy, they are malignant.

Monkey Island

Work like Phillips's helps us appreciate the awesome influence of the behavior of similar others. Once the enormity of that force is recognized, it becomes possible to understand perhaps the most spectacular act of compliance of our time—the mass suicide at Jonestown, Guyana. Certain crucial features of the event deserve review.

The People's Temple was a cultlike organization that was based in San Francisco and drew its recruits from the poor of that city. In 1977, the Reverend Jim Jones—who was the group's undisputed political, social, and spiritual leader—moved the bulk of the membership with him to a jungle settlement in Guyana, South America. There, the People's Temple existed in relative obscurity until November 18, 1978, when Congressmen Leo R. Ryan of California (who had gone to Guyana to investigate the cult), three members of Ryan's fact-finding party, and a cult defector were murdered as they tried to leave Jonestown by plane. Convinced that he would be arrested and implicated in the killings and that the demise of the People's Temple would result, Jones sought to control the end of the Temple in his own way. He gathered the entire community around him and issued a call for each person's death to be done in a unified act of self-destruction.

The first response was that of a young woman who calmly approached the now famous vat of strawberry-flavored poison, administered one dose to her baby, one to herself, and then sat down in a field, where she and her child died in convulsions within four minutes. Others followed steadily in turn. Although a handful of Jonestowners escaped and a few others are reported to have resisted, the survivors claim that the great majority of the 910 people who died did so in an orderly, willful fashion.

News of the event shocked us. The broadcast media and the papers provided a barrage of reports, updates, and analyses. For days, our conversations were full of the topic, "How many have they found dead now?" "A guy who escaped said they were drinking the poison like they were hypnotized or something." "What were they doing down in South America, anyway?" "It's so hard to believe. What caused it?"

Yes, "What caused it?"—the critical question. How are we to account for this most astounding of compliant acts? Various explanations have been offered. Some have focused on the charisma of Jim Jones, a man whose style allowed him to be loved like a savior, trusted like a father, and treated like an emperor. Other explanations have pointed to the kind of people who were attracted to the People's Temple. They were mostly poor and uneducated individuals who were willing to give up their freedoms of thought and action for the safety of a place where all decisions would be made for them. Still other explanations have emphasized the quasi-religious nature of the People's Temple, in which unquestioned faith in the cult's leader was assigned highest priority.

No doubt each of these features of Jonestown has merit in explaining what happened there, but I do not find them sufficient. After all, the world abounds with cults populated by dependent people who are led by a charismatic figure. What's more, there has never been a shortage of this combination of circumstances in the past. Yet virtually nowhere do we find evidence of an event even approximating the Jonestown incident among such groups. There must be something else that was critical.

One especially revealing question gives us a clue: "If the community had remained in San Francisco, would Reverend Jones's suicide command have been obeyed?" A highly speculative question to be sure, but the expert most familiar with the People's Temple had no doubt about the answer. Dr. Louis Jolyon West, then chairman of psychiatry and biobehavioral sciences at UCLA and director of its neuropsychiatric unit, was an authority on cults who had observed the People's Temple for eight years prior to the Jonestown deaths. When interviewed in the immediate aftermath, he made what strikes me as an inordinately instructive statement: "This wouldn't have happened in California. But they lived in total alienation from the rest of the world in a jungle situation in a hostile country."

Although lost in the welter of commentary following the tragedy, West's observation, together with what we know about the principle of social proof, seems to me quite important to a satisfactory understanding of the compliant suicides. To my mind, the single act in the history of the People's Temple that most contributed to the members' mindless compliance that day occurred a year earlier with the relocation of the Temple to a jungled country of unfamiliar customs and people. If we are to believe the stories of Jim Jones's malevolent genius, he realized fully the massive psychological impact such a move would have on his followers. All at once, they found themselves in a place they knew nothing about. South America, and the rain forests of Guyana, especially, were unlike anything they had experienced in San Francisco. The environment—both physical and social—into which they were dropped must have seemed dreadfully uncertain.

Bodies lay in orderly rows at Jonestown, displaying the most spectacular act of compliance of our time.

Ah, uncertainty—the right-hand man of the principle of social proof. We have already seen that when people are uncertain, they look to the actions of others to guide their own actions. In the alien, Guyanese environment, then, Temple members were very ready to follow the lead of others. As we have also seen, it is others of a special kind whose behavior will be most unquestioningly followed: similar others. Therein lies the awful beauty of Reverend Jones's relocation strategy. In a country like Guyana, there were no similar others for a Jonestown resident but the people of Jonestown itself.

What was right for a member of the community was determined to a disproportionate degree by what other community members—influenced heavily by Jones—did and believed. When viewed in this light, the terrible orderliness, the lack of panic, the sense of calm with which these people moved to the vat of poison and to their deaths seems more comprehensible. They hadn't been hypnotized by Jones; they had been convinced—partly by him but, more importantly, by the principle of social proof—that suicide was the correct conduct. The uncertainty they surely felt upon first hearing the death command must have caused them to look around them for a definition of the appropriate response.

It is worth particular note that they found two impressive pieces of social evidence, each pointing in the same direction. The first was the initial set of their compatriots, who quickly and willingly took the poison drafts. There will always be a few such fanatically obedient individuals in any strong leader-dominated group. Whether, in this instance, they had been specially instructed beforehand to serve as examples or whether they were just naturally the most compliant with Jones's wishes is difficult to know. No matter; the psychological effect of the actions of those individuals must have been potent. If the suicides of similar others in news stories can influence total strangers to kill themselves, imagine how enormously more compelling such an act would be when performed without hesitation by one's neighbors in a place like Jonestown. The second source of social evidence came from the reactions of the crowd itself. Given the conditions, I suspect that what occurred was a large-scale instance of the pluralistic ignorance phenomenon. Each Jonestowner looked to the actions of surrounding individuals to assess the situation and—finding calmness because everyone else, too, was surreptitiously assessing rather than reacting—"learned" that patient turntaking was the correct behavior. Such misinterpreted, but nonetheless convincing, social evidence would be expected to result precisely in the ghastly composure of the assemblage that waited in the tropics of Guyana for businesslike death.

From my own perspective, most attempts to analyze the Jonestown incident have focused too much on the personal qualities of Jim Jones. Although he was without question a man of rare dynamism, the power he wielded strikes me as coming less from his remarkable personal style than from his understanding of fundamental psychological principles. His real genius as a leader was his realization of the limitations of individual leadership. No leader can hope to persuade, regularly and single-handedly, all the members of the group. A forceful leader can reasonably expect, however, to persuade some sizable proportion of group members. Then the raw information that a substantial number of group members has been convinced can, by itself, convince the rest. Thus, the most influential leaders are those who know how to arrange group conditions to allow the principle of social proof to work in their favor.

It is in this that Jones appears to have been inspired. His masterstroke was the decision to move the People's Temple community from urban San Francisco to the remoteness of equatorial South America, where the conditions of uncertainty and exclusive similarity would make the principle of social proof operate for him as perhaps nowhere else. There a settlement of a thousand people, much too large to be held in persistent sway by the force of one man's personality, could be changed from a following into a *herd*. As slaughterhouse operators have long known, the mentality of a herd makes it easy to manage. Simply get some members moving in the desired direction and the others—responding not so much to the lead animal as to those immediately surrounding them—will peacefully and mechanically go along. The powers of the amazing Reverend Jones, then, are probably best understood not in terms of his dramatic personal style but in his profound knowledge of the art of social jujitsu.

DEFENSE

I began this chapter with an account of the relatively harmless practice of laugh tracking and moved on to stories of murder and suicide—all explained by the principle of social proof. How can we expect to defend ourselves against a weapon of influence that pervades such a vast range of behavior? The difficulty is compounded by the realization that, most of the time, we don't want to guard against the information that social proof provides. The evidence it offers about the way we should act is usually valid and valuable (Hill, 1982; Laughlin, 1980; Warnik & Sanders, 1980). With it we can cruise confidently through countless decisions without having to investigate the detailed pros and cons of each. In this sense, the principle of social proof equips us with a wonderful kind of automatic pilot device not unlike that aboard most aircraft.

Yet there are occasional, but real, problems with automatic pilots. Those problems appear whenever the flight information locked into the control mechanism is wrong. In these instances, we will be taken off course. Depending on the size of the error, the consequences can be severe; but, because the automatic pilot afforded by the principle of social proof is more often an ally than an enemy, we can't be expected to want simply to disconnect it. Thus, we are faced with a classic problem: how to make use of a piece of equipment that simultaneously benefits and imperils our welfare.

Fortunately, there is a way out of the dilemma. Because the disadvantages of automatic pilots arise principally when incorrect data have been put into the control system, our best defense against these disadvantages is to recognize when the data are in error. If we can become sensitive to situations in which the social proof automatic pilot is working with inaccurate information, we can disengage the mechanism and grasp the controls when we need to.

Sabotage

There are two types of situations in which incorrect data cause the principle of social proof to give us poor counsel. The first occurs when the social evidence has been purposely falsified. Invariably these situations are manufactured by exploiters intent on creating the *impression*—reality be damned—that a multitude is performing the way the exploiters want us to perform. The canned laughter of TV comedy shows is one variety of faked data of this sort, but there is a great deal more, and much of the fakery is strikingly obvious.

For instance, canned responses are not unique to the electronic media or even to the electronic age. In fact, the heavy-handed exploitation of the principle of social proof can be traced through the history of grand opera, one of our most venerable art forms. This is the phenomenon called claquing, said to have begun in 1820 by a pair of Paris opera-house habitués named Sauton and Porcher. The men were more than opera-goers, though. They were businessmen whose product was applause.

Organizing under the title L'Assurance des Succès Dramatiques, they leased themselves and their employees to singers and opera managers who wished to be assured of an appreciative audience response. So effective were Sauton and Porcher in stimulating genuine audience reaction with their rigged reactions that, before long, claques (usually consisting of a leader—*chef de claque*—and several individual *claqueurs*) had become an established and persistent tradition throughout the world of opera. As music historian Robert Sabin (1964) notes, "By 1830 the claque was a full-bloom institution, collecting by day, applauding by night, all in the honest open. . . . But it is altogether probable that neither Sauton, nor his ally Porcher, had a notion of the extent to which their scheme of paid applause would be adopted and applied wherever opera is sung."

As claquing grew and developed, its practitioners offered an array of styles and strengths. In the same way that laugh-track producers hire individuals who excel in titters, chuckles, or belly laughs, the claques spawned their own specialists—the *pleureuse,* chosen for her ability to weep on cue; the *bisseur,* who called *"bis"* (repeat) and "encore" in ecstatic tones; and, in direct kinship with today's laugh-track performer, the *rieur,* selected for the infectious quality of his laugh.

For our purposes, though, the most instructive parallel to modern forms of canned response is the conspicuous character of the fakery. No special need was seen to disguise or vary the claque, who often sat in the same seats, performance after performance, year after year, led by a *chef de claque* two decades into his position. Even the monetary transactions were not hidden from the public. Indeed, one hundred years after the birth of claquing, a reader of the London *Musical Times* could scan the advertised rates of the Italian *claqueurs* (see Figure 4.3). Whether in the world of *Rigoletto* or TV sit-coms, then, audiences have been successfully manipulated by those who use social evidence, even when that evidence has been openly falsified.

For applause on entrance, if a gentleman	25 lire
For applause on entrance, if a lady	15 lire
Ordinary applause during performance, each	10 lire
Insistent applause during performance, each	15 lire
Still more insistent applause	17 lire
For interruptions with "Bene!" or "Bravo!"	5 lire
For a "Bis" *at any cost*	50 lire
Wild enthusiasm—A special sum to be arranged	

FIGURE 4.3 Advertised Rates of the Italian Claque
From "ordinary applause" to "wild enthusiasm," *claqueurs* offered their services in an audaciously public fashion—in this case, in a newspaper read by many of the audience members they fully expected to influence. *Claque, whirr.*

What Sauton and Porcher realized about the mechanical way that we abide by the principle of social proof is understood as well by a variety of today's profiteers. They see no need to hide the manufactured nature of the social evidence they provide—witness the amateurish quality of the average TV laugh track. They seem almost smug in the recognition of our predicament: Either we must allow them to fool us or we must abandon the precious automatic pilots that make us so vulnerable to their tricks. In their certainty that they have us trapped, however, such exploiters have made a crucial mistake. The laxity with which they construct phony social evidence gives us a way to fight back.

Because automatic pilots can be engaged and disengaged at will, we can cruise along trusting in the course steered by the principle of social proof *until* we recognize that inaccurate data are being used. Then we can take the controls, make the necessary correction for the misinformation, and reset the automatic pilot. The transparency of the rigged social proof we get these days provides us with exactly the cue we need for knowing when to perform this simple maneuver. With no more cost than a bit of vigilance for plainly counterfeit social evidence, then, we can protect ourselves nicely.

Let's take an example. A bit earlier, I noted the proliferation of average person-on-the-street ads, in which a number of ordinary people speak glowingly of a product, often without knowing that their words are being recorded. As would be expected according to the principle of social proof, these testimonials from "average people like you and me" make for quite effective advertising campaigns. They have always included a relatively subtle kind of distortion: We hear only from those who like the product; as a result, we get an understandably biased picture of the amount of social support for it. More recently, though, a cruder and more unethical sort of falsification has been introduced. Commercial producers often don't bother to get genuine testimonials. They merely hire actors to play the roles of average people testifying in an unrehearsed fashion to an interviewer. It is amazing how bald-faced these "unrehearsed interview" commercials can be. The situations are obviously staged, the participants are clearly actors, and the dialogue is unmistakably prewritten.

I know that whenever I encounter an influence attempt of this sort, it sets off in me a kind of alarm with a clear directive: *Attention! Attention! Bad social proof in this situation. Temporarily disconnect automatic pilot.* It's so easy to do. We need only make a conscious decision to be alert to counterfeit social evidence. We can relax until the exploiters' evident fakery is spotted, at which time we can pounce.

And we should pounce with a vengeance. I am speaking of more than simply ignoring the misinformation, although this defensive tactic is certainly called for. I am speaking of aggressive counterattack. Whenever possible we ought to sting those responsible for the rigging of social evidence. We should purchase no products featured in phony "unrehearsed interview" commercials. Moreover, each manufacturer of the items should receive a letter explaining our response and recommending that they discontinue use of the advertising agency that produced so deceptive a presentation of their product.

Stay tuned, folks: Consumers from Mars are on next

By Dave Barry

Recently I was watching TV, and a commercial came on, and the announcer, in a tone of voice usually reserved for major developments in the Persian Gulf, said, "Now consumers can ask Angela Lansbury their questions about Bufferin!"

As a normal human, the natural reaction to this announcement is: "Huh?" Meaning, "What does Angela Lansbury have to do with Bufferin?" But this commercial featured several consumers who had apparently been stopped at random on the street, and *every one of them had a question for Angela Lansbury about Bufferin.* Basically,

what they asked was, "Miss Lansbury, is Bufferin a good product that I should purchase, or what?"

These consumers seemed very earnest. It was as if they had been going around for months wringing their hands and saying, "I have a question about Bufferin! If only I could ask Angela Lansbury!"

What we are seeing here is yet another example of a worsening problem that has been swept under the rug for too long in this nation: The invasion of Consumers From Mars. They *look* like humans, but they don't *act* like humans, and they are taking over.

FIGURE 4.4   Just Your Average Martian on the Street
Apparently I'm not alone in noticing the number of blatantly phony "unrehearsed" testimonial ads these days. Humorist Dave Barry has registered their prevalence too and has labeled their inhabitants *Consumers from Mars,* which is a term I like and have even begun using myself. It helps remind me that, as regards my buying habits, I should be sure to ignore the tastes of these individuals who, after all, come from another planet than I do.

Of course, we don't always want to trust the actions of others to direct our conduct—especially in a situation important enough to warrant our personal investigation of the pros and cons, or one in which we are experts—but we do want to be able to count on others' behavior as a source of valid information in a wide range of settings. If we find in such settings that we cannot trust the information to be valid because someone has tampered with the evidence, we ought to be ready to strike back. In such instances, I personally feel driven by more than an aversion to being duped. I bristle at the thought of being pushed into an unacceptable corner by those who would use one of my hedges against the decisional overload of modern life against me. And I get a genuine sense of righteousness by lashing out when they try. If you are like me, so should you.

Looking Up

In addition to the times when social evidence is deliberately faked, there is another time when the principle of social proof will regularly steer us wrong. In such an

"Well, so much for the safety-in-numbers theory."

"Shakin' Bacon"
The notion that there is safety in numbers can prove very
wrong once a herd mentality sets in.
By permission of Leigh Rubin and Creators Syndicate.

instance, an innocent, natural error will produce snowballing social proof that
pushes us to an incorrect decision. The pluralistic ignorance phenomenon, in which
everyone at an emergency sees no cause for alarm, is one example of this process.

The best illustration I know, however, comes from Singapore, where a few years
ago, for no good reason, customers of a local bank began drawing out their money
in a frenzy. The run on this respected bank remained a mystery until much later, when
researchers interviewing participants discovered its peculiar cause: An unexpected
bus strike had created an abnormally large crowd waiting at the bus stop in front of
the bank that day. Mistaking the gathering for a crush of customers poised to withdraw their funds from a failing bank, passersby panicked and got in line to withdraw
their deposits, which led more passersby to do the same. Soon after opening its doors,
the bank was forced to close to prevent a complete crash ("News," 1988).

This account provides certain insights into the way we respond to social proof. First, we seem to assume that if a lot of people are doing the same thing, they must know something we don't. Especially when we are uncertain, we are willing to place an enormous amount of trust in the collective knowledge of the crowd. Second, quite frequently the crowd is mistaken because its members are not acting on the basis of any superior information but are reacting, themselves, to the principle of social proof.

There is a lesson here: An automatic pilot device, like social proof, should never be trusted fully; even when no saboteur has slipped information into the mechanism, it can sometimes go haywire by itself. We need to check the machine from time to time to be sure that it hasn't worked itself out of sync with the other sources of evidence in the situation—the objective facts, our prior experiences, our own judgments. Fortunately, this precaution requires neither much effort nor much time. A quick glance around is all that is needed. And this little precaution is well worth it. The consequences of single-minded reliance on social evidence can be frightening. For instance, a serious international incident developed in 1983 when a Korean Airlines jet strayed deep into Soviet airspace and was shot down by Russian fighters. Subsequent analysis determined that during the flight, the jetliner's crew had never checked their progress manually, relying entirely on their autopilot, which had been fed the wrong magnetic heading at the flight's outset (Staff, 1993).

Certainly, a flier whose plane is locked into automatic pilot would be wise to glance occasionally at the instrument panel and out the window. In the same way, we need to look up and around periodically whenever we are locked into the evidence of the crowd. Without this simple safeguard against misguided social proof, our outcomes might well run parallel to those of the Korean Airliner and the Singapore bank: crash.

READER'S REPORT 4.2

From a Former Racetrack Employee

I became aware of one method of faking social evidence to one's advantage while working at a racetrack. In order to lower the odds and make more money, some bettors are able to sway the public to bet on bad horses.

Odds at a racetrack are based on where the money is being bet. The more money on a horse, the better the odds. Many people who play the horses have surprisingly little knowledge of racing or betting strategy. Thus, especially when they don't know much about the horses in a particular race, a lot of times they'll simply bet the favorite. Because tote boards display up-to-the-minute odds, the public can always tell who the current favorite is. The system that a high roller can use to alter the odds is actually quite simple. The guy has in mind a horse he feels has a good chance of winning. Next he chooses a horse that has long odds (say, 15 to 1) and doesn't have a realistic chance to win. The minute the mutual windows open, the guy puts down $100 on the inferior horse, creating an instant favorite whose odds on the board drop to about 2 to 1.

Now the elements of social proof begin to work. People who are uncertain of how to bet the race look to the tote board to see which horse the early bettors have decided is a favorite, and they follow. A snowballing effect now occurs as other people continue to bet the favorite. At this point, the high roller can go back to the window and bet heavily on his true favorite, which will have better odds now because the "new favorite" has been pushed down the board. If the guy wins, the initial $100 investment will have been worth it many times over.

I've seen this happen myself. I remember one time a person put down $100 on a pre-race 10 to 1 shot, making it the early favorite. The rumors started circulating around the track—the early bettors knew something. Next thing you know, everyone (myself included) was betting on this horse. It ended up running last and had a bad leg. Many people lost a lot of money. Somebody came out ahead, though. We'll never know who. But he is the one with all the money. He understood the theory of social proof.

Author's note: *Once again we can see that social proof is most telling for those who feel unfamiliar or unsure in a specific situation and who, consequently, must look outside of themselves for evidence of how best to behave there.*

SUMMARY

- The principle of social proof states that one important means that people use to decide what to believe or how to act in a situation is to look at what other people are believing or doing there. Powerful imitative effects have been found among both children and adults and in such diverse activities as purchase decisions, charity donations, and phobia remission. The principle of social proof can be used to stimulate a person's compliance with a request by informing the person that many other individuals (the more, the better) are or have been complying with it.

- Social proof is most influential under two conditions. The first is uncertainty. When people are unsure, when the situation is ambiguous, they are more likely to attend to the actions of others and to accept those actions as correct. In ambiguous situations, for instance, the decisions of bystanders to help are much more influenced by the actions of other bystanders than when the situation is a clear-cut emergency. The second condition under which social proof is most influential is similarity: People are more inclined to follow the lead of similar others. Evidence for the powerful effect of the actions of similar others on human behavior can be readily seen in the suicide statistics compiled by sociologist David Phillips. Those statistics indicate that after highly publicized suicide stories other troubled individuals, who are similar to the suicide-story victim, decide to kill themselves. An analysis of the mass suicide incident at Jonestown, Guyana, suggests that the group's leader, Reverend Jim Jones, used both of the factors of uncertainty and similarity to induce a herdlike suicide response from the majority of the Jonestown population.

- Recommendations to reduce our susceptibility to faulty social proof include a sensitivity to clearly counterfeit evidence of what similar others are doing and a recognition that the actions of similar others should not form the sole basis for our decisions.

STUDY QUESTIONS

Content Mastery

1. Describe the principle of social proof and how it can explain the effect of canned laughter on an audience's reaction to comedy material.

2. In the Festinger, Riecken, and Schachter study of the end-of-the-world cult, group members pushed to win new converts only after their doomsday predictions proved false. Why?

3. Which two factors maximize the influence of social proof on an individual? What was it about the Jonestown, Guyana, situation that allowed these two factors to operate forcefully?

4. What is pluralistic ignorance? How does it influence bystander intervention in emergencies?

5. Which naturally occurring conditions of city life reduce the chance of bystander intervention in an emergency?

6. What is the Werther effect? How does it explain the puzzling relationship between highly publicized suicide stories and startling increases in the number of airplane and automobile fatalities following publication of the stories?

Critical Thinking

1. If you had to deliver a lecture to heart patients concerning the best way to secure help should they experience heart trouble in a public place, which steps would you tell them to take?

2. In early 1986, someone injected cyanide into Tylenol capsules on store shelves, creating widespread publicity and a national furor after a New York woman died from ingesting one of the capsules. The weeks that followed saw a rash of product tampering incidents. Three other popular over-the-counter medications were found laced with poison; pieces of glass were inserted in packages of cereal and ice cream; even bathroom tissue was not immune— in one office building, the toilet paper in the public restrooms was sprayed with Mace. Although the Tylenol incident itself could not have been foreseen, explain why, after reading this chapter, you might have predicted the aftermath.

3. Suppose you were a TV producer given the delicate job of creating a series of public service programs designed to reduce teenage suicide. Knowing that research suggests that

previous programming may have inadvertently increased teen suicides via the principle of social proof, what would you do to use the same principle to make it likely that your shows would reduce the problem among those who watched? Who would you interview on-camera? Would any of them be troubled teenagers? Which questions would you ask them?

4. Describe a situation in your past in which you were tricked into compliance by someone who counterfeited the principle of social proof. How would you handle a similar situation today?

5. How does the ad that opens this chapter reflect the topic of the chapter?

CHAPTER

5 | *Liking*

The Friendly Thief

the crew that cooks together
stays together

People in a relationship this close are either very

disturbed or embrace a common vision.

We happen to embrace a common vision: that of

cooking good food and serving it in

a nice environment. We did it for years

in kind of a hep place back east.

Then we traveled here. In unison. Collectively.

As one. And no, we are not disturbed.

CREW
an eat place

480 488 8840
el Pedregal at the Boulders

> *The main work of a trial attorney is to make a jury like his client.*
>
> —CLARENCE DARROW

Few of us would be surprised to learn that, as a rule, we most prefer to say yes to the requests of people we know and like. What might be startling to note, however, is that this simple rule is used in hundreds of ways by total strangers to get us to comply with *their* requests.

The clearest illustration I know of the professional exploitation of the liking rule is the Tupperware party, which I consider a classic compliance setting. Anybody familiar with the workings of a Tupperware party will recognize the use of the various weapons of influence we have examined so far:

- *Reciprocity.* To start, games are played and prizes won by the party goers; anyone who doesn't win a prize gets to choose one from a grab bag so that everyone has received a gift before the buying begins.
- *Commitment.* Participants are urged to describe publicly the uses and benefits they have found for the Tupperware they already own.
- *Social proof.* Once the buying begins, each purchase builds the idea that other, similar people want the products; therefore, it must be good.

All the weapons of influence are present to help things along, but the real power of the Tupperware party comes from a particular arrangement that trades on the liking rule. Despite the entertaining and persuasive selling skills of the Tupperware demonstrator, the true request to purchase the product does not come from this stranger; it comes from a friend to every person in the room. Oh, the Tupperware representative may physically ask for each party goer's order, all right; but the more psychologically compelling requester is sitting off to the side, smiling, chatting, and serving refreshments. She is the party hostess, who has called her friends together for the demonstration in her home and who, everyone knows, makes a profit from each piece sold at the party.

By providing the hostess with a percentage of the take, the Tupperware Home Parties Corporation arranges for its customers to buy from and for a friend rather than from an unknown salesperson. In this way, the attraction, the warmth, the security, and the obligation of friendship are brought to bear on the sales setting (Taylor, 1978). In fact, consumer researchers who have examined the social ties between the hostess and the party goers in home party sales settings have affirmed the power of the company's approach: The strength of that social bond is twice as likely to determine product purchase as is preference for the product itself (Frenzen & Davis, 1990). The results have been remarkable. It was recently estimated that Tupperware sales now exceed 2.5 million dollars a day! Indeed, Tupperware's success has spread around the world to societies in Europe, Latin America, and Asia, where one's place in a network of friends and family is more socially significant than in the United States (Markus & Kitayama, 1991; Triandis, 1995). As a result, now less than a quarter of Tupperware sales take place in North America.

What is interesting is that the customers appear to be fully aware of the liking and friendship pressures embodied in the Tupperware party. Some don't seem to mind; others do, but don't seem to know how to avoid these pressures. One woman I spoke with described her reactions with more than a bit of frustration in her voice.

> *It's gotten to the point now where I hate to be invited to Tupperware parties. I've got all the containers I need; and if I wanted any more, I could buy another brand cheaper in the store. But when a friend calls up, I feel like I have to go. And when I get there, I feel like I have to buy something. What can I do? It's for one of my friends.*

With so irresistible an ally as friendship, it is little wonder that the Tupperware Corporation has abandoned retail sales outlets and is pushing the home party concept. Statistics reveal that a Tupperware party now starts somewhere every 2.7 seconds. Of course, all sorts of other compliance professionals recognize the pressure to say yes to someone we know and like. Take, for instance, the growing number of charity organizations that recruit volunteers to canvass for donations close to their own

The Tupperware Party
The Tupperware Home Party Corporation likes to boast about the air tight seal provided by its containers. But the bond that usually seals the sale is nothing that goes *pffftt* when you press on it. It's the bond that exists between the party goers and the party hostess.

homes. They understand perfectly how much more difficult it is for us to turn down a charity request when it comes from a friend or neighbor.

Other compliance professionals have found that the friend doesn't even have to be present to be effective; often, just the mention of the friends' name is enough. The Shaklee Corporation, which specializes in door-to-door sales of various home-related products, advises its salespeople to use the "endless chain" method for finding new customers. Once a customer admits that he or she likes a product, that customer can be pressed for the names of friends who would also appreciate learning about it. The individuals on that list can then be approached for sales *and* a list of their friends, who can serve as sources for still other potential customers, and so on in an endless chain.

The key to the success of this method is that each new prospect is visited by a salesperson armed with the name of a friend "who suggested I call on you." Turning the salesperson away under those circumstances is difficult; it's almost like rejecting the friend. The Shaklee sales manual insists that employees use this system: "It would be impossible to overestimate its value. Phoning or calling on a prospect and

"Louise, there's a gentleman here who says that you and he were in love in 1962 but you drifted apart and now he's come back in the hope that we might order a set of encyclopedias."

The Liking Rule
Love and encyclopedia sales are forever.

being able to say that Mr. So-and-so, a friend of his, felt he would benefit by giving you a few moments of his time is virtually as good as a sale 50 percent made before you enter."

READER'S REPORT 5.1

From a Chicago Man

Although I've never been to a Tupperware Party, I recognized the same kind of friendship pressures recently when I got a call from a long distance phone company saleswoman. She told me that one of my buddies had placed my name on something called the "MCI Friends and Family Calling Circle."

This friend of mine, Brad, is a guy I grew up with but who moved to New Jersey last year for a job. He still calls me pretty regularly to get the news on the guys we used to hang out with. The saleswoman told me that he could save 20 percent on all the calls he made to the people on his Calling-Circle list, provided they are MCI phone company subscribers. Then she asked me if I wanted to switch to MCI to get all the blah, blah, blah benefits of MCI service, and so that Brad could save 20 percent on his calls to me.

Well, I couldn't have cared less about the benefits of MCI service; I was perfectly happy with the long distance company I had. But the part about wanting to save Brad money on our calls really got to me. For me to say that I didn't want to be in his Calling Circle and didn't care about saving him money would have sounded like a real affront to our friendship when he heard about it. So, to avoid insulting him, I told her to switch me to MCI.

I used to wonder why women would go to a Tupperware Party just because a friend was holding it, and then buy stuff they didn't want once they were there. I don't wonder anymore.

Author's note: This reader is not alone in being able to testify to the power of the pressures embodied in MCI's Calling Circle idea. When Consumer Reports *magazine inquired into the practice, the MCI salesperson they interviewed was quite succinct: "It works 9 out of 10 times," he said.*

MAKING FRIENDS TO INFLUENCE PEOPLE

Compliance practitioners' widespread use of the liking bond between friends tells us much about the power of the liking rule to produce assent. In fact, we find that such professionals seek to benefit from the rule even when already formed friendships are not present for them to employ. Under these circumstances, the professionals still make use of the liking bond by employing a compliance strategy that is quite direct: They first get us to like *them*.

There is a man in Detroit, Joe Girard, who specialized in using the liking rule to sell Chevrolets. He became wealthy in the process, making over $200,000 a year.

With such a salary, we might guess that he was a high-level GM executive or perhaps the owner of a Chevrolet dealership. But no. He made his money as a salesman on the showroom floor. He was phenomenal at what he did. For twelve years straight, he won the title of "Number One Car Salesman"; he averaged more than five cars and trucks sold every day he worked; and he has been called the world's "greatest car salesman" by the *Guinness Book of World Records*.

For all his success, the formula he employed was surprisingly simple. It consisted of offering people just two things: a fair price and someone they liked to buy from. "And that's it," he claimed in an interview. "Finding the salesman you like, plus the price. Put them both together, and you get a deal."

Fine. The Joe Girard formula tells us how vital the liking rule is to his business, but it doesn't tell us nearly enough. For one thing, it doesn't tell us why customers liked him more than some other salesperson who offered a fair price. There is a crucial—and fascinating—general question that Joe's formula leaves unanswered. What are the factors that cause one person to like another? If we knew *that* answer, we would be a long way toward understanding how people such as Joe can so successfully arrange to have us like them and, conversely, how we might successfully arrange to have others like us. Fortunately, social scientists have been asking this question for decades. Their accumulated evidence has allowed them to identify a number of factors that reliably cause liking. As we will see, each is cleverly used by compliance professionals to urge us along the road to "yes."

WHY DO I LIKE YOU? LET ME LIST THE REASONS

Physical Attractiveness

Although it is generally acknowledged that good-looking people have an advantage in social interaction, recent findings indicate that we may have sorely underestimated the size and reach of that advantage. There seems to be a *click, whirr* response to attractive people. Like all *click, whirr* reactions, it happens automatically, without forethought. The response itself falls into a category that social scientists call *halo effects*. A halo effect occurs when one positive characteristic of a person dominates the way that person is viewed by others. The evidence is now clear that physical attractiveness is often such a characteristic.

Research has shown that we automatically assign to good-looking individuals such favorable traits as talent, kindness, honesty, and intelligence (for a review of this evidence, see Eagly, Ashmore, Makhijani, & Longo, 1991). Furthermore, we make these judgments without being aware that physical attractiveness plays a role in the process. Some consequences of this unconscious assumption that "good-looking equals good" scare me. For example, a study of the 1974 Canadian federal elections found that attractive candidates received more than two and a half times as many votes as unattractive candidates (Efran & Patterson, 1976). Despite such evidence of favoritism toward handsome politicians, follow-up research demonstrated that voters did not realize their bias. In fact, 73 percent of Canadian voters surveyed denied in the strongest possible terms that their votes had been influenced by physical appearance; only 14 percent even allowed for the possibility of such influence (Efran & Patterson, 1976). Voters can deny the impact of attractiveness on electability all they want, but evidence has continued to confirm its troubling presence (Budeshcim & DePaola, 1994).

A similar effect has been found in hiring situations. In one study, good grooming of applicants in a simulated employment interview accounted for more favorable hiring decisions than did job qualifications—this, even though the interviewers claimed that appearance played a small role in their choices (Mack & Rainey, 1990). The advantage given to attractive workers extends past hiring day to payday. Economists examining U.S. and Canadian samples have found that attractive individuals get paid an average of 12–14 percent more than their unattractive coworkers (Hammermesh & Biddle, 1994).

Equally unsettling research indicates that our judicial process is similarly susceptible to the influences of body dimensions and bone structure. It now appears that good-looking people are likely to receive highly favorable treatment in the legal system (see Castellow, Wuensch, & Moore, 1991; and Downs & Lyons, 1990, for reviews). For example, in a Pennsylvania study (Stewart, 1980), researchers rated the physical attractiveness of 74 separate male defendants at the start of their criminal trials. When, much later, the researchers checked court records for the results of these cases, they found that the handsome men had received significantly lighter sentences. In fact, attractive defendants were twice as likely to avoid jail as unattractive defendants.[1] In another study—this one on the damages awarded in a staged negligence trial—a defendant who was better looking than his victim was assessed an average amount of $5,623; but when the victim was more attractive of the two,

---

[1]This finding—that attractive defendants, even when they are found guilty, are less likely to be sentenced to prison—helps explain one fascinating experiment in criminology (Kurtzburg, Safar, & Cavior, 1968). Some New York City jail inmates with facial disfigurements underwent plastic surgery while incarcerated; other inmates with similar disfigurements did not. Furthermore, some members of each group received services (such as counseling, training, etc.) designed to rehabilitate them to society. One year after the inmates had been released from jail, a check of the records revealed that (except for heroin addicts) criminals given the cosmetic surgery were significantly less likely to have returned to jail. The most interesting feature of this finding was that it was equally true for those inmates who had not received the traditional rehabilitative services and for those who had. Apparently, some criminologists then argued that when it comes to ugly inmates, prisons would be better off to abandon the costly rehabilitation services they typically provide and offer plastic surgery instead; the surgery seems to be at least as effective and decidedly less expensive.

The importance of the Pennsylvania data (Stewart, 1980) is that it suggests that the argument for surgery as a means of rehabilitation may be faulty. Making ugly criminals more attractive may not reduce the chances that they will commit another crime; it may only reduce their chances of being sent to jail for it.

the average compensation was $10,051. What's more, both male and female jurors exhibited the attractiveness-based favoritism (Kulka & Kessler, 1978).

Other experiments have demonstrated that attractive people are more likely to obtain help when in need (Benson, Karabenic, & Lerner, 1976) and are more persuasive in changing the opinions of an audience (Chaiken, 1979). Here, too, both sexes respond in the same way. In the Benson et al. study on helping, for instance, the better-looking men and women received aid more often, even from members of their own sex. A major exception to this rule might be expected to occur, of course, if the attractive person is viewed as a direct competitor, especially a romantic rival. Short of this qualification, though, it is apparent that good-looking people enjoy an enormous social advantage in our culture. They are better liked, more persuasive, more frequently helped, and seen as possessing more desirable personality traits and greater intellectual capacities. It appears that the social benefits of good looks begin to accumulate quite early. Research on elementary school children shows that adults view aggressive acts as less naughty when performed by an attractive child (Dion, 1972) and that teachers presume good-looking children to be more intelligent than their less attractive classmates (Ritts, Patterson, & Tubbs, 1992).

It is hardly any wonder, then, that the halo of physical attractiveness is regularly exploited by compliance professionals. Because we like attractive people, and because we tend to comply with those we like, it makes sense that sales training programs include grooming hints, fashionable clothiers select their floor staffs from among the good-looking candidates, and con men and women are attractive.[2]

Similarity

What if physical appearance is not much at issue? After all, most people possess average looks. Are there other factors that can be used to produce liking? As both researchers and compliance professionals know, there are several, and one of the most influential is similarity.

We like people who are similar to us (Byrne, 1971). This fact seems to hold true whether the similarity is in the area of opinions, personality traits, background, or lifestyle. Consequently, those who want us to like them so that we will comply with

---

[2]Have you ever noticed that despite their good looks, many attractive people don't seem to share the positive impressions of their personalities and abilities that observers have? Research has not only confirmed the tenuous and inconsistent relationship between attractiveness and self-esteem (see Adams, 1977), it has also offered a possible explanation. One set of authors has produced evidence suggesting that good-looking people are aware that other people's positive evaluations of them are not based on their actual traits and abilities but are often caused by an attractiveness "halo" (Major, Carrington, & Carnevale, 1984). Consequently, many attractive people who are exposed to this confusing information may be left with an uncertain self-concept.

them can accomplish that purpose by appearing similar to us in a wide variety of ways.

Dress is a good example. Several studies have demonstrated that we are more likely to help those who dress like us. In one study, done in the early 1970s when young people tended to dress in either "hippie" or "straight" fashion, experimenters donned hippie or straight attire and asked college students on campus for a dime to make a phone call. When the experimenter was dressed in the same way as the student, the request was granted in more than two-thirds of the instances; when the student and requester were dissimilarly dressed, the dime was provided less than half the time (Emswiller, Deaux, & Willits, 1971). Another experiment showed how automatic our positive response to similar others can be. Marchers in an antiwar demonstration were found to be more likely to sign the petition of a similarly dressed requester *and* to do so without bothering to read it first (Suedfeld, Bochner, & Matas, 1971). *Click, whirr.*

Another way requesters can manipulate similarity to increase liking and compliance is to claim that they have backgrounds and interests similar to ours. Car salespeople, for example, are trained to look for evidence of such things while examining a customer's trade-in. If there is camping gear in the trunk, the salespeople might mention, later on, how they love to get away from the city whenever they can; if there are golf balls on the back seat, they might remark that they hope the rain will hold off until they can play the eighteen holes they scheduled for later in the day; if they notice that the car was purchased out of state, they might ask where a customer is from and report—with surprise—that they (or their spouse) were born there, too.

As trivial as these similarities may seem, they appear to work (Brewer, 1979; Tajfel, 1981). One researcher who examined the sales records of insurance companies found that customers were more likely to buy insurance when a salesperson was like them in age, religion, politics, and cigarette-smoking habits (Evans, 1963). Another researcher was able to significantly increase the percentage of people who responded to a mailed survey by changing one small feature of the request: On a cover letter, he modified the name of the survey-taker to be similar to that of the survey recipient. Thus, Robert Greer received the survey from a survey center official named Bob Gregar while Cynthia Johnston received hers from a survey center official named Cindy Johanson. In two separate studies, adding this little bit of similarity to the exchange nearly doubled survey compliance (Garner, 1999). These seemingly minor commonalties can affect decisions that go well beyond whose insurance to purchase or whose survey to complete. They can affect the decision of whose life to save. When asked to rank-order a waiting list of patients suffering from kidney disorder as to their deservingness for the next available treatment, people chose those whose political party preference matched their own (Furnham, 1996).

Because even small similarities can be effective in producing a positive response to another and because a veneer of similarity can be so easily manufactured, I would advise special caution in the presence of requesters who claim to be "just like you."[3] Indeed, it would be wise these days to be careful around salespeople who just *seem* to be just like you. Many sales training programs now urge trainees to "mirror and match" the customer's body posture, mood, and verbal style, as similarities along each of these dimensions have been shown to lead to positive results (Chartrand & Bargh, 1999; Locke & Horowitz, 1990; Woodside & Davenport, 1974).

Compliments

Actor McLean Stevenson once described how his wife tricked him into marriage: "She said she liked me." Although designed for a laugh, the remark is as instructive as it is humorous. The information that someone fancies us can be a bewitchingly effective device for producing return liking and willing compliance (Berscheid & Walster, 1978; Howard, Gengler, & Jain, 1995, 1997). So, often when people flatter us or claim affinity for us, they want something from us.

Remember Joe Girard, the world's "greatest car salesman," who says the secret of his success was getting customers to like him? He did something that, on the face of it, seems foolish and costly. Each month he sent every one of his more than 13,000 former customers a holiday greeting card containing a printed message. The holiday greeting card changed from month to month (Happy New Year, Happy Valentine's Day, Happy Thanksgiving, and so on), but the message printed on the face of the card never varied. It read, "I like you." As Joe explained it, "There's nothing else on the card, nothin' but my name. I'm just telling 'em that I like 'em."

"I like you." It came in the mail every year, 12 times a year, like clockwork. "I like you," on a printed card that went to 13,000 other people, too. Could a statement of liking so impersonal, obviously designed to sell cars, really work: Joe Girard thought so, and a man as successful as he was at what he did deserves our attention. Joe understood an important fact about human nature: we are phenomenal suckers for flattery. Although there are limits to our gullibility—especially when we can be sure that the flatterer is trying to manipulate us (Jones & Wortman, 1973)—we tend, as a rule, to believe praise and to like those who provide it, often when it is probably untrue (Byrne, Rasche, & Kelley, 1974).

An experiment done on a group of men in North Carolina shows how helpless we can be in the face of praise. The men in the study received comments about themselves from another person who needed a favor from them. Some of the men got only positive comments, some got only negative comments, and some got a mixture of good and bad. There were three interesting findings. First, the evaluator who provided only praise was liked best by the men. Second, this tendency held true even when

---

[3]Additional work suggests yet another reason for caution when dealing with similar requesters: we typically underestimate the degree to which similarity affects our liking for another (Gonzales, Davis, Loney, Lukens, & Junghans, 1983).

Cheep Real Estate

The potent influence of similarity on sales is something compliance professionals have long understood.

The Penguin Leunig, © 1983, by Michael Leunig, published by Penguin Books Australia Ltd.

the men fully realized that the flatterer stood to gain from their liking him. Finally, unlike the other types of comments, pure praise did not have to be accurate to work. Positive comments produced just as much liking for the flatterer when they were untrue as when they were true (Drachman, deCarufel, & Insko, 1978).

Apparently we have such an automatically positive reaction to compliments that we can fall victim to someone who uses them in an obvious attempt to win our favor. *Click, whirr.* When seen in this light, the expense of printing and mailing well over 150,000 "I like you" cards each year seems neither as foolish nor as costly as before.

Contact and Cooperation

For the most part, we like things that are familiar to us (Zajonc, 1968). To prove the point to yourself, try a little experiment. Get the negative of an old photograph that shows a front view of your face and have it developed into a pair of pictures—one that shows you as you actually look and one that shows a reverse image (so that the right and left sides of your face are interchanged). Now decide which version of your face you like better and ask a good friend to make the choice, too. If you are at all like the group of Milwaukee women on whom this procedure was tried, you should notice something odd: Your friend will prefer the true print, but you will prefer the reverse image. Why? Because you *both* will be responding favorably to the more familiar face—your friend to the one the world sees and you to the transposed one you find in the mirror every day (Mita, Dermer, & Knight, 1977).

Because of its effect on liking, familiarity plays a role in decisions about all sorts of things, including the politicians we elect (Grush, 1980; Grush, McKeough, & Ahlering, 1978). It appears that in an election booth voters often choose a candidate merely because the name seems familiar. In one controversial Ohio election a few years ago, a man given little chance of winning the state attorney-general race swept to victory when, shortly before the election, he changed his name to Brown—a family name of much Ohio political tradition.

How could such a thing happen? The answer lies partially in the unconscious way that familiarity affects liking. Often we don't realize that our attitude toward something has been influenced by the number of times we have been exposed to it in the past. For example, in one experiment, the faces of several individuals were flashed on a screen so quickly that, later on, the subjects who were exposed to the faces in this manner couldn't recall having seen any of them before. Yet, the more frequently a person's face was flashed on the screen, the more these subjects came to like that person when they met in a subsequent interaction. And because greater liking leads to greater social influence, these subjects were also more persuaded by the opinion statements of the individuals whose faces had appeared on the screen most frequently (Bornstein, Leone, & Galley, 1987).

On the basis of evidence that we are more favorably disposed toward the things we have had contact with, some people have recommended a "contact" approach to improving race relations. They argue that, simply by providing individuals of different ethnic backgrounds with more exposure to one another as equals, those individuals will naturally come to like each other better. However, when scientists have examined school integration—the area offering the single best test of the contact approach—they have discovered quite the opposite pattern. School desegregation is more likely to increase prejudice between blacks and whites than to decrease it (Stephan, 1978).

Let's stay with the issue of school desegregation for a while. However well intentioned the proponents of interracial harmony through simple contact are, their approach is unlikely to bear fruit because the argument on which it is based is terribly misinformed (Gerard, 1983; Maruyama, Miller, & Holtz, 1986). First of all, research has shown that the school setting is not a melting pot where children interact as readily with members of other ethnic groups as they do with their own. Years after formal school integration, there is little social integration. The students clot together ethnically, separating themselves, for the most part, from other groups (Rogers, Hennigan, Bowman, & Miller, 1984; Oskamp & Schultz, 1998). Second, even if there were much more interethnic interaction, research shows that becoming familiar with something through repeated contact doesn't necessarily cause greater liking (Gaertner et al., 1999). In fact, continued exposure to a person or object under unpleasant conditions such as frustration, conflict, or competition leads to less liking (Burgess & Sales, 1971; Swap, 1977; Zajonc, Markus, & Wilson, 1974). The typical American classroom fosters precisely these unpleasant conditions.

Consider the illuminating report of psychologist Elliot Aronson, called in to consult with school authorities on problems in the Austin, Texas, schools. His description of the way he found education proceeding in the standard classroom could apply to nearly any public school in the United States:

> *In general, here is how it works: The teacher stands in front of the class and asks a question. Six to ten children strain in their seats and wave their hands in the teacher's face, eager to be called on and show how smart they are. Several others sit quietly with eyes averted, trying to become invisible. When the teacher calls on one child, you see looks of disappointment and dismay on the faces of the eager students, who missed a chance to get the teacher's approval; and you will see relief on the faces of the others who didn't know the answer. . . . This game is fiercely competitive and the stakes are high, because the kids are competing for the love and approval of one of the two or three most important people in their world.*
>
> *Further, this teaching process guarantees that the children will not learn to like and understand each other. Conjure up your own experience. If you knew the right answer and the teacher called on someone else, you probably hoped that he or she would make a mistake so that you would have a chance to display your knowledge. If you were called on and failed, or if you didn't even raise your hand to compete, you probably envied and resented your classmates who knew the answer. Children who fail in this system become jealous and resentful of the successes, putting them down as teacher's pets or even resorting to violence against them in the school yard. The successful students, for their part, often hold the unsuccessful children in contempt, calling them "dumb" or "stupid." (Aronson, 1975, pp. 44, 47)*

Should we wonder, then, why strict school desegregation—whether by enforced busing, district rezoning, or school closures—so frequently produces increased rather than decreased prejudice? When our children find their pleasant social and friendship contacts within their ethnic boundaries and get repeated exposure to other groups only in the competitive cauldron of the classroom, we might expect as much.

Are there available solutions to this problem? One possibility might be to end our attempts at school integration, but that hardly seems workable. Even if we were to ignore the inevitable legal and constitutional challenges and the disruptive societal wrangle such a retreat would provide, there are solid reasons for pursuing classroom integration. For instance, although white students' achievement levels remain steady, it is 10 times more likely that the academic performance of minority students will significantly increase rather than significantly decline after desegregation (Stephan, 1978).

We must be cautious in our approach to school desegregation so that we do not throw out the baby with the bath water. The idea, of course, is to jettison just the water, leaving the baby shining from the bath. Right now, though, our baby is soaking in the *Schmutzwasser* of increased racial hostility. Fortunately, real hope for draining away that hostility is emerging from the research of education specialists into the concept of "cooperative learning." Because much of the heightened prejudice from classroom desegregation seems to stem from increased exposure to outside group members as rivals, these educators have experimented with forms of learning in which cooperation rather than competition with classmates is central.

Off to Camp

To understand the logic of the cooperative approach, it helps to reexamine the fascinating, four-decade-old research program of Turkish-born social scientist Muzafer Sherif and his colleagues (Sherif, Harvey, White, Hood, & Sherif, 1961). Intrigued with the issue of intergroup conflict, the research team decided to investigate the process as it developed in boys' summer camps. Although the boys never realized that they were participants in an experiment, Sherif and his associates consistently engaged in artful manipulations of the camp's social environment to observe the effects on group relations.

What the researchers learned is that it didn't take much to bring on certain kinds of ill will. Simply separating the boys into two residence cabins was enough to stimulate a "we versus they" feeling between the groups; letting the boys assign names to the two groups (the Eagles and the Rattlers) accelerated the sense of rivalry. The boys soon began to demean the qualities and accomplishments of the other group; however, these forms of hostility were minor compared to what occurred when the experimenters purposely introduced competitive activities into the groups' meetings with one another. Cabin-against-cabin treasure hunts, tugs-of-war, and athletic contests produced name-calling and confrontations. During the competitions, members of the opposing team were labeled "cheaters," "sneaks," and "stinkers." Afterward, cabins were raided, rival banners were stolen and burned, threatening signs were posted, and lunchroom scuffles were commonplace.

At this point, it was evident to Sherif that the recipe for disharmony was quick and easy: just separate the participants into groups and let them sit for a while in their own juices. Then mix together over the flame of continued competition. And there you have it: Cross-group hatred at a rolling boil.

A more challenging issue then faced the experimenters: how to remove the now entrenched hostility. They first tried the contact approach of bringing the bands together more often. Even when the joint activities were pleasant, such as movies and social events, the results were disastrous. Picnics produced food fights, entertainment programs gave way to shouting contests, dining-hall lines degenerated into shoving matches. Sherif and his research team began to worry that, in Dr. Frankenstein fashion, they might have created a monster they could no longer control. Then, at the height of the strife, they tried a strategy that was at once simple and effective.

They constructed a series of situations in which competition between the groups would have harmed everyone's interest; instead, cooperation was necessary for mutual benefit. On a day-long outing, the single truck available to go into town for food was "found" to be stuck. The boys were assembled and all pulled and pushed together until the vehicle was on its way. In another instance, the researchers arranged for an interruption of the camp's water supply, which came through pipes from a distant tank. Presented with the common crisis and realizing the need for unified action, the boys organized themselves harmoniously to find and fix the problem before day's end. In yet another circumstance requiring cooperation, the campers were informed that a desirable movie was available for rental but that the camp could not afford it. Aware that the only solution was to combine resources, the boys pooled their money for the film and spent a very congenial evening together enjoying it.

The consequences of these cooperative ventures though not instantaneous, were nonetheless striking. Successful joint efforts toward common goals steadily bridged the rift between the two groups. Before long, the verbal baiting had died, the jostling in lines had ended, and the boys had begun to intermix at the meal tables. Further, when asked to list their best friends, significant numbers changed from an earlier exclusive naming of in-group chums to a listing that included boys in the other group. Some even thanked the researchers for the opportunity to rate their friends again because they had changed their minds since the earlier evaluation. In one revealing episode, the boys were returning from a campfire on a single bus—something that would have produced bedlam before but, at that point, was specifically requested by the boys. When the bus stopped at a refreshment stand, the boys of one group, with $5 left in their treasury, decided to treat their former bitter adversaries to milkshakes!

We can trace the roots of this surprising turnabout to those times when the boys had to view one another as allies instead of opponents. The crucial procedure was the experimenters' imposition of common goals on the groups. It was the cooperation required to achieve these goals that finally allowed the rival group members to experience one another as reasonable fellows, valued helpers, friends, and friends of friends (Wright, Aaron, McLaughlin-Volpe, & Ropp, 1997). When success resulted from the mutual efforts, it became especially difficult to maintain feelings of hostility toward those who had been teammates in the triumph.[4]

---

[4]You should not assume from these descriptions that successful cooperation works to reduce intergroup hostility only among school-age children. Subsequent research has found similar results of similar procedures in college groups (Worchel, 1979) and business organizations (Blake & Mouton, 1979). In these and most all groups, cooperation not only leads to greater liking but to greater group success (Stanne, D. W. Johnson, & R. T. Johnson, 1999).

Back to School

In the welter of racial tensions that followed school desegregation, certain educational psychologists began to see the relevance to the classroom in Sherif et al.'s findings. If only the learning experience there could be modified to include at least occasional interethnic cooperation toward mutual successes, perhaps cross-group friendships would have a place to grow. Although similar projects have been under way in various states (S. W. Cook, 1990, DeVries & Slavin, 1978; D. W. Johnson & R. T Johnson, 1983; Oskamp & Schultz, 1998), an especially interesting approach in this direction—termed the jigsaw classroom—was developed by Elliot Aronson and his colleagues in Texas and California (Aronson, Stephan, Sikes, Blaney, & Snapp, 1978).

The essence of the jigsaw route to learning is to require that students work together to master the material to be tested on an upcoming examination. This end is accomplished by grouping students into cooperating teams and giving each student only part of the information—one piece of the puzzle—necessary to pass the test. Under this system the students must take turns teaching and helping one another. Everyone needs everyone else to do well. Like Sherif's campers working on tasks that could be successfully accomplished only jointly, the students become allies rather than enemies.

When tried in newly desegregated classrooms, the jigsaw approach has generated impressive results. Studies have shown that, compared to other classrooms in the same school using the traditional competitive method, jigsaw learning stimulated significantly more friendship and less prejudice among ethnic groups. Besides this vital reduction in hostility, there were other advantages: minority students' self-esteem, liking for school, and test scores improved. The white students benefited, too. Their self-esteem and liking for school went up, and their test performance was at least as high as that of whites in traditional classes (Aronson, Bridgeman, & Geffner, 1978a, 1978b).

There is a tendency when faced with positive results like those from the jigsaw classroom to become overly enthusiastic about a single, simple solution to a difficult problem. Experience should tell us that such problems rarely yield to a simple remedy. That is no doubt true in this case as well. Even within the boundaries of cooperative learning procedures, the issues are complex (Rosenfield & Stephan, 1981; Slavin, 1983). Before we can feel truly comfortable with the jigsaw, or any similar approach to learning and liking, much more research is needed to determine how frequently, in what size doses, at which ages, and in which sorts of groups cooperative strategies will work. We also need to know the best way for teachers to institute new methods—provided they will institute them at all. After all, not only are cooperative learning techniques a radical departure from the traditional, familiar routine of most teachers, but they may also threaten a teacher's sense of importance in the classroom by turning over much of the instruction to the students. Finally, we must realize that competition has its place, too. It can serve as a valuable motivator of desirable action and an important builder of self-concept. The task, then, is not to eliminate aca-

As studies reveal, the jigsaw classroom is not only an effective way to bring about friendship and cooperation among ethnic groups but it increases minority students' self-esteem, liking for school, and test scores as well.

demic competition but to break its monopoly in the classroom by introducing regular cooperative techniques that include members of all ethnic groups and lead to successful outcomes.

Despite these qualifications, I cannot help but be encouraged by the evidence to date. When I talk to my students, or even my neighbors and friends, about the prospects for cooperative learning approaches, I can feel the optimism rise in me. The public schools have for so long been sources of discouraging news—sinking test scores, teacher burnout, increasing crime, and of course, racial conflict. Now there is at least one crack in the gloom, and I find myself genuinely excited about it.

What's the point of this digression into the effects of school desegregation in race relations? The point is to make two points. First, although the familiarity produced by contact usually leads to greater liking, the opposite occurs if the contact carries distasteful experiences with it. Therefore, when children of different racial groups are thrown into the incessant, harsh competition of the standard American classroom, we ought to—and do—see hostilities worsen. Second, the evidence that team-oriented learning is an antidote to this disorder tells us about the heavy impact of cooperation on the liking process.

Before we assume that cooperation is a powerful cause of liking, we should first pass it through what, to my mind, is the acid test: Do compliance practitioners systematically use cooperation to get us to like them so that we will say yes to their requests? Do they point it out when it exists naturally in a situation? Do they try to amplify it when it exists only weakly? And, most instructive of all, do they manufacture it when it isn't there at all?

As it turns out, cooperation passes the test with flying colors. Compliance professionals are forever attempting to establish that we and they are working for the same goals, that we must "pull together" for mutual benefit, that they are, in essence, our *teammates*. A host of examples is possible. Most are familiar, such as the new-car salespeople who take our side and "do battle" with their bosses to secure us a good deal.[5] One rather spectacular illustration occurs in a setting few of us would recognize firsthand, because the professionals are police interrogators whose job is to induce suspects to confess to crime.

In recent years, the courts have imposed a variety of restrictions on the way police must behave in handling suspected criminals, especially in seeking confessions. Many procedures that, in the past, led to admissions of guilt can no longer be employed for fear that they will result in cases being dismissed. As yet, however, the courts have found nothing illegal in the police's use of subtle psychology. For this reason, criminal interrogations have taken increasingly to the use of such ploys as the one they call Good Cop/Bad Cop.

Good Cop/Bad Cop works as follows: A young robbery suspect, for example, who has been advised of his rights and is maintaining his innocence, is brought to a room to be questioned by a pair of officers. One of the officers, either because the part suits him or because it is merely his turn, plays the role of Bad Cop. Before the suspect even sits down, Bad Cop curses "the-son-of-a-bitch" for the robbery. For the rest of the session his words come only with snarls and growls. He kicks the prisoner's chair to emphasize his points. When he looks at the suspect, he seems to see a mound of garbage. If the suspect challenges Bad Cop's accusations or just refuses to answer them, Bad Cop becomes livid. His rage soars. He swears he will do everything possible to assure a maximum sentence. He says he has friends in the district attorney's office who will hear from him of the suspect's noncooperative attitude and will prosecute the case hard.

At the outset of Bad Cop's performance, his partner, Good Cop, sits in the background. Then, slowly, Good Cop starts to chip in. First he speaks only to Bad Cop,

---

[5] In truth, little in the way of combat takes place when the salesman enters the manager's office under such circumstances. Often, because the salesman knows exactly the price below which he cannot go, he and the boss don't even speak. In one car dealership I infiltrated while researching this book, it was common for a salesman to have a soft drink or cigarette in silence while the boss continued working. After a seemly time, the salesman would loosen his tie and return to his customers, looking weary but carrying the deal he had just "hammered out" for them—the same deal he had in mind before entering the boss' office.

trying to temper the burgeoning anger. "Calm down, Frank, calm down." But Bad Cop shouts back, "Don't tell me to calm down when he's lying right to my face! I hate these lying bastards!" A bit later, Good Cop actually says something in the suspect's behalf. "Take it easy, Frank, he's only a kid." Not much in the way of support, but compared to the rantings of Bad Cop, the words fall like music on the prisoner's ears. Still, Bad Cop is unconvinced. "Kid? He's no kid. He's a punk. That's what he is, a punk. And I'll tell you something else. He's over 18, and that's all I need to get his ass sent so far behind bars they'll need a flashlight to find him."

Now Good Cop begins to speak directly to the suspect, calling him by his first name and pointing out any positive details of the case. "I'll tell you, Kenny, you're lucky that nobody was hurt and you weren't armed. When you come up for sentencing, that'll look good." If the suspect persists in claiming innocence, Bad Cop launches into another tirade of curses and threats. This time Good Cop stops him, "Okay, Frank," handing Bad Cop some money, "I think we could all use some coffee. How about getting us three cups?"

When Bad Cop is gone, it's time for Good Cop's big scene: "Look, man, I don't know why, but my partner doesn't like you, and he's gonna try to get you. And he's gonna be able to do it, because we've got enough evidence right now. And he's right about the D.A.'s office going hard on guys who don't cooperate. You're looking at five years, man, five years! Now, I don't want to see that happen to you. So if you admit you robbed that place right now, before he gets back, I'll take charge of your case and put in a good word for you to the D.A. If we work together on this, we can cut that five years down to two, maybe one. Do us both a favor, Kenny. Just tell me how you did it, and let's start working on getting you through this." A full confession frequently follows.

Good Cop/Bad Cop works as well as it does for several reasons: The fear of long incarceration is quickly instilled by Bad Cop's threats; the perceptual contrast principle (see Chapter 1) ensures that compared to the raving, venomous Bad Cop, the interrogator playing Good Cop will seem like an *especially* reasonable and kind person (Kamisar, 1980); and because Good Cop has intervened repeatedly on the suspect's behalf—has even spent his own money for a cup of coffee—the reciprocity rule pressures for a return favor (Rafaeli & Sutton, 1991). The main reason that the technique is effective, though, is that it gives the suspect the idea that there is someone on his side, someone with his welfare in mind, someone working together with him, for him. In most situations, such a person would be viewed very favorably, but in the deep trouble our robbery suspect finds himself, that person takes on the character of a savior. And from savior, it is but a short step to trusted father confessor.

CONDITIONING AND ASSOCIATION

"Why do they blame *me*, Doc?" It was the shaky telephone voice of a local TV weatherman. He had been given my number when he called the psychology department at my university to find someone who could answer his question—a question that had always puzzled him but had recently begun to bother and depress him.

"I mean, it's crazy, isn't it? Everybody knows that I just report the weather, that I don't order it, right? So how come I get so much flak when the weather's bad? During the floods last year, I got hate mail! One guy threatened to shoot me if it didn't stop raining. Christ, I'm still looking over my shoulder from that one. And the people I work with at the station do it, too! Sometimes, right on the air, they'll zing me about a heat wave or something. They have to know that I'm not responsible, but that doesn't seem to stop them. Can you help me understand this, Doc? It's really getting me down."

We made an appointment to talk in my office, where I tried to explain that he was the victim of an ages-old *click, whirr* response that people have to things they perceive as merely connected to one another. Instances of this response abound in modern life. I felt that the example most likely to help the distressed weatherman would require a bit of ancient history. I asked him to consider the precarious fate of the imperial messengers of old Persia. Any such messenger assigned the role of military courier had special cause to hope mightily for Persian battlefield successes. With news of victory in his pouch, he would be treated as a hero upon his arrival at the palace. The food, drink, and women of his choice were provided gladly and sumptuously. Should his message tell of military disaster, though, the reception would be quite different: He was summarily slain.

I hoped that the point of this story would not be lost on the weatherman. I wanted him to be aware of a fact that is as true today as it was in the time of ancient Persia: The nature of bad news infects the teller. There is a natural human tendency to dislike a person who brings us unpleasant information, even when that person did not cause the bad news. The simple association with it is enough to stimulate our dislike (Manis, Cornell, & Moore, 1974).

There was something else I hoped the weatherman would get from the historical example. Not only was he joined in his predicament by centuries of other "tellers," but also, compared to some (such as the Persian messengers), he was very well-off. At the end of our session, he said something to convince me that he appreciated this point quite clearly. "Doc," he said on his way out, "I feel a lot better about my job now. I mean, I'm in Phoenix where the sun shines 300 days a year, right? Thank God I don't do the weather in Buffalo."

The weatherman's parting comment reveals that he understood more than I had told him about the principle that was influencing his viewers' liking for him. Being connected with bad weather does have a negative effect, but being connected with sunshine should do wonders for his popularity. And he was right. The principle of association is a general one, governing both negative and positive connections. *An innocent association with either bad things or good things will influence how people feel about us* (Lott & Lott, 1965).

Our instruction about the way negative association works seems to have been primarily undertaken by our parents. Remember how they are always warning us against

Weathermen pay price for nature's curve balls

by David L. Langford
Associated Press

Television weather forecasters make a good living talking about the weather, but when Mother Nature throws a curve ball, they duck for cover.

Conversations with several veteran prognosticators across the country this week turned up stories of their being whacked by old ladies with umbrellas, accosted by drunks in bars, pelted with snowballs and galoshes, threatened with death, and accused of trying to play God.

"I had one guy call and tell me that if it snowed over Christmas, I wouldn't live to see New Year's," said Bob Gregory, who has been the forecaster at WTHR-TV in Indianapolis for nine years.

Most of the forecasters claimed they are accurate 80 to 90 percent of the time on one-day forecasts, but longer-range predictions get tricky. And most conceded they are simply reporting information supplied by computers and anonymous meteorologists from the National Weather Service or a private agency.

But it's the face on the television screen that people go after.

Tom Bonner, 35, who has been with KARK-TV in Little Rock, AR, for 11 years, remembers the time a burly farmer from Lonoke, with too much to drink, walked up to him in a bar, poked a finger in his chest and said:

"You're the one that sent that tornado and tore my house up . . . I'm going to take your head off."

Bonner said he then looked for the bouncer, couldn't spot him, and replied, "That's right about the tornado, and I'll tell you something else. I'll send another one if you don't back off."

Several years ago, when a major flood left water 10 feet deep in San Diego's Mission Valley, Mike Ambrose of KGTV recalls that a woman walked up to his car, whacked the windshield with an umbrella and said, "This rain is your fault."

Chuck Whitaker of WSBT-TV in South Bend, IN, says, "One little old lady called the police department and wanted the weatherman arrested for bringing all the snow."

A woman upset that it had rained for her daughter's wedding called Tom Jolls of WKBW-TV in Buffalo, NY, to give him a piece of her mind. "She held me responsible and said if she ever met me she would probably hit me," he said.

Sonny Eliot of WJBK-TV, a forecaster in the Detroit area for 30 years, recalls predicting 2 to 4 inches of snow in the city several years ago and more than 8 came down. To retaliate, his colleagues at the station set up a contraption that rained about 200 galoshes on him while his was giving the forecast the next day.

"I've still got lumps to prove it," he says.

FIGURE 5.1   Weather-Beaten
Note the similarities between the account of the weatherman who came to my office and those of other TV weather reporters.

playing with the bad kids down the street? Remember how they said it didn't matter if we did nothing bad ourselves because, in the eyes of the neighborhood, we would be "known by the company we kept." Our parents were teaching us about guilt by association—and they were giving us a lesson in the negative side of the principle of association. And they were right. People do assume that we have the same personality traits as our friends (Miller, Campbell, Twedt, & O'Connell, 1966).

As for the positive associations, it is the compliance professionals who teach the lesson. They are incessantly trying to connect themselves or their products with the things we like. Did you ever wonder what all those good-looking models are doing standing around in the automobile ads? What the advertiser hopes they are doing is lending their positive traits—beauty and desirability—to the cars. The advertiser is betting that we will respond to the product in the same ways we respond to the attractive models merely associated with it—and we do.

In one study, men who saw a new-car ad that included a seductive female model rated the *car* as faster, more appealing, more expensive-looking, and better-designed than did men who viewed the same ad without the model. Yet when asked later, the men refused to believe that the presence of the young woman had influenced their judgments (Smith & Engel, 1968).

Although there are other examples (Bierley, McSweeney, & Vannieuwkerk, 1985; Gorn, 1982), perhaps the most intriguing evidence of the way the association principle can unconsciously stimulate us to part with our money comes from a series of investigations on credit cards and spending (Feinberg, 1986). Within modern life, credit cards are a relatively new device with a psychologically noteworthy characteristic: They allow us to get the immediate benefits of goods and services while deferring the costs weeks into the future. Consequently, we are more likely to associate credit cards and the insignias, symbols, and logos that represent them with the positive rather than the negative aspects of spending.

Consumer researcher Richard Feinberg wondered what effects the presence of such credit cards and credit card materials had on our tendencies to spend. In a set of studies done in West Lafayette, Indiana, he got some fascinating—and disturbing—results. First, restaurant patrons gave larger tips when paying with a credit card instead of cash. In a second study, college students were willing to spend an average of 29 percent more money for mail-order catalog items when they examined the items in a room that contained some MasterCard insignias; moreover, they had no awareness that the credit card insignias were part of the experiment. A final study showed that when asked to contribute to charity (the United Way), college students were markedly more likely to give money if the room they were in contained MasterCard insignias than if it did not (87 percent versus 33 percent). This last finding is simultaneously the most unsettling and instructive concerning the power of the association principle to generate compliance. Even though credit cards themselves were not used for the charity donation, the mere presence of their symbol (with its attendant positive associations) spurred people to spend more *cash*. This last phenomenon has been replicated in a pair of restaurant studies in which patrons received their bills on tip trays that either did or did not contain a credit card insignia. The diners tipped significantly more in the presence of the insignia, even when they paid with cash (McCall and Belmont, 1996).[6]

Because the association principle works so well—and so unconsciously—manufacturers regularly rush to connect their products with the current cultural rage. During the days of the first American moon shot, everything from breakfast drink to deodorant was sold with allusions to the American space program. In Olympiad years, we are told precisely the official hair sprays and facial tissue of our Olympic teams.[7] During the 1970s, when the magic cultural concept appeared to be "naturalness," the "natural" bandwagon was crowded to capacity. Sometimes the connections to naturalness didn't even make sense: "Change your hair color naturally" urged one popular TV commercial. Similarly, although it made great sense that sales of Mars Rover toys would jump after a U.S. Pathfinder rocket landed the real thing on the red planet in 1997, it made little sense that the same would happen for the sales of Mars Candy Bars, which have nothing to do with the space project but are named after the candy company's founder, Franklin Mars (White, 1997).

The linking of celebrities to products is another way advertisers cash in on the association principle. Professional athletes are paid to connect themselves to things that can be directly relevant to their roles (sports shoes, tennis racquets, golf balls) or wholly irrelevant (soft drinks, popcorn poppers, panty hose). The important thing for the advertiser is to establish the connection; it doesn't have to be a logical one, just a positive one.

Of course, popular entertainers provide another form of desirability that manufacturers have always paid dearly to tie to their goods. Recently, politicians have recognized the ability of a celebrity linkage to sway voters. According to Democratic Party consultant Tom Yamuda, who prepared a report titled "Celebrities = Sell-Ebrities," movie star endorsement is "the very best way to get your wish to become law" (Glass, 1997). Presidential candidates assemble stables of well-known nonpolitical figures who either actively participate in, or merely lend their names to, a campaign. Even at state and local levels, a similar game is played. Take as evidence

---

[6]Subsequent research by Feinberg (1990) strengthens the association explanation for his results. He has found that the presence of credit card insignias in a room only facilitates spending by people who have had a positive history with credit cards. Those who have had a negative history with credit cards—because they've paid an above-average number of interest charges in the previous year—do not show the facilitation effect. In fact, these individuals are more conservative in their spending tendencies when in the mere presence of credit card logos.

[7]The rights to such associations do not come cheaply. Corporate contributors spend millions to win sponsorships for the Olympics. But this amount pales in comparison to the many millions more these companies then spend to advertise their connection to the event. Yet it may be that the largest dollar figure of all for the corporate sponsors is the one on the profit line. A survey by *Advertising Age* magazine found that one-third of all consumers interviewed said they would be more likely to purchase an item if it were linked to the Olympics.

Star-Spangled Banter
On the campaign trail, presidential candidate Al Gore looks pleased to be linked with
Tonight Show host Jay Leno—no matter how Leno is dressed.

the comment of a Los Angeles woman I heard expressing her conflicting feelings
over a California referendum to limit smoking in public places. "It's a real tough
decision. They've got big stars speaking for it, and big stars speaking against it. You
don't know how to vote."

If politicians are relative newcomers to the use of celebrity endorsements, they
are old hands at exploiting the association principle in other ways. For example, congressional representatives invariably announce to the press the start of federal pro-

jects that will bring new jobs or benefits to their home states; this tradition continues even when the representative has had nothing to do with advancing the project or has, in some cases, voted against it.

Does the Name Pavlov Ring a Bell?

While politicians have long strained to associate themselves with the values of motherhood, country, and apple pie, it may be in the last of these connections—to food—that they have been most clever. For instance, it is White House tradition to try to sway the votes of balking legislators over a meal. It can be a picnic lunch, a sumptuous breakfast, or an elegant dinner; but when an important bill is up for grabs, out comes the silverware. Political fund-raising these days regularly involves the presentation of food. Notice, too, that at the typical fund-raising dinner the speeches and the appeals for further contributions and heightened effort never come before the meal is served, only during or after. There are several advantages to this technique. For example, time is saved and the reciprocity rule is engaged. The least recognized benefit, however, may be the one uncovered in research conducted in the 1930s by the distinguished psychologist Gregory Razran (1938).

Using what he termed the "luncheon technique," he found that his subjects become fonder of the people and things they experienced while they were eating. In the example most relevant for our purposes (Razran, 1940), subjects were presented with some political statements they had rated once before. At the end of the experiment, after all the political statements had been presented, Razran found that only certain of them had gained in approval—those that had been shown while food was being eaten. These changes in liking seem to have occurred unconsciously, since the subjects could not remember which of the statements they had seen while the food was being served.[8]

How did Razran come up with the luncheon technique? What made him think it would work? The answer may lie in the dual scholarly roles he played during his career. Not only was he a respected independent researcher, he was also one of the earliest translators into English of the pioneering psychological literature of Russia. It was a literature dedicated to the study of the association principle and dominated by the thinking of a brilliant man, Ivan Pavlov.

Although a scientist of broad and varied talent—he had, for instance, won a Nobel Prize years earlier for his work on the digestive system—Pavlov's most important experimental demonstration was simplicity itself. He showed that he could get an animal's typical response to food (salivation) to be directed toward something

---

[8]To demonstrate that the principle of association also works for unpleasant experiences, Razran (1940) included in his experiment a condition in which certain participants had putrid odors piped into the room while they were shown the political slogans. In this case, approval ratings for the slogans declined.

irrelevant to food (a bell) merely by connecting the two things in the animal's experience. If the presentation of food to a dog was always accompanied by the sound of a bell, soon the dog would salivate to the bell alone, even when there was no food to be had.

It is not a long step from Pavlov's classic demonstration to Razran's luncheon technique. Obviously, a normal reaction to food can be transferred to some other thing through the process of raw association. Razran's insight was that there are many normal responses to food besides salivation, one of them being a good and favorable feeling. Therefore, it is possible to attach this pleasant feeling, this positive attitude, to anything (political statements being only an example) that is closely associated with good food.

Nor is there a long step from the luncheon technique to the compliance professionals' realization that all kinds of desirable things can substitute for food in lending their likable qualities to the ideas, products, and people artificially linked to them. In the final analysis, then, that is why those good-looking models stand around in the magazine ads. That is why radio programmers are instructed to insert the station's call-letters jingle immediately before a big hit song is played. And that is even why the women playing Barnyard Bingo at a Tupperware party must yell the word *Tupperware* rather than *Bingo* before they can rush to the center of the floor for a prize. It may be Tupperware for the players, but it's *Bingo!* for the company.

Just because we are often unaware victims of compliance practitioners' use of the association principle doesn't mean that we don't understand how it works or don't use it ourselves. There is ample evidence, for instance, that we understand fully the predicament of a Persian imperial messenger or modern-day weatherman announcing the bad news. In fact, we can be counted on to take steps to avoid putting ourselves in any similar positions. Research done at the University of Georgia shows just how we operate when faced with the task of communicating good or bad news (Rosen & Tesser, 1970). Students waiting for an experiment to begin were given the job of informing a fellow student that an important phone call had come in for him. Half the time the call was supposed to bring good news and half the time, bad news. The researchers found that the students conveyed the information very differently depending on its quality. When the news was positive, the tellers were sure to mention that feature: "You just got a phone call with great news. Better see the experimenter for the details." When the news was unfavorable, they kept themselves apart from it: "You just got a phone call. Better see the experimenter for the details." Obviously, the students had previously learned that, to be liked, they should connect themselves to good news but not bad news.

From the News and Weather to the Sports

A lot of strange behavior can be explained by the fact that people understand the association principle well enough to try to link themselves to positive events and separate themselves from negative events—even when they have not caused the events.

Some of the strangest of such behavior takes place in the great arena of sports. The actions of the athletes are not the issue, though. After all, in the heated contact of the game, they are entitled to an occasional eccentric outburst. Instead, it is the often raging, irrational, boundless fervor of sports fans that seems, on its face, so puzzling. How can we account for wild sports riots in Europe, or the murder of players and referees by South American soccer crowds gone berserk, or the unnecessary lavishness of gifts provided by local fans to already wealthy American ballplayers on the special "day" set aside to honor them? Rationally, none of this makes sense. It's just a game! Isn't it?

Hardly. The relationship between sport and earnest fan is anything but gamelike. It is serious, intense, and highly personal. An apt illustration comes from one of my favorite anecdotes. It concerns a World War II soldier who returned to his home in the Balkans after the war and shortly thereafter stopped speaking. Medical examinations could find no physical cause for the problem. There was no wound, no brain damage, no vocal impairment. He could read, write, understand a conversation, and follow orders. Yet he would not talk—not for his doctors, not for his friends, not even for his pleading family.

Perplexed and exasperated, his doctors moved him to another city and placed him in a veterans' hospital where he remained for 30 years, never breaking his self-imposed silence and sinking into a life of social isolation. Then one day, a radio in his ward happened to be tuned to a soccer match between his hometown team and a traditional rival. When at a crucial point of play the referee called a foul against a player from the mute veteran's home team, he jumped from his chair, glared at the radio, and spoke his first words in more than three decades: "You dumb ass!" he cried. "Are you trying to *give* them the match?" With that, he returned to his chair and to a silence he never again violated.

There are two important lessons to be derived from this true story. The first concerns the sheer power of the phenomenon. The veteran's desire to have his hometown team succeed was so strong that it alone produced a deviation from his solidly entrenched way of life. The second lesson reveals much about the nature of the union of sports and sports fans, something crucial to its basic character: It is a personal thing. Whatever fragment of an identity that ravaged, mute man still possessed was engaged by soccer play. No matter how weakened his ego may have become after 30 years of wordless stagnation in a hospital ward, it was involved in the outcome of the match. Why? Because he, personally, would be diminished by a hometown defeat, and he, personally, would be enhanced by a hometown victory. How? Through the principle of association. The mere connection of birthplace hooked him, wrapped him, tied him to the approaching triumph or failure.

This phenomenon helps explain the tragic event that befell tennis superstar Monica Seles in April of 1993. In the midst of a match at the Citizen Cup Tournament in Hamburg, Germany, a spectator lunged out of the stands and buried a boning knife in her back. In one sense, Seles and the tournament security crew had been worried about just such an occurrence. It happened at the time of the brutal civil war in Bosnia

between the Serbs and the Croats when accusations of Serbian atrocities were making worldwide headlines. Seles, Serbian by birth, had been the subject of various
death threats and political attacks for months before the incident, causing her to travel
frequently under another name, to make multiple plane reservations, and even to wear
a disguise. When her assailant struck, everyone assumed that his act was connected
to the bloody strife in Seles' homeland. But, no; her attacker, an unemployed lathe
operator from eastern Germany, was not a political or ethnic terrorist. He was a sports
fan. His intent was not to kill Seles but only to injure her so that her rival—and his
countrywoman—Steffi Graf could regain the No. 1 ranking that she had previously
lost to Seles. What centuries-old ethnic hatreds and a raging war had not been able
to do to Monica Seles, the power of sports accomplished.

As distinguished author Isaac Asimov (1975) put it in describing our reactions
to the contests we view, "All things being equal, you root for your own sex, your own
culture, your own locality . . . and what you want to prove is that *you* are better than
the other person. Whomever you root for represents *you;* and when he [or she] wins,
you win." When viewed in this light, the passion of a sports fan begins to make sense.
The game is no light diversion to be enjoyed for its inherent form and artistry. The
self is at stake. That is why hometown crowds are so adoring and, more tellingly, so
grateful toward those regularly responsible for home-team victories. That is also why
the same crowds are often ferocious in their treatment of players, coaches, and officials implicated in athletic failures.[9]

So we want our affiliated sports teams to win to prove our own superiority, but
to whom are we trying to prove it? Ourselves, certainly, but to everyone else, too.
According to the association principle, if we can surround ourselves with success that
we are connected with in even a superficial way (for example, place of residence), our
public prestige will rise.

All this tells me is that we purposefully manipulate the visibility of our connections with winners and losers in order to make ourselves look good to anyone who
views these connections. By showcasing the positive associations and burying the
negative ones, we are trying to get observers to think more highly of us and to like
us more. There are many ways we go about this, but one of the simplest and most
pervasive is in the pronouns we use. Have you noticed for example, how often after
a home-team victory fans crowd into the range of a TV camera, thrust their index
fingers high, and shout, "We're number one! We're number one!" Note that the call
is not "They're number one" or even "Our team is number one." The pronoun is *we,*
designed to imply the closest possible identity with the team.

---

[9]Take, for example, the case of Andres Escobar who, as a member of the Colombian national
team, accidentally tipped a ball into his own team's net during a World Cup soccer match in
1994. The "auto-goal" led to a U.S. team victory and to the elimination of the favored Colom-
bians from the competition. Back home two weeks later, Escobar was executed in a restaurant by two gunmen, who shot him 12 times for his mistake.

The Agony of Victory

Monica Seles grimaces from a stab wound while her attacker, Guenther
Parche, is subdued. Parche later testified that his motivation was not politi-
cal or symbolic. He was only trying to advance the career of fellow German
Steffi Graf, who was Seles's chief rival at the time. Perhaps in recognition
that sports fanaticism can lead to temporary insanity, a Hamburg court gave
Parche a two-year suspended sentence and allowed him to go free.

Sports Fan(atic)s
Team spirit goes a step beyond wearing the school sweatshirt as these
Stanford University students wear their school letters a different way
and cheer their team to victory.

Note also that nothing similar occurs in the case of failure. No television viewer
will ever hear the chant, "We're in last place! We're in last place!" Home-team defeats are the times for distancing oneself. Here *we* is not nearly as preferred as the
insulating pronoun *they*. To prove the point, I once did a small experiment in which
students at Arizona State University were phoned and asked to describe the outcome
of a football game their school team had played a few weeks earlier (Cialdini et al.,
1976). Some of the students were asked the outcome of a certain game their team
had lost; the other students were asked the outcome of a different game—one their
team had won. My fellow researcher, Avril Thorne, and I simply listened to what
was said and recorded the percentage of students who used the word *we* in their descriptions. When the results were tabulated, it was obvious that the students had tried
to connect themselves to success by using the pronoun *we* to describe their school-
team victory—"We beat Houston, 17 to 14," or "We won." In the case of the lost
game, however, *we* was rarely used. Instead, the students used terms designed to
keep themselves separate from their defeated team—"They lost to Missouri, 30 to
20," or "I don't know the score, but Arizona State got beat." Perhaps the twin desires to connect ourselves to winners and to distance ourselves from losers were
combined consummately in the remarks of one particular student. After dryly recounting the score of the home-team defeat—"Arizona State lost it, 30 to 20"—he
blurted in anguish, "*They* threw away *our* chance for a national championship!"

Although the desire to bask in reflected glory exists to a degree in all of us, there seems to be something special about people who would take this normal tendency too far. Just what kind of people are they? Unless I miss my guess, they are not merely great sports aficionados; they are individuals with hidden personality flaws: poor self-concepts. Deep inside is a sense of low personal worth that directs them to seek prestige not from the generation or promotion of their own attainments but from the generation or promotion of their associations with others' attainments. There are several varieties of this species that bloom throughout our culture. The persistent name-dropper is a classic example. So, too, is the rock-music groupie, who trades sexual favors for the right to tell friends that she or he was "with" a famous musician for a time. No matter which form it takes, the behavior of such individuals shares a similar theme—the rather tragic view of accomplishment as deriving from outside the self.

Certain of these people work the association principle in a slightly different way. Instead of striving to inflate their visible connections to others of success, they strive to inflate the success of others they are visibly connected to. The clearest illustration is the notorious "stage mother," obsessed with securing stardom for her child. Of course, women are not alone in this regard. In 1991, a Davenport, Iowa, obstetrician cut off service to the wives of three school officials, reportedly because his son had not been given enough playing time in school basketball games. One of the wives was eight months pregnant at the time.

READER'S REPORT 5.2

From a Los Angeles Movie Studio Employee

Because I work in the industry, I'm a huge film buff. The biggest night of the year for me is the night of the Academy Awards. I even tape the shows so I can replay the acceptance speeches of the artists I really admire. One of my favorite speeches was what Kevin Costner said after his film *Dances with Wolves* won best picture in 1991. I liked it because he was responding to critics who say that the movies aren't important. In fact, I liked it so much that I copied it down. But there is one thing about the speech that I never understood before. Here's what he said about winning the best picture award:

"While it may not be as important as the rest of the world situation, it will always be important to us. My family will never forget what happened here; my Native American brothers and sisters, especially the Lakota Sioux, will never forget, and the people I went to high school with will never forget."

OK, I get why Kevin Costner would never forget this enormous honor. And I also get why his family would never forget it. And I even get why Native Americans would remember it, since the film is about them. But I never understood why he mentioned the people he went to high school with. Then, I read about how sports fans think they can "bask in the reflected glory" of their hometown stars and teams. And, I realized that it's the same thing. Everyone who went to school with Kevin Costner would be telling everyone about their connection the day after he won the Oscar, thinking that they would get some prestige out of it even though they had zero to do with the film. They would be right, too, because that's how it works. You don't have to be a star to get the glory. Sometimes you only have to be associated with the star somehow. How interesting.

Author's note: I've seen this sort of thing work in my own life when I've told architect friends that I was born in the same place as the great Frank Lloyd Wright. Please understand, I can't even draw a straight line; but I can see the favorable reaction in my friends' eyes. "Wow," they seem to say, "You and Frank Lloyd Wright?"

DEFENSE

Because liking can be increased by many means, a list of the defenses against compliance professionals who employ the liking rule must, oddly enough, be a short one. It would be pointless to construct a horde of specific countertactics to combat each of the countless versions of the various ways to influence liking. There are simply too many routes to be blocked effectively with such a one-on-one strategy. Besides, several of the factors leading to liking—physical attractiveness, familiarity, association—have been shown to work unconsciously to produce their effects on us, making it unlikely that we could muster a timely protection against them anyway.

Instead we need to consider a general approach, one that can be applied to any of the liking-related factors to neutralize their unwelcome influence on our compliance decisions. The secret to such an approach may lie in its timing. Rather than trying to recognize and prevent the action of liking factors before they have a chance to work on us, we might be well advised to let them work. Our vigilance should be directed not toward the things that may produce undue liking for a compliance practitioner but toward the fact that undue liking has been *produced*. The time to call out the defense is when we feel ourselves liking the practitioner more than we should under the circumstances.

By concentrating our attention on the effects rather than the causes, we can avoid the laborious, nearly impossible task of trying to detect and deflect the many psychological influences on liking. Instead, we have to be sensitive to only one thing related to liking in our contacts with compliance practitioners: the feeling that we have come to like the practitioner more quickly or more deeply than we would have expected. Once we *notice* this feeling, we will have been tipped off that there is probably some tactic being used, and we can start taking the necessary countermeasures. Note that the strategy I am suggesting borrows much from the jujitsu style favored by the compliance professionals themselves. We don't attempt to restrain the influence of the factors that cause liking. Quite the contrary. We allow those factors to exert their force, and then we use that force in our campaign against those who would profit by them. The stronger the force, the more conspicuous it becomes and, consequently, the more subject to our alerted defenses.

Suppose, for example, we find ourselves bargaining on the price of a new car with Dealin' Dan, a candidate for Joe Girard's vacated "Greatest Car Salesman" title. After talking a while and negotiating a bit, Dan wants to close the deal: he wants us to decide to buy the car. Before any such decision is made, we should ask ourselves the crucial question, "In the 25 minutes I've known this guy, have I come to like him more than I would have expected?" If the answer is yes, we might want to reflect on the ways Dan behaved during those few minutes. We might recall that he has fed us (coffee and doughnuts), complimented us on our choice of options and color combinations, made us laugh, and cooperated with us against the sales manager to get us a better deal.

Although such a review of events might be informative, it is not a necessary step in protecting ourselves from the liking rule. Once we discover that we have come to like Dan more than we would have expected, we don't have to know why. The simple recognition of unwarranted liking should be enough to get us to react against it. One possible reaction would be to reverse the process and actively dislike Dan, but that might be unfair to him and contrary to our own interests. After all, some individuals are naturally likeable, and Dan might just be one of them. It wouldn't be right to turn automatically against those compliance professionals who happen to be most likeable. Besides, for our own sakes, we wouldn't want to shut ourselves off from business interactions with such nice people, especially when they may be offering us the best available deal.

I recommend a different reaction. If our answer to the crucial question is "Yes, under the circumstances, I like this guy peculiarly well," this should be the signal that the time has come for a quick countermaneuver: Mentally separate Dan from that Chevy or Toyota he's trying to sell. It is vital to remember at this point that, should we choose Dan's car, we will be driving *it,* not him, off the dealership lot. It is irrelevant to a wise automobile purchase that we find Dan likeable because he is good-looking, claims an interest in our favorite hobby, is funny, or has relatives living where we grew up.

Our proper response, then, is a conscious effort to concentrate exclusively on the merits of the deal and the car Dan has for us. Of course, when we make a compliance decision, it is always a good idea to separate our feelings about the requester from the request. Once immersed in even a brief personal and sociable contact with a requester, however, we may easily forget that distinction. In those instances when we don't care one way or the other about a requester, forgetting to make the distinction won't steer us very far wrong. The big mistakes are likely to come when we like the person making the request.

That's why it is so important to be alert to a sense of undue liking for a compliance practitioner. The recognition of that feeling can serve as our reminder to separate the dealer from the merits of the deal and to make our decision based on considerations related only to the latter. Were we all to follow this procedure, I am certain we would be much more pleased with the results of our exchanges with compliance professionals—though I suspect that Dealin' Dan would not.

SUMMARY

- *People prefer to say yes to individuals they know and like.* Recognizing this rule, compliance professionals commonly increase their effectiveness by emphasizing several factors that increase their overall attractiveness and likability.
- One feature of a person that influences overall liking is physical attractiveness. Although it has long been suspected that physical beauty provides an advantage in social interaction, research indicates that the advantage may be greater than supposed. Physical attractiveness seems to engender a halo effect that extends to favorable impressions of other traits such as talent, kindness, and intelligence. As a result, attractive people are more persuasive both in terms of getting what they request and in changing others' attitudes.
- A second factor that influences liking and compliance is similarity. We like people who are like us, and we are more willing to say yes to their requests, often in an unthinking manner. Another factor that produces liking is praise. Although they can sometimes backfire when crudely transparent, compliments generally enhance liking and, thus, compliance.
- Increased familiarity through repeated contact with a person or thing is yet another factor that normally facilitates liking. This relationship holds true principally when the contact takes place under positive rather than negative circumstances. One positive circumstance that works especially well is mutual and successful cooperation. A fifth factor linked to liking is association. By connecting themselves or their products with positive things, advertisers, politicians, and merchandisers frequently seek to share in the positivity through the process of association. Other individuals as well (sports fans, for example) appear to recognize the effect of simple connections and try to associate themselves with favorable events and distance themselves from unfavorable events in the eyes of observers.
- A potentially effective strategy for reducing the unwanted influence of liking on compliance decisions requires a special sensitivity to the experience of undue liking for a requester. Upon recognizing that we like a requester inordinately well under the circumstances, we should step back from the social interaction, mentally separate the requester from his or her offer, and make any compliance decision based solely on the merits of the offer.

STUDY QUESTIONS

Content Mastery

1. To what does the term *halo effect* refer? How can it help explain the relationship between a person's physical attractiveness and that person's general attractiveness in the eyes of others?

2. We tend to like people who say they like us (that is, who give us compliments). We also tend to like people who say they *are* like us (that is, similar to us). In the latter case, what is the evidence that we tend to say yes to similar others in an automatic fashion?

3. A series of studies on the creation and reduction of hostility between groups was conducted at boys' summer camps. After hostility was generated, which procedures successfully reduced the hostility? Which were unsuccessful?

4. To what does the tendency to bask in reflected glory refer? Under which conditions and for which kind of person is this tendency most likely to appear?

Critical Thinking

1. In a letter to her sister, Jane Austen wrote, "I do not want people to be very agreeable, as it saves me the trouble of liking them a great deal." To which trouble associated with liking people could she have been referring?

2. Will Rogers, who boasted, "I never met a man I didn't like," obviously felt differently than Austen about the advantages of liking others. What would be the consequences of Rogers's more expansive approach to interpersonal relations? Think about your own interpersonal style. Is it closer to Rogers's or Austen's? Why?

3. What parallels can you see between the findings of the boys' camp studies and those of studies on the effects of (a) school desegregation and (b) cooperative learning in the classroom?

4. Suppose you wanted the person sitting next to you in class to like you more. Using the factors discussed in this chapter, describe how you would arrange your next encounter to accomplish your goal.

5. How does the ad that opens this chapter reflect the topic of the chapter?

CHAPTER

6 *Authority*

Directed Deference

Your bones may be in jeopardy.

One in five osteoporosis victims is male. Luckily, fat free milk has the calcium bones need to help beat it. Beating your Harvard Ph.D. opponents? Well, that's another story.

got milk?

Suppose while leafing through your local newspaper, you notice an ad for volunteers to take part in a "study of memory" being done in the psychology department of a nearby university. Suppose further that, finding the idea of such an experiment intriguing, you contact the director of the study, Professor Stanley Milgram, and make arrangements to participate in an hour-long session. When you arrive at the laboratory suite, you meet two men. One is the researcher in charge of the experiment, clearly evidenced by the grey lab coat he wears and the clipboard he carries. The other is a volunteer like yourself who seems quite average in all respects.

After initial greetings and pleasantries are exchanged, the researcher begins to explain the procedures to be followed. He says that the experiment is a study of how punishment affects learning and memory. Therefore, one participant will have the task of learning pairs of words in a long list until each pair can be recalled perfectly; this person is to be called the Learner. The other participant's job will be to test the Learner's memory and to deliver increasingly strong electric shocks for every mistake; this person will be designated the Teacher.

Naturally, you get a bit nervous at this news. Your apprehension increases when, after drawing lots with your partner, you find that you are assigned the Learner role. You hadn't expected the possibility of pain as part of the study, so you briefly consider leaving. But no, you think, there's plenty of time for that if need be and, besides how strong a shock could it be?

After you have had a chance to study the list of word pairs, the researcher straps you into a chair and, with the Teacher looking on, attaches electrodes to your arm. More worried now about the effect of the shock, you inquire into its severity. The researcher's response is hardly comforting. He says that although the shocks can be extremely painful, they will cause you "no permanent tissue damage." With that, the researcher and Teacher leave you alone and go to the next room where the Teacher asks you the test questions through an intercom system and delivers electric punishment for every wrong response.

As the test proceeds, you quickly recognize the pattern that the Teacher follows: He asks the question and waits for your answer over the intercom. Whenever you err, he announces the voltage of the shock you are about to receive and pulls a lever to deliver the punishment. The most troubling thing is that, with each error you make, the shock increases by 15 volts.

The first part of the test progresses smoothly. The shocks are annoying but tolerable. Later on, though, as you make more mistakes and the shock voltages climb, the punishment begins to hurt enough to disrupt your concentration, which leads to more errors and ever more disruptive shocks. At the 75-, 90-, and 105-volt levels, the pain makes you grunt audibly. At 120 volts, you exclaim into the intercom that the shocks are *really* starting to hurt. You take one more punishment with a groan and decide that you can't take much more pain. After the Teacher delivers the 150-volt shock, you shout back into the intercom "That's all. Get me out of here. Get me out of here, please. Let me out."

Instead of the assurance you expect from the Teacher, that he and the researcher are coming to release you, he merely gives you the next test question to answer. Surprised and confused you mumble the first answer to come into your head. It's wrong, of course, and the Teacher delivers a 165-volt shock. You scream at the Teacher to stop, to let you out. He responds only with the next test question—and with the next slashing shock, when your frenzied answer is incorrect. You can't hold down the panic any longer, the shocks are so strong now they make you writhe and shriek. You kick the wall, demand to be released, and beg the Teacher to help you. However, the test questions continue as before and so do the dreaded shocks—in searing jolts of 195, 210, 225, 240, 255, 270, 285, and 300 volts. You realize that you can't possibly answer the questions correctly now, so you shout to the Teacher that you won't answer his questions anymore. Nothing changes; the Teacher interprets your failure to respond as an incorrect response and sends another bolt. The ordeal continues in this way until, finally, the power of the shocks stuns you into near-paralysis. You can no longer cry out, no longer struggle. You can only feel each terrible electric bite. Perhaps, you think, this total inactivity will cause the Teacher to stop. There can be no reason to continue this experiment, but he proceeds relentlessly, calling out the test questions, announcing the horrid shock levels (above 400 volts now), and pulling the levers. What must this man be like, you wonder in confusion. Why doesn't he help me? Why won't he stop?

THE POWER OF AUTHORITY PRESSURE

For most of us, the previous scenario reads like a bad dream. To recognize how nightmarish it is, though, we should understand that, in most respects, it is real. There was such an experiment—actually, a whole series—run by a psychology professor named Milgram (1974) in which participants in the Teacher role were willing to deliver continued, intense, and dangerous levels of shock to a kicking, screeching, pleading Learner. Only one major aspect of the experiment was not genuine. No real shock was delivered; the Learner, who repeatedly cried out in agony for mercy and release, was not a true subject but an actor who only pretended to be shocked. The actual purpose of Milgram's study, then, had nothing to do with the effects of punishment on learning and memory. Rather, it involved an entirely different question: When it is their job, how much suffering will ordinary people be willing to inflict on an entirely innocent other person?

The answer is most unsettling. Under circumstances mirroring precisely the features of the "bad dream," the typical Teacher was willing to deliver as much pain as was available to give. Rather than yield to the pleas of the victim, about two-thirds of the subjects in Milgram's experiment pulled every one of the 30 shock switches in front of them and continued to engage the last switch (450 volts) until the researcher ended the experiment. More alarming still, almost none of the 40 subjects in this study quit his job as Teacher when the victim first began to demand his release, nor later when he began to beg for it, nor even later when his reaction to each shock had become, in Milgram's words, "definitely an agonized scream."

These results surprised everyone associated with the project, Milgram included. In fact, before the study began, he asked groups of colleagues, graduate students, and psychology majors at Yale University (where the experiment was performed) to read a copy of the experimental procedures and estimate how many subjects would go all the way to the last (450-volt) shock. Invariably, the answers fell in the 1–2 percent range. A separate group of 39 psychiatrists predicted that only about one person in a thousand would be willing to continue to the end. No one, then, was prepared for the behavior pattern that the experiment actually produced.

How can we explain that alarming pattern? Perhaps, as some have argued, it has to do with the fact that the subjects were all males who are known as a group for

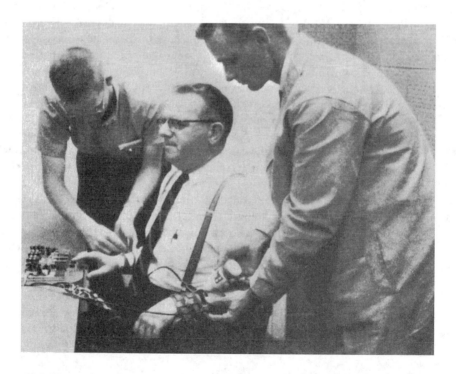

The Milgram Study
The picture shows the Learner (victim) being strapped into a chair and fitted with electrodes by the lab-coated experimenter and the true subject.

their aggressive tendencies, or that the subjects didn't recognize the potential harm that such high shock voltages could cause, or that the subjects were a freakish collection of moral cretins who enjoyed the chance to inflict misery. There is good evidence against each of these possibilities. First, a later experiment showed that the subjects' sex was irrelevant to their willingness to give all the shocks to the victim; female Teachers were just as likely to do so as were the males in Milgram's initial study.

Another experiment investigated the explanation that subjects weren't aware of the potential physical danger to the victim. In this experiment the victim was instructed to announce that he had a heart condition and to declare that his heart was being affected by the shock: "That's all. Get me out of here. I told you I had heart trouble. My heart's starting to bother me. I refuse to go on. Let me out." Once again the results were the same; 65 percent of the subjects carried out their duties faithfully through to the maximum shock.

Finally, the explanation that Milgram's subjects were a twisted, sadistic bunch not at all representative of average citizens has proven unsatisfactory as well. The people who answered Milgram's newspaper ad to participate in his "memory" experiment represented a standard cross section of ages, occupations, and educational levels within our society. What's more, later on, a battery of personality scales showed these people to be quite normal psychologically, with not a hint of psychosis as a group. They were, in fact, just like you and me; or, as Milgram likes to term it, they *are* you and me. If he is right that his studies implicate us in their grisly findings, the unanswered question becomes an uncomfortably personal one, "What could make *us* do such things?"

Milgram is sure he knows the answer. It has to do, he says, with a deep-seated sense of duty to authority. According to Milgram, the real culprit in the experiments was his subjects' inability to defy the wishes of the boss, the lab-coated researcher who urged and, if necessary, directed the subjects to perform their duties, despite the emotional and physical mayhem they were causing.

The evidence supporting Milgram's obedience-to-authority explanation is strong. First, it is clear that, without the researcher's directives to continue, the subjects would have ended the experiment quickly. They hated what they were doing and agonized over their victim's anguish. They implored the researcher to let them stop. When he refused, they went on, but in the process they trembled, they perspired, they shook, they stammered protests and additional pleas for the victim's release. Their fingernails dug into their own flesh; they bit their lips until they bled; they held their heads in their hands; some fell into fits of uncontrollable nervous laughter. An outside observer to Milgram's initial experiment described one subject.

I observed a mature and initially poised businessman enter the laboratory smiling and confident. Within 20 minutes he was reduced to a twitching,

stuttering wreck, who was rapidly approaching a point of nervous collapse.
He constantly pulled on his earlobe and twisted his hands. At one point he
pushed his fist into his forehead and muttered: "Oh, God, let's stop it." And
yet he continued to respond to every word of the experimenter and obeyed
to the end. (Milgram, 1963, p. 377)

In addition to these observations, Milgram has provided even more convincing evidence for the obedience-to-authority interpretation of his subjects' behavior. In a later experiment, for instance, he had the researcher and the victim switch scripts so that the researcher told the Teacher to stop delivering shocks to the victim, while the victim insisted bravely that the Teacher continue. The result couldn't have been clearer; 100 percent of the subjects refused to give one additional shock when it was merely the fellow subject who demanded it. The identical finding appeared in another version of the experiment in which the researcher and fellow subject switched roles so that it was the researcher who was strapped into the chair and the fellow subject who ordered the Teacher to continue—over the protests of the researcher. Again, not one subject touched another shock lever.

The extreme degree to which subjects in Milgram's studies obeyed the orders of authority was documented in yet another variation of the basic experiments. In this case, the Teacher faced two researchers who issued contradictory orders; one ordered the Teacher to terminate the shocks when the victim cried out for release, while the other maintained that the experiment should go on. These conflicting instructions reliably produced what may have been the project's only humor: In tragicomic befuddlement and with eyes darting from one researcher to another, subjects would beseech the pair to agree on a single command to follow, "Wait, wait. Which is it going to be? One says stop, one says go. . . . Which is it!?" When the researchers remained at loggerheads, the subjects tried frantically to determine who was the bigger boss. Failing this route to obedience with *the* authority, every subject finally followed his better instincts and ended the shocks. As in the other experimental variations, such a result would hardly be expected had the subjects' motivations involved some form of sadism or neurotic aggressiveness.[1]

To Milgram's mind, evidence of a chilling phenomenon emerges repeatedly from his accumulated data. "It is the extreme willingness of adults to go to almost any lengths on the command of an authority that constitutes the chief finding of the study" (Milgram, 1974). There are sobering implications of this finding for those concerned about the ability of another form of authority—government—to extract frightening

---

[1] The basic experiment, as well as all these and other variations on it, is presented in Milgram's highly readable *Obedience to Authority*, 1974. A review of much of the subsequent research on obedience can be found in Blass (1991, 1999) and in Miller, Collins, & Brief (1995).

levels of obedience from ordinary citizens.[2] Furthermore, the finding tells us something about the sheer strength of authority pressures in controlling our behavior. After witnessing Milgram's subjects squirming and sweating and suffering at their task, could anyone doubt the power of the force that held them there?

For those whose doubts remain, the story of S. Brian Willson might prove instructive. On September 1, 1987, to protest U.S. shipments of military equipment to Nicaragua, Mr. Willson and two other men stretched their bodies across the railroad tracks leading out of the Naval Weapons Station in Concord, California. The protesters were confident that their act would halt the scheduled train's progress that day, as they had notified navy and railroad officials of their intent three days before. But the civilian crew, which had been given orders not to stop, never even slowed the train, despite being able to see the protesters 600 feet ahead. Although two of the men managed to scramble out of harm's way, Mr. Willson was not quick enough to avoid being struck and having both legs severed below the knee. Because navy medical corpsmen at the scene refused to treat him or allow him to be taken to the hospital in their ambulance, onlookers—including Mr. Willson's wife and son—were left to try to staunch the flow of blood for 45 minutes until a private ambulance arrived.

Amazingly, Mr. Willson, who served four years in Vietnam, does not blame either the crewmen or the corpsmen for his misfortune; he points his finger, instead, at a system that constrained their actions through the pressure to obey. "They were just doing what I did in 'Nam. They were following orders that are part of an insane policy. They're the fall guys." Although the crew members shared Mr. Willson's assessment of them as victims, they did not share his magnanimity. In what is perhaps the most remarkable aspect of the incident, the train crew filed suit against *him,* requesting punitive damages for the "humiliation, mental anguish, and physical stress" they suffered because he hadn't allowed them to carry out their orders without cutting off his legs.

---

[2]In fact, Milgram first began his investigations in an attempt to understand how the German citizenry could have participated in the concentration camp destruction of millions of innocents during the years of Nazi ascendancy. After testing his experimental procedures in the United States, he had planned to take them to Germany, a country whose populace he was sure would provide enough obedience for a full-flown scientific analysis of the concept. The first eye-opening experiment in New Haven, Connecticut, however, make it clear that he could save his money and stay close to home. "I found so much obedience," he said, "I hardly saw the need of taking the experiment to Germany."

More telling evidence, perhaps, of a willingness to submit to authorized command within the American character comes from a national survey taken after the trial of Lieutenant William Calley, who ordered his soldiers to kill the inhabitants—infants and toddlers as well as their parents and grandparents—of My Lai, Vietnam (Kelman & Hamilton, 1989). A majority of Americans (51 percent) responded that if so ordered, they too would shoot all the residents of a Vietnamese village. But Americans have no monopoly on the need to obey authority. When Milgram's basic procedure was eventually repeated in Holland, Germany, Spain, Italy, Australia, and Jordan, the results were similar (see Meeus & Raaijmakers, 1986, for a review).

THE ALLURES AND DANGERS
OF BLIND OBEDIENCE

Whenever we are faced with a potent motivator of human action, it is natural to expect that good reasons exist for the motivation. In the case of obedience to authority, even a brief consideration of human social organization offers justification aplenty. A multilayered and widely accepted system of authority confers an immense advantage upon a society. It allows the development of sophisticated structures for production of resources, trade, defense, expansion, and social control that would otherwise be impossible. At the opposite end, the alternative is anarchy, a state hardly known for its beneficial effects on cultural groups and one that the social philosopher Thomas Hobbes assures us would render life "solitary, poor, nasty, brutish, and short." Consequently, we are trained from birth to believe that obedience to proper authority is right and disobedience is wrong. This message fills the parental lessons, the schoolhouse rhymes, stories, and songs of our childhood and is carried forward in the legal, military, and political systems we encounter as adults. Notions of submission and loyalty to legitimate rule are accorded much value in each.

Religious instruction contributes as well. The very first book of the Bible, for example, describes how failure to obey the ultimate authority resulted in the loss of paradise for Adam, Eve, and the rest of the human race. Should that particular metaphor prove too subtle, just a bit further into the Old Testament, we can read—in what might be the closest biblical representation of the Milgram experiment—the respectful account of Abraham's willingness to plunge a dagger through the heart of his young son because God, without any explanation, ordered it. We learn in this story that the correctness of an action was not judged by such considerations as apparent senselessness, harmfulness, injustice, or usual moral standards, but by the mere command of a higher authority. Abraham's tormented ordeal was a test of obedience, and he—like Milgram's subjects, who perhaps had learned an early lesson from him—passed.

Stories like those of Abraham and Milgram's subjects can tell us a great deal about obedience's power and value in our culture. In another sense, however, the stories may be misleading. We rarely agonize to such a degree over the pros and cons of authority demands. In fact, our obedience frequently takes place in a *click, whirr* fashion with little or no conscious deliberation. Information from a recognized authority can provide us a valuable shortcut for deciding how to act in a situation.

After all, as Milgram suggests, conforming to the dictates of authority figures has always had genuine practical advantages for us. Early on, these people (parents, teachers) knew more than we did, and we found that taking their advice proved beneficial—partly because of their greater wisdom and partly because they controlled our rewards and punishments. As adults, the same benefits persist for the same reasons, though the authority figures are now employers, judges, and government leaders. Because their positions speak of greater access to information and power, it makes sense to comply with the wishes of properly constituted authorities. It makes so much sense, in fact, that we often do so when it makes no sense at all.

This paradox is, of course, the same one that attends all major weapons of influence. In this instance, once we realize that obedience to authority is mostly rewarding, it is easy to allow ourselves the convenience of automatic obedience. The simultaneous blessing and curse of such blind obedience is its mechanical character. We don't have to think, therefore we don't. Although such mindless obedience leads us to appropriate action most of the time, there will be conspicuous exceptions because we are reacting, not thinking.

Let's take an example from one facet of our lives in which authority pressures are visible and strong: medicine. Health is enormously important to us. Thus, physicians, who possess great knowledge and influence in this vital area, hold the position of respected authorities. In addition, the medical establishment has a clearly terraced power and prestige structure. The various kinds of health workers well understand the level of their jobs in this structure, and they well understand, too, that M.D.s sit at the top. No one may overrule a doctor's judgment in a case, except, perhaps, another doctor of higher rank. Consequently, a long-established tradition of automatic obedience to doctors' orders has developed among health care staffs.

The worrisome possibility arises, then, that when a physician makes a clear error, no one lower in the hierarchy will *think* to question it—precisely because, once a legitimate authority has given an order, subordinates stop *thinking* in the situation and start reacting. Mix this kind of *click, whirr* response into a complex hospital environment and mistakes are inevitable. Indeed, a study by the U.S. Health Care Financing Administration shows that, for patient medication alone, the average hospital has a 12 percent daily error rate.

Errors in the medicine patients receive can occur for a variety of reasons. However, in their book *Medication Errors: Causes and Prevention* (1981), Temple University professors of pharmacy Michael Cohen and Neil Davis attribute much of the problem to the mindless deference given to the "boss" of a patient's case: the attending physician. According to Cohen, "in case after case, patients, nurses, pharmacists, and other physicians do not question the prescription." Take, for example, the strange case of the "rectal earache" reported by Cohen and Davis. A physician ordered ear drops to be administered to the right ear of a patient suffering pain and infection there. Instead of writing out completely the location "Right ear" on the prescription, the doctor abbreviated it so that the instructions read "place in R ear." Upon receiving the prescription, the duty nurse promptly put the required number of ear drops into the patient's anus.

Obviously, rectal treatment of an earache made no sense, but neither the patient nor the nurse questioned it. The important lesson of this story is that in many situations in which a legitimate authority has spoken, what would otherwise make sense is irrelevant. In these instances, we don't consider the situation as a whole but attend and respond to only one aspect of it.

We are not the only species to give sometimes single-minded deference to those in authority positions. In monkey colonies, where rigid dominance hierarchies exist, beneficial innovations (for example, learning how to use a stick to bring food into

Who's Really the King?

Communication researchers have learned that, in conversations, people unconsciously shift their voice and speech styles toward the styles of individuals in positions of power and authority. One study explored this phenomenon by analyzing interviews on the *Larry King Live* television show. When King interviewed guests having great social standing and prestige (for instance, Bill Clinton, George Bush, and Barbara Streisand), his voice style changed to match theirs. But when he interviewed guests of lower status (for instance, Dan Quayle, Spike Lee, and Julie Andrews), he remained unmoved, and their voice styles shifted to match his (Gregory & Webster, 1996).

the cage area) do not spread quickly through the group unless they are taught first to a dominant animal. When a lower animal is taught the new concept first, the rest of the colony remains mostly oblivious to its value. One study, cited by Ardry (1970), on the introduction of new food tastes to Japanese monkeys provides a nice illustration. In one troop, a taste for caramels was developed by introducing this new food into the diet of young peripherals, low on the status ladder. The taste for caramels inched slowly up the ranks: A year and a half later, only 51 percent of the colony had acquired it, but still none of the leaders. Contrast this with what happened in a second troop where wheat was introduced first to the leader: Wheat eating—to this point unknown to these monkeys—spread through the whole colony within four hours. Very much the same thing happened in 1995 on the Chicago Bulls basketball team when the acknowledged leader and star, Michael Jordan, began eating three Energy Booster bars before each game. According to substitute player Steve Kerr, "B. J. Armstrong [another non-star player] and I were the only ones eating them before. Then Michael eats some, and now everybody's eating them" (Shappell, 1995).

Wherever our behaviors are governed in such an unthinking manner, we can be confident that there will be compliance professionals trying to take advantage. Returning to the field of medicine, we can see that advertisers have frequently commissioned the respect accorded doctors in our culture by hiring actors to play the roles of doctors speaking on behalf of the product. My favorite example was a TV commercial featuring the actor Robert Young warning people against the dangers of caffeine and recommending caffeine-free Sanka brand coffee. The commercial was highly successful, selling so much Sanka that it was played for years in several versions. Why should this commercial prove so effective? Why on earth would we take Robert Young's word for the health consequences of decaffeinated coffee? Because— as the advertising agency that hired him knew perfectly well—he was associated in the minds of the American public with Marcus Welby, M.D., the role he played in an earlier long-running television series. Objectively, it doesn't make sense to be swayed by the comments of a man we know to be just an actor who used to play a doctor; but, practically, that man sold the Sanka.

CONNOTATION NOT CONTENT

From the first time I saw it, I found the most intriguing feature of Robert Young's Sanka commercial to be its ability to use the influence of the authority principle without ever providing a real authority. The appearance of authority was enough. This tells us something important about unthinking reactions to authority figures. When in a *click, whirr* mode, we are often as vulnerable to the symbols of authority as to the substance.

Several of these symbols can reliably trigger our compliance in the absence of the genuine substance of authority. Consequently, these symbols are employed extensively by those compliance professionals who are short on substance. Con artists, for example, drape themselves with the titles, the clothes, and the trappings of authority. They love nothing more than to emerge elegantly dressed from a fine automobile and to introduce themselves to their prospective "marks" as Doctor or Judge or Professor or Commissioner Someone. They understand that when they are so adorned their chances for compliance are greatly increased. Each of these three types of symbols of authority—titles, clothes, and trappings—has its own story and is worth a separate look.

Titles

Titles are simultaneously the most difficult and the easiest symbols of authority to acquire. To earn a title normally takes years of work and achievement. Yet, it is possible for somebody who has put in none of this effort to adopt the mere label and receive a kind of automatic deference. As we have seen, actors in TV commercials and con artists do it successfully all the time.

I recently talked with a friend—a faculty member at a well-known eastern university—who provided a telling illustration of the way our actions are frequently more influenced by a title than by the nature of the person claiming it. My friend travels quite a bit and often finds himself chatting with strangers in bars, restaurants, and airports. He says that he has learned through much experience during these conversations never to use his title of professor. When he does, he finds that the tenor of the interaction changes immediately. People who have been spontaneous and interesting conversation partners for the previous half hour become respectful, accepting, and dull. His opinions that before may have produced a lively exchange now generate extended (and highly grammatical) statements of accord. Annoyed and slightly bewildered by the phenomenon—because as he says, "I'm still the same guy they've been talking to for the last 30 minutes, right?"—my friend now regularly lies about his occupation in such situations.

What an eccentric shift from the more typical pattern in which certain compliance practitioners lie about titles they *don't* truly have. Either way, however, such practiced dishonesty makes the same point about the ability of a symbol of authority to influence behavior.

I wonder whether my professor friend—who is somewhat short—would be so eager to hide his title if he knew that, besides making strangers more accommodating, it also makes them see him as taller. Studies investigating the way in which authority status affects perceptions of size have found that prestigious titles lead to height distortions. In one experiment conducted on five classes of Australian college students, a man was introduced as a visitor from Cambridge University in England. However, his status at Cambridge was represented differently in each of the classes. To one class, he was presented as a student; to a second class, a demonstrator; to another, a lecturer; to yet another, a senior lecturer; to a fifth, a professor. After he left the room, the class was asked to estimate his height. It was found that with each increase in status, the same man grew in perceived height by an average of a half-inch, so that as the "professor" he was seen as 2½ inches taller than as the "student" (P. R. Wilson, 1968). Another study found that after winning an election, politicians become taller in the eyes of the citizenry (Higham & Carment, 1992).

It is worth the time for a small detour to pursue this interesting connection between status and perceived size, as it shows up in a variety of ways. In one study in which children were asked to judge the size of coins, for example, they most overestimated the size of the more valuable coins (Bruner & Goodman, 1947). Adults are just as guilty of such distortions. In a study by Dukes and Bevan (1952), college students drew cards on which were printed monetary values ranging from $3.00 to –$3.00; the students won or lost the amount shown on the cards they picked. Afterward, they were asked to rate the size of each card. Although all the cards were exactly the same size, those that had the extreme values—positive or negative—were seen as physically larger. Thus, it is not necessarily the pleasantness of a thing that makes it seem bigger, it is its importance.

Because we see size and status as related, it is possible for certain individuals to benefit by substituting the former for the latter. In some animal societies, in which the status of an animal is assigned on the basis of dominance, size is an important factor in determining which animal will achieve which status level in the group.[3]

Usually, in combat with a rival, the larger and more powerful animal wins. To avoid the harmful effects to the group of such physical conflict, however, many species employ methods that frequently involve more form than fracas. The two rivals confront each other with showy aggression displays that invariably include size-enhancing tricks. Various mammals arch their backs and bristle their coats; fish extend their fins and puff themselves up with water; birds unfurl and flutter their wings. Very often, this exhibition alone is enough to send one of the histrionic warriors into retreat leaving the contested status position to the seemingly larger and stronger rival.

Fur, fins, and feathers. Isn't it interesting how these most delicate of parts can be exploited to give the impression of substance and weight? There are two lessons for us here. One is specific to the association between size and status: The connection of those two features can be profitably employed by individuals who are able to

DILBERT

High Expectations

Cartoonist Scott Adams's depiction is not so far-fetched. Research indicates that tall men earn more than their shorter contemporaries and are more likely to rise to positions of leadership (Chaiken, 1986; Stogdill, 1948). And, although there are no data directly to the point, I would guess that Adams is right about silver hair, too.

© DILBERT reprinted by permission of United Feature Syndicate, Inc.

---

[3]Subhumans are not alone in this regard, even in modern times. For example, since 1900 the U.S. presidency has been won by the taller of the major party candidates in nearly 90 percent of the elections. Research suggests that the height advantage may also apply to candidates for affection in contests of the heart: women are significantly more likely to respond to a man's published personal ad when he describes himself as tall. Interestingly for female ad-runners, size works in the opposite direction. Women who report being short and weighing less get more male/mail action (Lynn & Shurgot, 1984; Shepperd & Strathman, 1989).

fake the first to gain the appearance of the second. This possibility is precisely why con artists, even those of average or slightly above average height, commonly wear lifts in their shoes. The other lesson is more general: The outward signs of power and authority frequently may be counterfeited with the flimsiest of materials. Let's return to the realm of titles for an example—an example that involves what, in several ways, is the scariest experiment I know. A group of researchers, composed of doctors and nurses with connections to three midwestern hospitals, became increasingly concerned with the extent of mechanical obedience to doctors' orders on the part of nurses. It seemed to the researchers that even highly trained and skilled nurses were not using that training or skill sufficiently to check on a doctor's judgment; instead, when confronted with a physician's directives, they would simply defer.

We saw how this process accounted for the case of the rectally administered ear drops, but the midwestern researchers took things several steps further. First, they wanted to find out whether such cases were isolated incidents or representative of a widespread phenomenon. Second, they wanted to examine the problem in the context of a serious treatment error: the gross over-prescription of an unauthorized drug to a hospital patient. Finally, they wanted to see what would happen if they physically removed the authority figure from the situation and substituted an unfamiliar voice on the phone, offering only the frailest evidence of authority—the claimed title "doctor."

One of the researchers made an identical phone call to 22 separate nurses' stations on various surgical, medical, pediatric, and psychiatric wards. He identified himself as a hospital physician and directed the answering nurse to give 20 milligrams of a drug (Astrogen) to a specific ward patient. There were four excellent reasons for the nurse's caution in response to this order: (1) the prescription was transmitted by phone, in direct violation of hospital policy; (2) the medication itself was unauthorized. Astrogen had not been cleared for use nor placed on the ward stock list; (3) the prescribed dosage was obviously and dangerously excessive. The medication containers clearly stated that the "maximum daily dose" was only 10 milligrams, half of what had been ordered; (4) the directive was given by a man the nurse had never met, seen, or even talked with before on the phone. Yet, in 95 percent of the instances, the nurses went straight to the ward medicine cabinet where they secured the ordered dosage of Astrogen and started for the patient's room to administer it. It was at this point that they were stopped by a secret observer, who revealed the nature of the experiment (Hofling, Brotzman, Dalrymple, Graves, & Pierce, 1966).

The results are frightening indeed. That 95 percent of regular staff nurses complied unhesitatingly with a patently improper instruction of this sort must give us all as potential hospital patients great reason for concern. Given the U.S. Health Financing Care Administration estimate of a 12 percent daily medication error rate in American hospitals, stays of longer than a week make it likely that we will be recipients of such an error. What the midwestern study shows is that the mistakes are hardly limited to the trivial slips in the administration of harmless ear drops or the like, but extend to grave and dangerous blunders.

In interpreting their unsettling findings, the researchers came to an instructive conclusion:

> *In a real-life situation corresponding to the experimental one, there would, in theory, be two professional intelligences, the doctor's and the nurse's, working to ensure that a given procedure be undertaken in a manner beneficial to the patient or, at the very least, not detrimental to him [or her]. The experiment strongly suggests, however, that one of these intelligences is, for all practical purposes, nonfunctioning. (Hofling et al., 1966, p. 176)*

It seems that, in the face of a physician's directives, the nurses unhooked their "professional intelligences" and moved to a *click, whirr* form of responding. None of their considerable medical training or knowledge was engaged in the decision about what to do. Instead, because obedience to legitimate authority had always been the most preferred and efficient action in their work setting, they were willing to err on the side of automatic obedience. It is all the more instructive that they have traveled so far in this direction that their error had come in response not to genuine authority but to its most easily falsified symbol—a bare title.[4]

Perhaps as dismaying as the mechanical deference given to individuals whose titles bespeak authority is the evidence for a mechanical resistance to the ideas of individuals whose titles suggest a lack of authority. In the realm of scholarly publication, a revealing study was done by psychologists Douglas Peters and Stephen Ceci (1982). They took 12 articles that had been published 18 to 32 months earlier by authors from prestigious universities and, changing nothing but the names and affiliations of the authors to those of unknowns from "Tri-Valley Center for Human Potential," they resubmitted the articles in manuscript form to the journals that had already published them. Nine of the doctored articles went through the review process undetected and, remarkably, eight were rejected, even though each had been published shortly before by the same journal when it had been submitted by researchers with more prestigious reputations and affiliations. A similar, but less scientific, experiment was tried by a popular writer who typed word-for-word Jerzy Kosinski's novel *Steps* and sent the manuscript to 28 literary agencies and publishing houses 10 years after the book had sold nearly a half million copies and had won the National Book Award. The manuscript, now carrying the name of an unknown, was rejected as inadequate by all 28 organizations including Random House, the novel's original publisher (C. Ross, 1979).

---

[4]Additional data collected in the Hofling et al. study suggest that nurses may not be conscious of the extent to which the title "doctor" sways their judgments and actions. A separate group of 33 nurses and student nurses were asked what they would have done in the experimental situation. Contrary to the actual findings, only two predicted that they would have given the medication as ordered.

READER'S REPORT 6.1

From a Texas-Based University Professor

I grew up in an Italian ghetto in Warren, Pennsylvania. I occasionally return home to visit family and the like. As in most places these days, most of the small Italian specialty stores are gone, having been replaced by larger supermarkets. My mother sent me supermarket shopping during a visit for a load of canned tomatoes, and I noticed that nearly all the cans of Furmano Italian diced tomatoes were sold out. Searching a bit on the shelf immediately beneath the almost empty shelf, I found a full shelf (loaded, even!) of Furman brand diced tomatoes. Looking closely at the labels, I realized that Furmano is Furman. The company had just added an "o" to its name when distributing some of its products. I guess it must be because, when selling Italian-style foods, you're perceived as more of an authority if your name ends in a vowel.

Author's note: The man who wrote this report also commented that the added letter "o" was doing double duty as an influence trigger in that store. Not only did it lend authority to the manufacturer, in an "Italian ghetto," it made the company appear similar to its customers.

Clothes

A second kind of authority symbol that can trigger our mechanical compliance is clothing. Though more tangible than a title, the cloak of authority is every bit as fakeable. Police bunco files bulge with records of con artists whose methods include the quick change. In chameleon style, they adopt the hospital whites, priestly black, army green, or police blue that the situation requires for maximum advantage. Only too late do their victims realize that the garb of authority is hardly its guarantee.

A series of studies by social psychologist Leonard Bickman (1974) indicates how difficult it can be to resist requests that come from figures in authority attire. Bickman's basic procedure was to ask passersby on the street to comply with some sort of odd request (for example, to pick up a discarded paper bag or to stand on the other side of a bus-stop sign). In half of the instances, the requester—a young man— was dressed in ordinary street clothes: the rest of the time, he wore a security guard's uniform. Regardless of the type of request, many more people obeyed the requester when he was wearing the guard costume. Similar results have been obtained when the uniformed requester was female (Bushman, 1988).

Especially revealing was one version of the experiment in which the requester stopped pedestrians and pointed to a man standing by a parking meter 50 feet away. The requester, whether dressed normally or as a security guard, always said the same thing to the pedestrian, "You see that guy over there by the meter? He's overparked but doesn't have any change. Give him a dime!" The requester then turned a corner and walked away so that by the time the pedestrian reached the meter, the requester was out of sight. The power of his uniform lasted, however, even after he was long gone: Nearly all of the pedestrians complied with his directive when he wore the guard costume, but fewer than half did so when he was dressed normally.[5]

It is interesting to note that, later on, Bickman found college students guessed with considerable accuracy the percentage of compliance that occurred in the experiment when the requester wore street clothes (50 percent versus the actual 42 percent); yet, the students greatly underestimated the percentage of compliance when he was in uniform—63 percent versus the actual 92 percent (Bickman, 1974).

Less blatant in its connotation than a uniform, but nonetheless effective, is another kind of attire that has traditionally indicated authority status in our culture: the well-tailored business suit. It, too, can evoke a telling form of deference from total strangers. In a study conducted in Texas, for instance, researchers arranged for a 31-year-old man to violate the law by crossing the street against the traffic light on a variety of occasions. In half of the cases, he was dressed in a freshly pressed business suit and tie; on the other occasions, he wore a work shirt and trousers. The researchers watched from a distance and counted the number of pedestrians waiting at the corner who followed the man across the street. Like the children of Hamlin who crowded after the Pied Piper, 3½ times as many people swept into traffic behind the suited jaywalker (Lefkowitz, Blake, & Mouton, 1955). In this case, though, the magic came not from his pipe but from his pinstripes.

It is noteworthy that the two types of authority apparel shown by these studies to be influential—the guard uniform and the business suit—are combined deftly by confidence artists in a fraud called the *bank examiner scheme.* The target of the swindle can be anyone, but elderly persons living alone are preferred. The con begins when a man dressed in a properly conservative three-piece business suit appears at the door of a likely victim. Everything about the con man's clothing speaks of propriety and respectability. The white shirt is starched; the wingtip shoes glow darkly. His suit is not trendy but classic: the lapels are three inches wide—no more, no less; the cloth is heavy and substantial, even in July; the tones are muted—business blue, business gray, business black.

He explains to his intended victim—perhaps a widow he secretly followed home from the bank a day or two earlier—that he is a professional bank examiner who, in the course of auditing the books of her bank, has found some seeming irregularities. He thinks he has spotted the culprit, a bank officer who is regularly doctoring reports of transactions in certain accounts. He says that the widow's account may be one of these, but he can't be sure until he has hard evidence; therefore, he has come to ask

---

[5]A study by Mauro (1984) may explain why the requester in uniform was effective, even after he had left the scene. Police officers dressed in their traditional uniforms, versus more conventional clothing (blazers and slacks), were rated by observers as more fair, helpful, intelligent, honest, and good.

for her cooperation. Would she help out by withdrawing her savings so a team of ex aminers and responsible bank officials can trace the record of the transaction as it passes across the suspect's desk?

Often, the appearance and presentation of "bank examiner" are so impressive that the victim never thinks to check on their validity with even a simple phone call. Instead, she drives to the bank, withdraws all her money, and returns home with it to wait with the examiner for word on the success of the trap. When the message comes, it is delivered by a uniformed "bank guard" who arrives after closing hours to announce that all is well—apparently, the widow's account was not one of those being tampered with. Greatly relieved, the examiner offers gracious thanks and, since the bank is now conveniently closed, instructs the guard to return the widow's money to the vault, to save her the trouble of doing so the next day. With smiles and hand-shakes all around, the guard leaves with the funds while the examiner expresses a few more minutes of thanks before he, too, exits. Naturally, as the victim eventually discovers, the "guard" is no more a guard than the "examiner" is an examiner. What they are is a pair of bunco artists who have recognized the capacity of carefully coun-terfeited uniforms to click us into mesmerized compliance with "authority."

Trappings

Aside from its function in uniforms, clothing can symbolize a more generalized type of authority when it serves an ornamental purpose. Finely styled and expen-sive clothes carry an aura of status and position, as do similar trappings such as jewelry and cars. The last of these status symbols is particularly interesting in the United States where "the American love affair with the automobile" gives it unusual significance.

According to the findings of a study done in the San Francisco Bay area, own-ers of prestige autos receive a special kind of deference from others. The experi-menters discovered that motorists would wait significantly longer before honking their horns at a new, luxury car stopped in front of a green traffic light than at an older, economy model. The motorists had little patience with the economy-car driver: Nearly all sounded their horns, and the majority of these did so more than once; two simply rammed into the rear bumper. So intimidating was the aura of the prestige automobile, however, that 50 percent of the motorists waited respectfully behind it, never touching their horns until it moved on (Doob & Gross, 1968).

Later the researchers asked college students what they would have done in such situations. Compared to the actual findings of the experiment, the students consistently underestimated the time it would take them to honk at the luxury car. The male stu-dents were especially inaccurate, feeling that they would honk faster at the prestige-than at the economy-car driver; of course, the study itself showed just the opposite. Note the similarity of this pattern to much other research on authority pressures. As in Milgram's research, the midwestern hospital nurses' study, and the security guard uniform experiment, people were unable to predict correctly how they or others would react to authority influence. In each instance, the effect of such influence was grossly underestimated. This property of authority status may account for much of its success as a compliance device. Not only does it work forcefully on us, but it does so unexpectedly.

DEFENSE

One protective tactic we can use against authority status is to remove its element of surprise. Because we typically misperceive the profound impact of authority (and its symbols) on our actions, we become insufficiently cautious about its presence in compliance situations. A fundamental form of defense against this problem, there-fore, is a heightened awareness of authority power. When this awareness is coupled with a recognition of how easily authority symbols can be faked, the benefit will be a properly guarded approach to situations involving authority influence attempts.

Sounds simple, right? And in a way it is. A better understanding of the workings of authority influence should help us resist it. Yet, there is a perverse complication—the familiar one inherent in all weapons of influence: We shouldn't want to resist au-thority altogether or even most of the time. Generally, authority figures know what they are talking about. Physicians, judges, corporate executives, legislative leaders, and the like have typically gained their positions through superior knowledge and judgment. Thus, as a rule, their directives offer excellent counsel.

Authorities, then, are frequently experts; indeed, one dictionary definition of an authority is an expert. In most cases, it would be foolish to try to substitute our less informed judgments for those of an expert, an authority. At the same time, we have seen in settings ranging from street corners to hospitals that it would be fool-ish to rely on authority direction in all cases. The trick is to be able to recognize without much strain or vigilance when authority directives are best followed and when they are not.

Authoritative Authority

Posing two questions to ourselves can help enormously to determine when author-ity directives should and should not be followed. The first question to ask when we are confronted with what appears to be an authority figure's influence attempt is "Is this authority truly an expert?" This question focuses our attention on two crucial pieces of information: the authority's credentials and the relevance of those creden-tials to the topic at hand. By turning in this simple way to the *evidence* for authority status, we can avoid the major pitfalls of automatic deference. An illustration or two is in order.

Let's examine the highly successful Robert Young Sanka commercial in this light. If, rather than responding to his "Marcus Welby, M.D." association, people had focused on Young's actual status as an authority, I am confident that the commercial would not have had so long and productive a run. Obviously, Robert Young did not possess a physician's training or knowledge. We all know that. What he did possess, however, was a physician's *title*, "M.D." Now, clearly, it was an empty title, connected to him in our minds through the device of playacting. We all know that, but isn't it fascinating how, when we are *whirring* along, what is obvious often doesn't matter unless we pay specific attention to it?

That is why the "Is this authority truly an expert?" question can be so valuable—it brings our attention to the obvious. It moves us effortlessly away from a focus on possibly meaningless symbols toward a consideration of genuine authority credentials. What's more, the question forces us to distinguish between relevant authorities and irrelevant authorities. This distinction is easy to forget when the push of authority pressure is combined with the rush of modern life. The Texas pedestrians who bustled into city traffic behind a business-suited jaywalker are prime examples. Even if the man were the business authority his clothes suggested he might be, he was unlikely to be a greater authority on crossing the street than those who followed him into traffic.

Still, they did follow, as if his label, *authority,* overwhelmed the vital difference between relevant and irrelevant forms. Had they bothered to ask themselves whether he represented a true expert in the situation, someone whose actions indicated superior knowledge, I expect the result would have been quite different. The same process applies to Robert Young, a man who was not without expertise. He had a long career with many achievements in a difficult business. However, his skills and knowledge were as an actor, not a doctor. When, in viewing the famous coffee commercial, we focus on his true credentials, we realize quickly that he should be no more believed than would be any other successful actor who claims that Sanka is healthful.

Sly Sincerity

Suppose, though, that we are confronted with an authority who we determine *is* a relevant expert. Before submitting to authority influence, we should ask a second simple question, "How truthful can we expect the expert to be?" Authorities, even the best informed, may not present their information honestly to us; therefore, we need to consider their trustworthiness in the situation. Most of the time we do. We allow ourselves to be swayed more by experts who seem to be impartial than by those who have something to gain by convincing us (Eagly, Wood, & Chaiken, 1978); research has shown this to be true around the world (McGuinnies & Ward, 1980). By wondering how an expert stands to benefit from our compliance, we give ourselves another safety net against undue and automatic influence. Even knowledgeable authorities in a field will not persuade us until we are satisfied that their messages represent the facts faithfully.

When asking ourselves about an authority's trustworthiness, we should keep in mind a little tactic compliance practitioners often use to assure us of their sincerity: They will argue somewhat against their own interests. Correctly practiced, this approach can be a subtle yet effective device for "proving" their honesty. Perhaps they will mention a small shortcoming in their position or product ("Oh, the disadvantages of Benson & Hedges"). Invariably though, the drawback will be a secondary one that is easily overcome by more significant advantages—"Listerine, the taste you hate three times a day"; "Avis: We're number two, but we try harder"; "L'Oreal, a bit more expensive and worth it." By establishing their basic truthfulness on minor issues, the compliance professionals who use this ploy can then be more believable when stressing the important aspects of their argument (Hunt, Domzal, & Kernan, 1981; Settle & Gorden, 1974; Smith & Hunt, 1978).

I have seen this approach used with devastating effect in a place that few of us recognize as a compliance setting—a restaurant. It is no secret that, because of shamelessly low wages, servers in restaurants must supplement their earnings with tips. Leaving the *sine qua non* of good service aside, the most successful waiters and waitresses know certain tricks for increasing tips. They also know that the larger a customer's bill, the larger the amount of money they are likely to receive in a standard gratuity. In these two regards, then—building the size of the customer's charge and building the percentage of that charge that is given as a tip—servers regularly act as compliance agents.

Hoping to find out how they operate, I applied for a position as a waiter at several fairly expensive restaurants. Without experience, though, the best I could do was to land a busboy job that, as things turned out, provided me a propitious vantage point from which to watch and analyze the action. Before long, I realized what the other employees already knew: that the most successful waiter in the place was Vincent who somehow arranged for patrons to order more and tip higher. The other servers were not even close to him in weekly earnings.

So I began to linger in my duties around Vincent's tables to observe his technique. I quickly learned that his style was to have no single style. He had a repertoire of approaches, each ready to be used under the appropriate circumstances. When the customers were a family, he was effervescent—even slightly clownish—directing his remarks as often to the children as the adults. With a young couple on a date, he became formal and a bit imperious in an attempt to intimidate the young man (to whom he spoke exclusively) into ordering and tipping lavishly. With an older, married couple, he retained the formality but dropped the superior air in favor of a respectful orientation to both members of the couple. Should the patron be dining alone, Vincent selected a friendly demeanor—cordial, conversational, and warm.

Vincent reserved the trick of seeming to argue against his own interests for large parties of 8 to 12 people. His technique was veined with genius. When it was time for the first person, normally a woman, to order, he went into his act. No matter what she elected, Vincent reacted identically: His brow furrowed, his hand hovered above his order pad, and after looking quickly over his shoulder for the manager, he leaned conspiratorially toward the table to report for all to hear "I'm afraid that is not as good tonight as it normally is. Might I recommend instead the ___ or the ___?" (At this point, Vincent suggested a pair of menu items that were slightly less expensive than the dish the patron had selected initially.) "They are both excellent tonight."

With this single maneuver, Vincent engaged several important principles of influence. First, even those who did not take his suggestions felt that Vincent had done them a favor by offering valuable information to help them order. Everyone felt grateful, and consequently, the rule for reciprocity would work in his favor when it came time for them to decide on his gratuity. Besides hiking the percentage of his tip, Vincent's maneuver also placed him in a favorable position to increase the size of the party's order. It established him as an authority on the current stores of the house: he clearly knew what was and wasn't good that night. Moreover— and here is where seeming to argue against his own interests comes in— it proved him to be a trustworthy informant because he recommended dishes that were slightly *less* expensive than the one originally ordered. Rather than trying to line his own pockets, he seemed to have the customers' best interests at heart.

To all appearances, he was at once knowledgeable and honest, a combination that gave him great credibility. Vincent was quick to exploit the advantage of this credible image. When the party had finished giving their food orders, he would say, "Very well, and would you like me to suggest or select wine to go with your meals?" As I watched the scene repeated almost nightly, there was a notable consistency to the customer's reaction—smiles, nods, and, for the most part, general assent.

Even from my vantage point, I could read their thoughts from their faces. "Sure," the customers seemed to say, "You know what's good here, and you're obviously on our side. Tell us what to get." Looking pleased, Vincent, who did know his vintages, would respond with some excellent (and costly) choices. He was similarly persuasive when it came time for dessert decisions. Patrons who otherwise would have passed up the dessert course or shared with a friend were swayed to partake fully by Vincent's rapturous descriptions of the baked Alaska and chocolate mousse. Who, after all, is more believable than a demonstrated expert of proven sincerity?

By combining the factors of reciprocity and credible authority into a single, elegant maneuver, Vincent was able to inflate substantially both the percentage of his tip and the base charge on which it was figured. His proceeds from this trick were handsome indeed. Notice, though, that much of his profit came from an apparent lack of concern for personal profit. Seeming to argue against his financial interests served those interests extremely well.[6]

---

[6]This same strategy can be used effectively in a variety of other situations as well. For example, one researcher found that letters of recommendation sent to the personnel directors of major corporations produced the most favorable results for job candidates when the letters contained one unflattering comment about the candidates in an otherwise wholly positive set of specific remarks (Knouse, 1983).

READER'S REPORT 6.2

From a Young Businessman

About two years ago, I was trying to sell my old car. One day I passed a used car lot with a sign reading, "We will sell your car for more." Just what I wanted, I thought; so, I stopped in to talk with the owner. I told him I wanted to get about $3,000 for my old car, and he said he thought I should be asking for a lot more because it was worth at least $3,500. This came as a real surprise to me because the way their consignment system worked the larger my asking price for the car, the less money was left over for them to keep after they sold it to somebody. By telling me to ask for more than $3,000, they were cutting off their own profits. Just like your Vincent the waiter example, they were seeming to argue against their own interests so I'd see them as trustworthy authorities, but I didn't realize this until much later. Anyway, I went along with the owner's idea that my car was worth more than I'd first thought, and set my asking price at $3,500.

After they'd had my car on their lot for a couple of days, they called saying that someone was really interested in it but that the price was a little too high. Would I be willing to drop my price by $200 to sell the car? Convinced that they had my interests at heart, I agreed. The next day they called back to say the buyer's financing had fallen through and that he couldn't buy the car. In the next two weeks, I got two more calls from the dealership, each asking me to drop my price $200 to seal a sale to some customer. Both times I OK'd it because I still believed they were trustworthy. But each time, the alleged deal fell through. I was suspicious enough to call a friend whose family was in the car business. He said this was an old trick designed to get sellers like me to reduce their asking prices to super low levels, giving the dealership big profits when they finally sold the car.

So, I went over there and took my car. As I was leaving, they were still trying to persuade me to let them keep it because they had a "hot prospect" they were sure would buy it if I'd only knock off another $200.

Author's note: Once again, we see the influence of the contrast principle combining with the principle of primary interest. In this case, after the $3,500 figure was set, each $200 nick seemed small in comparison.

SUMMARY

- In the Milgram studies of obedience we can see evidence of strong pressure in our society for compliance with the requests of an authority. Acting contrary to their own preferences, many normal, psychologically healthy individuals were willing to deliver dangerous and severe levels of pain to another person because they were directed to do so by an authority figure. The strength of this tendency to obey legitimate authorities comes from systematic socialization practices designed to instill in members of society the perception that such obedience constitutes correct conduct. In addition, it is frequently adaptive to obey the dictates of genuine authorities because such individuals usually possess high levels of knowledge, wisdom, and power. For these reasons, deference to authorities can occur in a mindless fashion as a kind of decision-making shortcut.

- When reacting to authority in an automatic fashion, there is a tendency to do so in response to the mere symbols of authority rather than to its substance. Three kinds of symbols that have been shown by research to be effective in this regard are titles, clothing, and automobiles. In separate studies investigating the influence of these symbols, individuals possessing one or another of them (and no other legitimizing credentials) were accorded more deference or obedience by those they encountered. Moreover, in each instance, individuals who deferred or obeyed underestimated the effect of authority pressures on their behaviors.

- It is possible to defend ourselves against the detrimental effects of authority influence by asking two questions: Is this authority truly an expert? How truthful can we expect this expert to be? The first question directs our attention away from symbols and toward evidence for authority status. The second advises us to consider not just the expert's knowledge in the situation but also his or her trustworthiness. With regard to this second consideration, we should be alert to the trust-enhancing tactic in which communicators first provide some mildly negative information about themselves. Through this strategy they create a perception of honesty that makes all subsequent information seem more credible to observers.

STUDY QUESTIONS

Content Mastery

1. What, in your opinion, is Milgram's most persuasive evidence for his argument that the willingness of subjects in his experiments to harm another results from a strong tendency to obey authority figures?

2. What does the research indicate about our ability to recognize the influence of authority pressures on our actions? Cite evidence to support your position.

3. Which are the three most influential symbols of authority, according to the research discussed in the chapter? Give examples from your own experience of the way you have seen at least two of these symbols work.

Critical Thinking

1. In Chapter 1, we came across a disturbing phenomenon called *Captainitis,* in which junior members of a flight crew pay no attention to the captain's errors or are reluctant to mention them. If you were an airplane captain what would you do to reduce this potentially disastrous tendency?

2. Why do you suppose the relationship between size and status developed as it has in human society? Do you see any reason why this relationship might change in the future? If so, by what processes?

3. Suppose you held a position in an advertising agency in which your job was to create a TV commercial for a product that had several good features and one weak feature. If you wanted the audience to believe in the good features, would you mention the weak one? If you did mention it, would you do so at the beginning, middle, or end of the commercial? What is the reason for your choice?

4. How does the ad that opens this chapter reflect the topic of the chapter?

7 *Scarcity*

The Rule of the Few

> *The way to love anything is to realize that it might be lost.*
>
> —G. K. CHESTERTON

The city of Mesa, Arizona, is a suburb in the Phoenix area where I live. Perhaps the most notable features of Mesa are its sizable Mormon population—next to Salt Lake City, the largest in the world—and a huge Mormon temple located on exquisitely kept grounds in the center of the city. Although I had appreciated the landscaping and architecture from a distance, I had never been interested enough in the temple to go inside, until the day I read a newspaper article that told of a special inner sector of Mormon temples to which no one has access but faithful members of the church. Even potential converts must not see it; however, there is one exception to the rule. For a few days immediately after a temple is newly constructed, non-members are allowed to tour the entire structure, including the otherwise restricted section.

The newspaper story reported that the Mesa temple had been recently refurbished and that the renovations had been extensive enough to classify it as "new" by church standards. Thus, for the next several days only, non-Mormon visitors could see the temple area traditionally banned to them. I remember quite well the effect this article had on me: I immediately resolved to take a tour; but when I phoned a friend to ask if he wanted to come along, I came to understand something that changed my decision just as quickly.

After declining the invitation, my friend wondered why *I* seemed so intent on a visit. I was forced to admit that, no, I had never been inclined toward the idea of a temple tour before, that I had no questions about the Mormon religion I wanted answered, that I had no general interest in church architecture, and that I expected to find nothing more spectacular or stirring than what I might see at a number of other churches in the area. It became clear as I spoke that the special lure of the temple had a sole cause: If I did not experience the restricted sector soon, I would never again have the chance. Something that, on its own merits, held little appeal for me had become decidedly more attractive merely because it was rapidly becoming less available.

LESS IS BEST AND LOSS IS WORST

I count myself far from alone in this weakness. Almost everyone is vulnerable to the scarcity principle in some form. Take as evidence the experience of Florida State University students who, like most undergraduates when surveyed, rated the quality of their campus cafeteria food unsatisfactory. Nine days later, according to a second survey, they had changed their minds. Something had happened to make them like their cafeteria's food significantly better than before. Interestingly, the event that caused them to shift their opinions had nothing to do with the quality of the food service, which had not changed a whit. But its availability had. On the day of the second survey, the students had learned that, because of a fire, they could not eat at the cafeteria for the next two weeks (West, 1975).

204

Collectors of everything from baseball cards to antiques are keenly aware of the scarcity principle's influence in determining the worth of an item. As a rule, if an item is rare or becoming rare, it is more valuable. Especially enlightening on the importance of scarcity in the collectibles market is the phenomenon of the "precious mistake." Flawed items—a blurred stamp or double-struck coin—are sometimes the most valued of all. Thus, a stamp carrying a three-eyed likeness of George Washington is anatomically incorrect, aesthetically unappealing, and yet highly sought after. There is instructive irony here: Imperfections that would otherwise make for rubbish make for prized possessions when they bring along an abiding scarcity.

Since my own encounter with the scarcity principle—*that opportunities seem more valuable to us when they are less available*—I have begun to notice its influence over a whole range of my actions. For instance, I routinely will interrupt an interesting face-to-face conversation to answer the ring of an unknown caller. In such a situation, the caller possesses a compelling feature that my face-to-face partner does not—potential unavailability. If I don't take the call, I might miss it (and the information it carries) for good. Never mind that the present conversation may be highly engaging or important—much more than I could reasonably expect an average phone call to be. With each unanswered ring, the phone interaction becomes less retrievable. For that reason and for that moment, I want it more than the other conversation.

People seem to be more motivated by the thought of losing something than by the thought of gaining something of equal value. For instance, college students experienced much stronger emotions when asked to imagine losses as opposed to gains in their romantic relationships or in their grade point averages (Ketelaar, 1995). Especially under conditions of risk and uncertainty, the threat of potential loss plays a powerful role in human decision making (Tversky & Kahneman, 1981; De Dreu & McCusker, 1997). Health researchers Alexander Rothman and Peter Salovey have applied this insight to the medical arena, where individuals are frequently urged to undergo tests to detect existing illnesses (e.g., mammography procedures, HIV screenings, cancer self-examinations). Because such tests involve the risk that a disease will be found and the uncertainty that it will be cured, messages stressing potential losses are most effective (Rothman & Salovey, 1997; Rothman, Martino, Bedell, Detweiler, & Salovey, 1999). For example, pamphlets advising young women to check for breast cancer through self-examinations are significantly more successful if they state their case in terms of what stands to be lost rather than gained (Meyerwitz & Chaiken, 1987). In a similar vein, physicians' letters to smokers describing the number of years of life that will be lost if they don't quit are more effective than letters describing the number of years that will be gained if they do quit (Wilson, Kaplan, & Schneiderman, 1987; Wilson, Purdon, & Wallston, 1988).

Limited Numbers

With the scarcity principle operating so powerfully on the worth we assign things, it is natural that compliance professionals will do some similar operating of their own. Probably the most straightforward use of the scarcity principle occurs in the "limited-number" tactic in which a customer is informed that a certain product is in short supply that cannot be guaranteed to last long. During the time I was researching compliance strategies by infiltrating various organizations, I saw the limited-number tactic employed repeatedly in a range of situations: "There aren't more than five convertibles with this engine left in the state. And when they're gone, that's it, 'cause we're not making 'em anymore." "This is one of only two unsold corner lots in the entire development. You wouldn't want the other one; it's got a nasty east-west exposure." "You may want to think seriously about buying more than one case today because production is backed way up and there's no telling when we'll get any more in."

Sometimes the limited-number information was true, sometimes it was wholly false. In each instance, however, the intent was to convince customers of an item's scarcity and thereby increase its immediate value in their eyes. I admit to developing a grudging admiration for the practitioners who made this simple device work in a multitude of ways and styles. I was most impressed, however, with a particular version that extended the basic approach to its logical extreme by selling a piece of merchandise at its scarcest point—when it seemingly could no longer be had. The tactic was played to perfection in one appliance store I investigated where 30 to 50 percent of the stock was regularly listed on sale. Suppose a couple in the store seemed, from a distance, to be moderately interested in a certain sale item. There are all sorts of cues that tip off such interest—closer-than-normal examination of the appliance, a casual look at any instruction booklets associated with the appliance, discussions held in front of the appliance, but no attempt to seek out a salesperson for further information. After observing the couple so engaged, a salesperson might approach and say, "I see you're interested in this model here, and I can understand why: it's a great machine at a great price. But, unfortunately, I sold it to another couple not more than 20 minutes ago. And, if I'm not mistaken, it was the last one we had."

The customers' disappointment registers unmistakably. Because of its lost availability, the appliance suddenly becomes more attractive. Typically, one of the customers asks if there is any chance that an unsold model still exists in the store's back room or warehouse or other location. "Well," the salesperson allows, "that is possible, and I'd be willing to check. But do I understand that this is the model you want and if I can get it for you at this price, you'll take it?" Therein lies the beauty of the technique. In accord with the scarcity principle the customers are asked to commit to buying the appliance when it looks least available and therefore most desirable. Many customers do agree to purchase at this singularly vulnerable time. Thus, when the salesperson (invariably) returns with the news that an additional supply of the appliance has been found, it is also with a pen and sales contract in hand. The information that the desired model is in good supply actually may make some customers find it less attractive again (Schwarz, 1984), although by then the business transaction has progressed too far for most people to renege. The purchase decision made and committed to publicly at an earlier, crucial point still holds. They buy.

COLGATE TOTAL®
WORKS ALL DAY TO FIGHT
GINGIVITIS, PLAQUE, TARTAR,
CAVITIES AND BAD BREATH.
(And you thought fluoride was a big breakthrough.)

If you thought fluoride was big, wait until you try Colgate Total.® With its unique formula that fights gingivitis, plaque, cavities, tartar, even bad breath. All day. All night. For up to 12 hours between brushings.

There's nothing else like it.
Colgate Total's formula of triclosan and gantrez is patented until 2008. So there's nothing like it now. And there'll be no formula exactly like it for a long time to come.

It's proven to work.

Rare Value
Marketers frequently use the scarcity principle in their appeals. In the present instance, they emphasize the uniqueness of the Colgate Total brand.

Time Limits

Related to the limited-number technique is the "deadline" tactic in which some official time limit is placed on the customer's opportunity to get what the compliance professional is offering. Much like my experience with the Mormon temple's inner sanctum, people frequently find themselves doing what they wouldn't much care to do simply because the time to do so is running out. The adept merchandiser makes this tendency pay off by arranging and publicizing customer deadlines that generate interest where none may have existed before. Concentrated instances of this approach often occur in movie advertising. In fact, I recently noticed that one theater owner, with remarkable singleness of purpose, had managed to invoke the scarcity principle three separate times in just five words of copy: "Exclusive, limited engagement ends soon!"

A variant of the deadline tactic is much favored by some face-to-face, high-pressure sellers because it carries the ultimate decision deadline: right now. Customers are often told that unless they make an immediate decision to buy, they will have to purchase the item at a higher price later or they will be unable to purchase it at all. A prospective health-club member or automobile buyer might learn that the deal offered by the salesperson is good for that one time only; should the customer leave the premises, the deal is off. One large child-portrait photography company urges parents to buy as many poses and copies as they can afford because "stocking limitations force us to burn the unsold pictures of your children within 24 hours." A door-to-door magazine solicitor might say that salespeople are in the customer's area for just a day; after that, they, and the customer's chance to buy their magazine package, will be long gone. A home vacuum cleaner operation I infiltrated instructed its sales trainees to claim that, "I have so many other people to see that I have the time to visit a family only once. It's company policy that even if you decide later that you want this machine, I can't come back and sell it to you." This, of course, is nonsense; the company and its representatives are in the business of making sales, and any customer who called for another visit would be accommodated gladly. As the company sales manager impressed on his trainees, the true purpose of the "can't come back" claim has nothing to do with reducing overburdened sales schedules. It is to "keep the prospects from taking the time to think the deal over by scaring them into believing they can't have it later, which makes them want it now."

PSYCHOLOGICAL REACTANCE

The evidence, then, is clear. Compliance practitioners' reliance on scarcity as a weapon of influence is frequent, wide-ranging, systematic, and diverse. Whenever this is the case with a weapon of influence, we can be assured that the principle involved has notable power in directing human action. With the scarcity principle, that power comes from two major sources. The first is familiar. Like the other weapons of influence, the scarcity principle trades on our weakness for shortcuts. The weakness is, as before, an *enlightened* one. We know that the things that are difficult to get are typically better than those that are easy to get (Lynn, 1989). As such, we can often use an item's availability to help us quickly and correctly decide on its quality. Thus, one reason for the potency of the scarcity principle is that, by following it, we are usually and efficiently right.[1] In addition, there is a unique, secondary source of power within the scarcity principle: As opportunities become less available, we lose freedoms. And we *hate* to lose the freedoms we already have. This desire to preserve our established

---

[1] Without wishing to minimize the advantage of this type of shortcut or the dangers associated with it, I should note that these advantages and dangers are essentially the same ones that we have examined in previous chapters. Accordingly, I will not focus on this theme in the remainder of the present chapter, except to say at this point that the key to properly using the shortcut feature of scarcity is to be alert to the distinction between naturally occurring, honest scarcity and the fabricated variety favored by certain compliance practitioners.

Don't Wait!
Last chance to read this now before you turn the page.

prerogatives is the centerpiece of psychological reactance theory, developed by psychologist Jack Brehm to explain the human response to diminishing personal control (J. W. Brehm, 1966; S. S. Brehm & J. W. Brehm, 1981). According to the theory, whenever free choice is limited or threatened, the need to retain our freedoms makes us want them (as well as the goods and services associated with them) significantly more than before. Therefore, when increasing scarcity—or anything else—interferes with our prior access to some item, we will *react against* the interference by wanting and trying to possess the item more than we did before.

As simple as the kernel of the theory seems, its shoots and roots curl extensively through much of the social environment. From the garden of young love to the jungle of armed revolution to the fruits of the marketplace, impressive amounts of our behavior can be explained by examining the tendrils of psychological reactance. Before beginning such an examination, though, it would be helpful to determine when people first show the desire to fight against restrictions of their freedoms.

Child psychologists have traced the tendency back to the age of 2—a time identified as a problem by parents and widely known to them as "the terrible twos." Most parents attest to seeing more contrary behavior in their children around this period. Two-year-olds seem masters of the art of resistance to outside pressure, especially from their parents. Tell them one thing, they do the opposite; give them one toy, they want another; pick them up against their will, they wriggle and squirm to be put down; put them down against their will, they claw and struggle to be carried.

One Virginia-based study nicely captured the style of terrible twos among boys who averaged 24 months in age (S. S. Brehm & Weintraub, 1977). The boys accompanied their mothers into a room containing two equally attractive toys. The toys were always arranged so that one stood next to a transparent Plexiglas barrier and the other stood behind the barrier. For some of the boys, the Plexiglas sheet was only a foot high—forming no real barrier to the toy behind it, since the boys could easily reach over the top. For the other boys, however, the Plexiglas was 2 feet high, effectively blocking their access to one toy unless they went around the barrier. The researchers wanted to see how quickly the toddlers would make contact with the toys under these conditions. Their findings were clear. When the barrier was too short to restrict access to the toy behind it, the boys showed no special preference for either of the toys; on the average, the toy next to the barrier was touched just as quickly as the one behind it. When the barrier was high enough to be a true obstacle, however, the boys went directly to the obstructed toy, making contact with it three times faster than with the unobstructed toy. In all, the boys in this study demonstrated the classic terrible-twos response to a limitation of their freedom: outright defiance.[2]

Why should psychological reactance emerge at the age of 2? Perhaps the answer has to do with a crucial change that most children go through about this time. It is then that they first come to a recognition of themselves as individuals. No longer do they view themselves as mere extensions of the social milieu but rather as identifiable, singular, and separate beings (Levine, 1983; Lewis & Brooks-Gunn, 1979; Mahler, Pine, & Bergman, 1975). This developing concept of autonomy brings naturally with it the concept of freedom. An independent being is one with choices; a child with the newfound realization that he or she is such a being will want to explore the length and breadth of the options. Perhaps we should be neither surprised

---

[2] Two-year-old girls in this study did not show the same resistant response to the large barrier as did the boys. Another study suggested this to be the case not because girls don't oppose attempts to limit their freedoms. Instead, it appears that they are primarily reactant to restrictions that come from other persons rather than from physical barriers (S. S. Brehm, 1981).

Swindled

By Peter Kerr

New York Times

NEW YORK—Daniel Gulban doesn't remember how his life savings disappeared.

He remembers the smooth voice of a salesman on the telephone. He remembers dreaming of a fortune in oil and silver futures. But to this day, the 81-year-old retired utility worker does not understand how swindlers convinced him to part with $18,000.

"I just wanted to better my life in my waning days," said Gulban, a resident of Holder, FL. "But when I found out the truth, I couldn't eat or sleep. I lost 30 pounds. I still can't believe I would do anything like that."

Gulban was the victim of what law enforcement officials call a "boiler room operation," a ruse that often involves dozens of fast-talking telephone salesmen crammed into a small room where they call thousands of customers each day. The companies snare hundreds of millions of dollars each year from unsuspecting customers, according to a U.S. Senate subcommittee on investigations, which issued a report on the subject last year.

"They use an impressive Wall Street address, lies and deception to get individuals to sink their money into various glamorous-sounding schemes," said Robert Abrams, the New York State attorney general, who has pursued more than a dozen boiler-room cases in the past four years. "The victims are sometimes persuaded to invest the savings of a lifetime."

Orestes J. Mihaly, the New York assistant attorney general in charge of the bureau of investor protection and securities, said the companies often operate in three stages. First, Mihaly said, comes the "opening call," in which a salesman identifies himself as representing a company with an impressive-sounding name and address. He will simply ask the potential customer to receive the company's literature.

A second call involves a sales pitch, Mihaly said. The salesman first describes the great profits to be made and then tells the customer that it is no longer possible to invest. The third call gives the customer a chance to get in on the deal, he said, and is offered with a great deal of urgency.

"The idea is to dangle a carrot in front of the buyer's face and then take it away," Mihaly said. "The aim is to get someone to buy it quickly, without thinking too much about it." Sometimes, Mihaly said, the salesman will be out of breath on the third call and will tell the customer that he "just came off the trading floor."

Such tactics convinced Gulban to part with his life savings. In 1979, a stranger called him repeatedly and convince Gulban to wire $1,756 to New York to purchase silver, Gulban said. After another series of telephone calls the salesman cajoled Gulban into wiring more than $6,000 for crude oil. He eventually wired an additional $9,740, but his profits never arrived.

"My heart sank," Gulban recalled, "I was not greedy. I just hoped I would see better days." Gulban never recouped his losses.

FIGURE 7.1 The Scarcity Scam

Note how the scarcity principle was employed during the second and third phone calls to cause Mr. Gulban to "buy quickly without thinking too much about it." *Click, Blur.*

nor distressed, then, when our 2-year-olds strain incessantly against our will. They have come to a recent and exhilarating perspective of themselves: they are free-standing human entities. Vital questions of choice, rights, and control now need to be asked and answered within their small minds. The tendency to fight for every liberty and against every restriction might be best understood, then, as a quest for information. By testing severely the limits of their freedoms (and, coincidentally, the patience of their parents), the children are discovering where in their worlds they can expect to be controlled and where to be in control. As we will see later, it is the wise parent who provides highly consistent information.

Adult Reactance: Love, Guns, and Suds

Although the terrible twos may be the most noticeable age of psychological reactance, we show the strong tendency to react against restrictions on our freedoms of action throughout our lives. One other age does stand out, however, as a time when this tendency takes an especially rebellious form: the teenage years. An enlightened neighbor once advised me, "If you really want to get something done, you've got three options: do it yourself, pay top dollar, or forbid your teenagers to do it." Like the twos, this period is characterized by an emerging sense of individuality. For teenagers, the emergence is out of the role of child, with all of its attendant parental control, and toward the role of adult, with all of its attendant rights and duties. Not surprisingly, adolescents tend to focus less on the duties than on the rights they feel they have as young adults. Not surprisingly, again, imposing traditional parental authority at these times is often counterproductive; teenagers will sneak, scheme, and fight to resist such attempts at control.

Nothing illustrates the boomerang quality of parental pressure on adolescent behavior quite so clearly as a phenomenon known as the "Romeo and Juliet effect." As we know, Romeo Montague and Juliet Capulet were the ill-fated Shakespearean characters whose love was doomed by a feud between their families. Defying all parental attempts to keep them apart, the teenagers won a lasting union in their tragic act of twin suicide, an ultimate assertion of free will.

The intensity of the couple's feelings and actions has always been a source of wonderment and puzzlement to observers of the play. How could such inordinate devotion develop so quickly in a pair so young? A romantic might suggest rare and perfect love. A social scientist, though, might point to the role of parental interference and the psychological reactance it can produce. Perhaps the passion of Romeo and Juliet was not initially so consuming that it transcended the extensive barriers erected by the families. Perhaps, instead, it was fueled to a white heat by the placement of those barriers. Could it be that had the youngsters been left to their own devices, their inflamed devotion would have amounted to no more than a flicker of puppy love?

Because the story is a work of fiction, such questions are, of course, hypothetical and any answer to them speculative. However, it is possible to ask and answer with more certainty similar questions about modern-day Romeos and Juliets.

Do couples suffering parental interference react by committing themselves more firmly to the partnership and falling more deeply in love? According to a study done with 140 Colorado teenage couples, that is exactly what they do. The researchers in this study found that although parental interference was linked to some problems in the relationship—the partners viewed one another more critically and reported a greater number of negative behaviors in the other—that interference also made the pair feel greater love for each other and desire for marriage. During the course of the study, as parental interference intensified, so did the love experience. When the interference weakened, romantic feelings actually cooled (Driscoll, Davis, & Lipetz, 1972).[3]

READER'S REPORT 7.1

From a Blacksburg, Virginia, Woman

Last Christmas I met a 27-year-old man. I was 19. Although he really wasn't my type, I went out with him—probably because it was a status thing to date an older man— but I really didn't become interested in him until my folks expressed their concern about his age. The more they got on my case about it, the more in love I became. It only lasted five months, but this was about four months longer than it would have lasted if my parents hadn't said anything.

Author's note: Although Romeo and Juliet have long since passed away, it appears that the Romeo and Juliet *effect is alive and well and making regular appearances in places like Blacksburg, Virginia.*

For twos and teens, then, psychological reactance flows across the broad surface of experience, always turbulent and forceful. For most of the rest of us, the pool of reactant energy lies quiet and covered, erupting geyserlike only on occasion (Ruback & Juieng, 1997). Still, these eruptions manifest themselves in a variety of

---

[3]The occurrence of the Romeo and Juliet effect should not be interpreted as a warning to parents to be always accepting of their teenagers' romantic choices. New players at this delicate game are likely to err often and, consequently, would benefit from the direction of an adult with greater perspective and experience. In providing such direction, parents should recognize that teenagers, who see themselves as young adults, will not respond well to control attempts that are typical of parent-child relationships. Especially in the clearly adult arena of mating, adult tools of influence (preference and persuasion) will be more effective than traditional forms of parental control (prohibitions and punishments). Although the experience of the Montague and Capulet families is an extreme example, heavy-handed restrictions on a young romantic alliance may well turn it clandestine, torrid, and sad.

fascinating ways that are of interest not only to the student of human behavior but to lawmakers and policymakers as well.

For instance, there's the odd case of Kennesaw, Georgia, the town that enacted a law requiring every adult resident to own a gun and ammunition, under penalty of six months in jail and a $200 fine. All the features of the Kennesaw gun law make it a prime target for psychological reactance. The freedom that the law restricts is an important, longstanding one to which most American citizens feel entitled. Furthermore, the law was passed by the Kennesaw City Council with a minimum of public input. Reactance theory would predict that under these circumstances few of the adults in the town of 5,400 would obey. Yet, the newspaper reports testified that three to four weeks after passage of the law, firearms sales in Kennesaw were—no pun intended—booming.

How are we to make sense of this apparent contradiction of the reactance principle? The answer is by looking a bit closer at those who were buying Kennesaw's guns. Interviews with Kennesaw store owners revealed that the gun buyers were not town residents at all, but visitors, many of them lured by publicity to purchase their initial guns in Kennesaw. Donna Green, proprietor of a shop described in one newspaper article as a virtual "grocery store of firearms," summed it up: "Business is great. But they're almost all being bought up by people from out of town. We've only had two or three local people buy a gun to comply with the law." After passage of the law, then, gun buying had become a frequent activity in Kennesaw, but not among those it was intended to cover; they were massively noncompliant. Only those individuals whose freedom in the matter had not been restricted by the law had the inclination to live by it.

A similar situation arose a decade earlier several hundred miles south of Kennesaw, when, to protect the environment, Dade County (Miami), Florida, imposed an antiphosphate ordinance prohibiting the use—and possession!—of laundry or cleaning products containing phosphates. A study done to determine the social impact of the law discovered two parallel reactions on the part of Miami residents. First, in what seems a Florida tradition, many Miamians turned to smuggling. Sometimes with neighbors and friends in large "soap caravans," they drove to nearby counties to load up on phosphate detergents. Hoarding quickly developed and, in the rush of obsession that frequently characterizes hoarders, families boasted of having 20-year supplies of phosphate cleaners.

The second reaction to the law was more subtle and more general than the deliberate defiance of the smugglers and hoarders. Spurred by the tendency to want what they could no longer have, the majority of Miami consumers came to see phosphate cleaners as better products than before. Compared to Tampa residents, who were not affected by the Dade County ordinance, the citizens of Miami rated phosphate detergents gentler, more effective in cold water, better whiteners and fresheners, and more powerful on stains. After passage of the law, they had even come to believe that phosphate detergents poured more easily (Mazis, 1975; Mazis, Settle, & Leslie, 1973).

This sort of response is typical of individuals who have lost an established freedom; and recognizing that it is typical is crucial to understanding how psychological reactance and the principle of scarcity work. When something becomes less available our freedom to have it is limited, and we experience an increased desire for it. We rarely recognize, however, that psychological reactance has caused us to want the item more; all we know is that we *want* it. To make sense of our heightened desire for the item, we begin to assign it positive qualities. In the case of the Dade County antiphosphate law—and in other instances of newly restricted availability—assuming a cause-and-effect relationship between desire and merit is a faulty supposition. Phosphate detergents clean, whiten, and pour no better after they are banned than they do before. We just assume they do because we find that we desire them more.

Censorship

The tendency to want what has been banned, and, therefore, to presume that it is more worthwhile is not limited to commodities such as laundry soap; it also extends to restrictions on information. In an age when the ability to acquire, store, and manage information increasingly affects access to wealth and power, it is important to understand how we typically react to attempts to censor or otherwise constrain our access to information. Although much data exist concerning our reactions to observing various kinds of potentially censorable material—media violence, pornography, radical political rhetoric—there is surprisingly little evidence on our reactions to the censoring of this material. Fortunately, the results of the few studies that have been done on censorship are highly consistent. Almost invariably, our response to banned information is to want to receive that information to a greater extent and to become more favorable toward it than we were before the ban. (Ashmore, Ramchandra, & Jones, 1971; Wicklund & Brehm, 1974; Worchel & Arnold, 1973; Worchel, Arnold, & Baker, 1975; Worchel, 1992).

The intriguing finding about the effects of censored information on an audience is not that audience members want to have the information more than before; that seems natural. Rather, it is that they come to believe in the information more, even though they haven't received it. For example, when University of North Carolina students learned that a speech opposing coed dorms on campus would be banned, they became more opposed to the idea of coed dorms (Worchel, Arnold, & Baker, 1975). Thus, without ever hearing the speech, the students became more sympathetic to its argument. This raises the worrisome possibility that especially clever individuals holding a weak or unpopular position on an issue can get us to agree with that position by arranging to have their message restricted. The irony is that for such people—members of fringe political groups, for example—the most effective strategy may not be to publicize their unpopular views but to get those views officially censored and then to publicize the censorship. Perhaps the authors of this country's Constitution were acting as much as sophisticated social psychologists as staunch civil libertarians when they wrote the remarkably permissive free speech provision of the First Amendment. By refusing to restrain freedom of speech, they may have been trying to minimize the chance that new political notions would win support via the irrational course of psychological reactance.[4]

Of course, political ideas are not the only kind that are susceptible to restriction. Access to sexually oriented material is also frequently limited. Although not as sensational as the occasional police crackdown on "adult" bookstores and theaters, regular pressure is applied by parents and citizens groups to censor the sexual content of educational material ranging from sex education and hygiene texts to school library books. Both sides in the struggle seem to be well intentioned and the issues are not simple, as they involve such matters as morality, art, parental control over the schools, and freedoms guaranteed by the First Amendment. From a purely psychological point of view, however, those favoring strict censorship may wish to examine closely the results of a study done on Purdue University undergraduates (Zellinger, Fromkin, Speller, & Kohn, 1974). In this study, students were shown some advertisements for a novel. For half the students, the advertising copy included the statement "a book for adults only, restricted to those 21 years and over"; the other half of the students read no such age restriction on the book. When the researcher later asked the students to indicate their feelings toward the book, they discovered the same pair of reactions we have noted with other bans: Those who learned of the age restriction wanted to read the book more and believed that they would like the book more than did those who thought their access to the book was unlimited.

It might be argued that, although these results may be true for a small sample of sexually inclined college students, they would not apply to students in junior and senior high schools, where the sex curricula battles are actually being waged. Two factors make me doubt such an argument. First, developmental psychologists report that the desire to oppose adult control generally begins quite early in adolescence, around the start of the teenage years. Nonscientific observers have also noted the early rise of these strong oppositional tendencies. Shakespeare, scholars tell us, placed Romeo and Juliet at the ages of 15 and 13 years, respectively. Second, the pattern of reactions exhibited by the Purdue students is not unique to the topic of sex and thus can't be attributed to any great preoccupation with sex that college students may have (Bushman & Stack, 1996). In fact, the pattern is common to externally imposed restrictions in general. Limiting access to the book had the same effects as did banning phosphate detergents in Florida or censoring a speech in North Carolina: The people involved wanted the restricted item more and, as a result, felt more favorable toward it.

Those who support the official banning of sexually relevant materials from school curricula have the avowed goal of reducing the orientation of the society, es-

---

[4]Evidence that reactance can cause people to take political action they would otherwise not have taken comes from a study by Heilman (1976). Supermarket shoppers were most likely to sign a petition favoring federal price controls after they had been informed that a federal official had opposed the distribution of the petition.

pecially of its youth, toward eroticism. In the light of the Purdue study and in the context of other research on the effects of imposed restraints, one must wonder whether official censorship as a means may not be antithetical to the goal. If we are to believe the implications of the research, then censorship is likely to increase the desire of students for sexual material and, consequently, to cause them to view themselves as the kind of individuals who like such material.

The term *official censorship* usually makes us think of bans on political or sexually explicit material, yet there is another common sort of official censorship that we don't think of in the same way, probably because it occurs after the fact. Often in a jury trial, a piece of evidence or testimony will be introduced, only to be ruled inadmissible by the presiding judge, who may then admonish the jurors to disregard that evidence. From this perspective, the judge may be viewed as a censor, though the form of the censorship is odd. The presentation of the information to the jury is not banned—too late for that—it's the jury's use of the information that is banned. How effective are such instructions from a judge? Is it possible that, for jury members who feel it is their right to consider all the available information, declarations of inadmissibility may actually cause psychological reactance, leading the jurors to use the evidence to a greater extent?

These were some of the questions asked in a large-scale jury research project conducted by the University of Chicago Law School (Broeder, 1959). One reason the results of the Chicago jury project are informative is that the participants were individuals who were actually on jury duty at the time and who agreed to be members of "experimental juries" formed by the researchers. These experimental juries then heard tapes of evidence from previous trials and deliberated as if they were deciding the case. In the study most relevant to our interest in official censorship, 30 such juries heard the case of a woman who was injured by a car driven by a careless male defendant. The first finding of the study was no surprise: When the driver said he had liability insurance, the jurors awarded his victim an average of $4,000 more than when he said he had no insurance ($37,000 versus $33,000). Thus, as insurance companies have long suspected, juries make larger awards to victims if an insurance company will have to pay. The second finding of the study is the fascinating one, though. If the driver said he was insured *and* the judge ruled that evidence inadmissible (directing the jury to disregard it), the instruction to disregard had a boomerang effect, causing an average award of $46,000. So, when certain juries learned that the driver was insured, they increased the damage payment by $4,000. When other juries were told officially that they must disregard the information, they used it still more, increasing the damage payment by $13,000. It appears, then, that even the proper, official censorship of a courtroom setting creates problems for the censor. We react to information restriction there, as we do in other areas, by valuing the banned information more than ever (for additional evidence, see Wolf & Montgomery, 1977).

The realization that we value limited information allows us to apply the scarcity principle to realms beyond material commodities. The principle works for messages, communications, and knowledge, too. Taking this perspective, we can see that *information may not have to be censored for us to value it more; it need only be scarce.* According to the scarcity principle, we will find a piece of information more persuasive if we think that we can't get it elsewhere. This idea—that exclusive information is more persuasive information—is central to the thinking of two psychologists, Timothy Brock and Howard Fromkin, who have developed a "commodity theory" analysis of persuasion (Brock, 1968; Fromkin & Brock, 1971).

The strongest support I know for Brock and Fromkin's theory comes from a small experiment done by a student of mine (Knishinsky, 1982). At the time, the student was also a successful businessman, the owner of a beef-importing company, who had returned to school to get advanced training in marketing. After we talked in my office one day about scarcity and exclusivity of information, he decided to do a study using his sales staff. The company's customers—buyers for supermarkets and other retail food outlets—were called on the phone as usual by a salesperson and asked for a purchase in one of three ways. One set of customers heard a standard sales presentation before being asked for their orders. Another set of customers heard the standard sales presentation plus information that the supply of imported beef was likely to be scarce in the upcoming months. A third group received the standard sales presentation and the information about a scarce supply of beef, too; however, they also learned that the scarce supply news was not generally available information—it had come, they were told, from certain exclusive contacts that the company had.[5] Thus, the customers who received this last sales presentation learned that not only was the availability of the product limited, so too was the news concerning it—the scarcity double-whammy.

The results of the experiment quickly became apparent when the company salespeople began to urge the owner to buy more beef because there wasn't enough in the inventory to keep up with all the orders they were receiving. Compared to the customers who got only the standard sales appeal, those who were also told about the future scarcity of beef bought more than twice as much. The real boost in sales, however, occurred among the customers who heard of the impending scarcity via "exclusive" information. They purchased six times the amount that the customers who received only the standard sales pitch did. Apparently, the fact that the news about the scarcity information was itself scarce made it especially persuasive.

OPTIMAL CONDITIONS

Much like the other effective weapons of influence, the scarcity principle is more effective at some times than at others. An important practical defense, then, is to find out when scarcity works best on us. A great deal can be learned from an experiment

---

[5]For ethical reasons, the information provided to the customers was always true. There *was* an impending foreign beef shortage and this news had, indeed, come to the company through its exclusive sources.

devised by social psychologist Stephen Worchel and his colleagues (Worchel, Lee, & Adewole, 1975). The basic procedure used by Worchel and his research team was simple: Participants in a consumer preference study were given a chocolate chip cookie from a jar and asked to taste and rate its quality. For half of the raters, the jar contained ten cookies; for the other half, it contained just two. As we might expect from the scarcity principle, when the cookie was one of only two available, it was rated more favorably than when it was one of ten. The cookie in short supply was rated as more desirable to eat in the future, more attractive as a consumer item, and more costly than the identical cookie in abundant supply.

Although this pattern of results provides a rather striking validation of the scarcity principle, it doesn't tell us anything we don't already know. Once again, we see that a less available item is more desired and valued. The real worth of the cookie study comes from two additional findings. Let's take them one at a time, as each deserves thorough consideration.

New Scarcity: Costlier Cookies and Civil Conflict

The first of these noteworthy results involved a small variation in the experiment's basic procedure. Rather than rating the cookies under conditions of constant scarcity, some participants were first given a jar of ten cookies that was then replaced by a jar of two cookies. Thus, before taking a bite, certain of the participants saw their abundant supply of cookies reduced to a scarce supply. Other participants, however, knew only scarcity of supply from the onset, as the number of cookies in their jars was left at two. With this procedure, the researchers were seeking to answer a question about types of scarcity: Do we value more those things that have become recently less available to us or those things that have always been scarce? In the cookie experiment, the answer was plain. The drop from abundance to scarcity produced a decidedly more positive reaction to the cookies than did constant scarcity.

The idea that newly experienced scarcity is the more powerful kind applies to situations well beyond the bounds of the cookie study. For example, social scientists have determined that such scarcity is a primary cause of political turmoil and violence. Perhaps the most prominent proponent of this argument is James C. Davies (1962, 1969) who states that we are most likely to find revolutions at a time when a period of improving economic and social conditions is followed by a short, sharp reversal in those conditions. Thus, it is not the traditionally most downtrodden people— those who have come to see their deprivation as part of the natural order of things—who are especially likely to revolt. Instead, revolutionaries are more likely to be those who have been given at least some taste of a better life. When the economic and social improvements they have experienced and come to expect suddenly become less available, they desire them more than ever and often rise up violently to secure them. For instance, it is little recognized that at the time of the American Revolution, the colonists had the highest standard of living and the lowest taxes in the Western World. According to historian Thomas Fleming (1997), it wasn't until the

British sought a cut of this widespread prosperity (by levying taxes) that the Americans revolted.

Davies has gathered persuasive evidence for his novel thesis from a range of revolutions, revolts, and internal wars, including the French, Russian, and Egyptian revolutions, as well as such domestic uprisings as Dorr's Rebellion in nineteenth-century Rhode Island, the American Civil War, and the urban black riots of the 1960s. In each case, a time of increasing well-being preceded a tight cluster of reversals that burst into violence.

The racial conflict in America's cities during the mid-1960s represents a case in point that many of us can recall. At the time, it was not uncommon to hear the question, "Why now?" It didn't seem to make sense that within their 300-year history, most of which had been spent in servitude and much of the rest in privation, American blacks would choose the socially progressive sixties as the time to revolt. Indeed, as Davies points out, the two decades after the start of World War II had brought dramatic political and economic gains to the black population. In 1940, blacks faced stringent legal restrictions in such areas as housing, transportation and education; moreover, even when the amount of education was the same, the average black family earned only a bit more than half the amount its counterpart white family earned. Fifteen years later, much had changed. Federal legislation had struck down as unacceptable formal and informal attempts to segregate blacks in schools, public places, housing, and employment settings. Economic advances had been made, too; black family income had risen from 56 to 80 percent of that of a comparably educated white family.

Then, according to Davies' analysis of social conditions, this rapid progress was stymied by events that soured the heady optimism of previous years. First, political and legal change proved substantially easier to enact than social change. Despite all the progressive legislation of the 1940s and 1950s, blacks perceived that most neighborhoods, jobs, and schools remained segregated. Thus, the Washington-based victories came to feel like defeats at home. For example, in the four years following the Supreme Court's 1954 decision to integrate all public schools, blacks were the targets of 530 acts of violence (direct intimidation of black children and parents, bombings and burnings) designed to prevent school integration. This violence generated the perception of another sort of setback in black progress. For the first time since well before World War II, when lynchings had occurred at an average rate of 78 per year, blacks had to be concerned about the basic safety of their families. The new violence was not limited to the education issue, either. Peaceful civil rights demonstrations of the time were frequently confronted by hostile crowds—and police.

Still another type of downturn occurred within the black populace in economic progress. In 1962, the income of a black family had slid back to 74 percent of that of a similarly educated white family. By Davies's argument, the most illuminating aspect of this 74 percent figure is not that it represented a long-term increase in prosperity from prewar levels, but that it represented a short-term decline from the flush levels of the mid-1950s. In 1963 came the Birmingham riots and, in staccato succession, scores of violent demonstrations, building toward the major upheavals of Watts, Newark, and Detroit.

In keeping with a distinct historical pattern of revolution, blacks in the United States were more rebellious when their prolonged progress was somewhat curtailed than they were before it began. This pattern offers a valuable lesson for would-be rulers: When it comes to freedoms, it is more dangerous to have given for a while than never to have given at all. The problem for a government that seeks to improve the political and economic status of a traditionally oppressed group is that, in so doing, it establishes freedoms for the group where none existed before. Should these now *established* freedoms become less available, there will be an especially hot variety of hell to pay.

We can look to more recent events in the former Soviet Union for evidence that this basic rule still holds. After decades of repression, Mikhail Gorbachev began granting the Soviet populace new liberties, privileges, and choices via the twin policies of *glasnost* and *perestroika*. Alarmed by the direction their nation was taking, a small group of government, military, and KGB officials staged a coup, placing Gorbachev under house arrest and announcing on August 19, 1991, that they had assumed power and were moving to reinstate the old order. Most of the world imagined that the Soviet people, known for their characteristic acquiescence to subjugation, would passively yield as they had always done. *Time* magazine editor, Lance Morrow, described his own reaction similarly: "At first the coup seemed to confirm the norm. The news administered a dark shock, followed immediately by a depressed sense of resignation: of course, of course, the Russians must revert to their essential selves, to their own history. Gorbachev and *glasnost* were an aberration; now we are back to fatal normality" (1991).

But these were not to be normal times. For one thing, Gorbachev had not governed in the tradition of the czars or Stalin or any of the line of oppressive post-War rulers who had not allowed even a breath of freedom to the masses. He had ceded them certain rights and choices. And when these now established freedoms were threatened, the people lashed out the way a dog would if someone tried taking a fresh bone from its mouth. Within hours of the junta's announcement, thousands were in the streets erecting barricades, confronting armed troops, surrounding tanks, and defying curfews. The uprising was so swift, so massive, so unitary in its opposition to any retreat from the gains of *glasnost* that after only three riotous days, the astonished officials relented, surrendering their power and pleading for mercy from Chairman Gorbachev. Had they been students of history—or of psychology—the failed plotters would not have been so surprised by the tidal wave of popular resistance that swallowed their coup. From the vantage point of either discipline, they could have learned an invariant lesson: Freedoms once granted will not be relinquished without a fight.

The lesson applies to the politics of family as well as country. The parent who grants privileges or enforces rules erratically invites rebellion by unwittingly establishing freedoms for the child. The parent who only sometimes prohibits between-meal sweets may create for the child the freedom to have such snacks. At that point,

Tanks, but No Tanks
Incensed by the news that then Soviet President Mikhail Gorbachev had been replaced in favor of plotters planning to cancel the newly instituted freedoms, Moscow residents confronted the tanks, defied the coup, and won the day.

enforcing the rule becomes a much more difficult and explosive matter because the child is no longer merely lacking a never-possessed right but is losing an established one. As we have seen in the case of political freedoms and (especially pertinent to the present discussion) chocolate chip cookies, people see a thing as more desirable when it recently has become less available than when it has been scarce all along. We should not be surprised, then, that research shows that parents who enforce and discipline inconsistently produce generally rebellious children (Lytton, 1979; O'Leary, 1995).[6]

---

[6]To avoid this problem, parents needn't be severe or unduly rigid rulekeepers. For example, a child who unavoidably misses lunch can be given a before-dinner snack because this would not violate the normal rule against such snacks and, consequently, would not establish a general freedom. The difficulty comes when the child is capriciously allowed a treat on some days but not on others and can see no good reason for the difference. It is this arbitrary approach that can build perceived freedoms and provoke rebellion.

READER'S REPORT 7.2

From a New York Investment Manager

I recently read a story in the *Wall Street Journal* that illustrates the scarcity principle and how people want whatever is taken away from them. The article described how Procter & Gamble tried an experiment in upstate New York by eliminating all savings coupons for their products and replacing the coupons with lower everyday prices. This produced a big consumer revolt—with boycotts, and protests, and a firestorm of complaints—even though Procter & Gamble's data showed that only 2 percent of coupons are used and that, on average during the no-coupon experiment, consumers paid the same for P&G products with less inconvenience. According to the article, the revolt happened because of something that P&G didn't recognize: "Coupons, to many people, are practically an inalienable right." It is amazing how strongly people react when you try to take things away, even if they never use them.

Author's note: *Although Procter & Gamble executives may have been perplexed by this seemingly irrational consumer response, they inadvertently contributed to it. Discount coupons have been part of the American scene for over a century, and P&G had actively "couponed" its products for decades, thereby helping to establish coupons as something consumers had a right to expect. And it's always the long-established rights that people fight most ferociously to preserve.*

Competition for Scarce Resources: Foolish Fury

Let's look back to the cookie study for another insight into the way we react to scarcity. We've already seen from the results of that study that scarce cookies were rated higher than abundant cookies and that newly scarce cookies were rated higher still. Staying with the newly scarce cookies now, we find that certain cookies were the highest rated of all—those that became less available because of a demand for them.

Remember that in the experiment the participants who experienced new scarcity had been given a jar of ten cookies that was then replaced with a jar of only two cookies. Actually, the researchers created this scarcity in one of two ways. Certain participants were told that some of their cookies had to be given away to other raters in order to supply the demand for cookies in the study. Another set of participants was told that the number of their cookies had to be reduced because the researcher had simply made a mistake and given them the wrong jar initially. The results showed that those whose cookies became scarce through the process of social demand liked the cookies significantly more than did those whose cookies became scarce by mistake. In fact, the cookies made less available through social demand were rated the most desirable of any in the study.

This finding highlights the importance of competition in the pursuit of limited resources. Not only do we want the same item more when it is scarce, we want it most when we are in competition for it. Advertisers often try to exploit this tendency in us. In their ads, we learn that "popular demand" for an item is so great that we must "hurry to buy"; we see a crowd pressing against the doors of a store before the start of a sale; we watch a flock of hands quickly deplete a supermarket shelf of a product. There is more to such images than the idea of ordinary social proof. The message is not just that the product is good because other people think so, but also that we are in direct competition with those people for it.

The feeling of being in competition for scarce resources has powerful motivating properties. The ardor of an indifferent lover surges with the appearance of a rival. It is often for reasons of strategy, therefore, that romantic partners reveal (or invent) the attentions of a new admirer. Salespeople are taught to play the same game with indecisive customers. For example, a realtor who is trying to sell a house to a "fence-sitting" prospect sometimes will call the prospect with news of another potential buyer who has seen the house, liked it, and is scheduled to return the following day to talk about terms. When wholly fabricated, the new bidder is commonly described as an outsider with plenty of money: "an out-of-state investor buying for tax purposes" and "a physician and his wife moving into town" are favorites. The tactic, called in some circles "goosing 'em off the fence," can work devastatingly well. The thought of losing out to a rival frequently turns a buyer from hesitant to zealous.

There is something almost physical about the desire to have a contested item. Shoppers at big close-out or bargain sales report being caught up emotionally in the event. Charged by the crush of competitors, they swarm and struggle to claim merchandise they would otherwise disdain. Such behavior brings to mind the "feeding frenzy" phenomenon of wild, indiscriminate eating among animal groups. Commercial fishermen exploit the phenomenon by throwing a quantity of loose bait to large schools of certain fish. Soon the water is a roiling expanse of thrashing fins and snapping mouths competing for the food. At this point, the fishermen save time and money by dropping unbated lines into the water, since the crazed fish will bite ferociously at anything, including bare metal hooks.

There is a noticeable parallel between the ways that commercial fishermen and department stores generate a competitive fury among those they wish to hook. To attract and arouse the catch, fishermen scatter some loose bait called chum. For similar purposes, department stores holding a bargain sale toss out a few especially good deals on prominently advertised items called loss leaders. If the bait—of either form—has done its job, a large and eager crowd forms to snap it up. Soon, in the rush to score, the group becomes agitated, nearly blinded, by the adversarial nature of the situation. Human beings and fish alike lose perspective on what they want and begin striking at whatever is being contested. One wonders whether the tuna flapping on a dry deck with only a bare hook in its mouth shares the what-hit-me bewilderment of the shopper arriving home with a load of department store bilge.

Lest we believe that the competition-for-limited-resources fever occurs only in such unsophisticated forms of life as tuna and bargain basement shoppers, we should examine the story behind a remarkable purchase decision made in 1973 by Barry Diller, who was vice president for prime-time programming of the American Broad-

Contagious Competitiveness
The struggle is intense in the china department of Harrod's as shoppers compete to grab the best bargains during the famous London department store's summer sale.

casting Company and who went on to head Paramount Pictures and the Fox Television Network. He agreed to pay $3.3 million for a single television showing of the movie *The Poseidon Adventure.* The figure is noteworthy in that it greatly exceeded the highest price ever before paid for a one-time movie showing—$2 million for *Patton.* In fact, the payment was so excessive that ABC figured to lose $1 million on the *Poseidon* showing. As NBC vice president for special programs, Bill Storke, declared at the time, "There's no way they can get their money back, no way at all."

How could an astute and experienced businessman like Diller go for a deal that would produce an expected loss of $1 million? The answer may lie in a second note-worthy aspect of the sale: It was the first time that a motion picture had been offered to the networks in an open-bid auction. Never before had the three networks been forced to battle for a scarce resource in quite this way. The novel idea of a competitive auction was the brainchild of the movie's flamboyant showman producer, Irwin Allen, and 20th Century-Fox vice president, William Self, who must have been ecstatic about the outcome. How can we be sure that it was the auction format that generated the spectacular sales price rather than the blockbluster quality of the movie itself?

Some comments from the auction participants provide impressive evidence. First came a statement from the victor, Barry Diller, intended to set future policy for his network. In language sounding like it could have escaped only from between clenched teeth, he said, "ABC has decided regarding its policy for the future that it would never again enter into an auction situation." Even more instructive are the remarks of Diller's rival, Robert Wood, then president of CBS Television, who nearly lost his head and outbid his competitors at ABC and NBC:

> *We were very rational at the start. We priced the movie out, in terms of what it could bring in for us, then allowed a certain value on top of that for exploitation.*
>
> *But then the bidding started. ABC opened with $2 million. I came back with $2.4. ABC went $2.8. And the fever of the thing caught us. Like a guy who had lost his mind, I kept bidding. Finally, I went to $3.2; and there came a moment when I said to myself, "Good grief, if I get it, what the heck am I going to do with it?" When ABC finally topped me, my main feeling was relief.*
>
> *It's been very educational. (MacKenzie, 1974, p. 4)*

According to interviewer Bob MacKenzie, when Wood said, "It's been very educational," he was smiling. We can be sure that when ABC's Diller vowed "never again," he was not. Both men had clearly learned a lesson from the "Great *Poseidon* Auction." The reason that both could not smile as a consequence was that, for one, there had been a $1 million tuition charge. Fortunately, there is a valuable but drastically less expensive lesson here for us, too. It is instructive to note that the smiling man was the one who had *lost* the highly sought-after prize. As a general rule, when the dust settles and we find losers looking and speaking like winners (and vice versa), we should be especially wary of the conditions that kicked up the dust—in the present case, open competition for a scarce resource. As the TV executives learned, extreme caution is advised whenever we encounter the devilish construction of scarcity plus rivalry.

Does the Vest Come with That?

To the astonishment of all concerned, a leisure suit worn by John Travolta in the movie *Saturday Night Fever* recently sold for $145,000. Perhaps we can help explain the astronomical price by noting two features of the sale. First, the suit is a special, one-of-a-kind item. Second, it was purchased at auction, where two buyers became locked into a competitive bidding spiral. When asked later whether he thought the final figure was excessive, the auctioneer remarked graciously, "Well, it certainly was a record for polyester."

DEFENSE

It is easy enough to feel properly warned against scarcity pressures, but it is substantially more difficult to act on that warning. Part of the problem is that our typical reaction to scarcity hinders our ability to think. When we watch as something we want becomes less available, a physical agitation sets in. Especially in those cases involving direct competition, the blood comes up, the focus narrows, and emotions rise. As this visceral current advances, the cognitive, rational side retreats. In the rush of arousal, it is difficult to be calm and studied in our approach. As CBS-TV president Robert Wood commented in the wake of his *Poseidon* adventure, "you get caught up in the mania of the thing, the acceleration of it. Logic goes right out the window" (MacKenzie, 1974).

Here's our predicament, then: Knowing the causes and workings of scarcity pressures may not be sufficient to protect us from them because knowing is a cognitive act, and cognitive processes are suppressed by our emotional reaction to scarcity pressures. In fact, this may be the reason for the great effectiveness of scarcity tactics. When they are employed properly, our first line of defense against foolish behavior—a thoughtful analysis of the situation—becomes less likely.

If, because of brain-clouding arousal, we can't rely on our knowledge about the scarcity principle to stimulate properly cautious behavior, what can we use? Perhaps, in fine jujitsu style, we can use the arousal itself as our prime cue. In this way, we can turn the enemy's strength to our advantage. Rather than relying on a considered, cognitive analysis of the entire situation, we might well tune ourselves to just the internal, visceral sweep for our warning. By learning to flag the experience of heightening arousal in a compliance situation, we can alert ourselves to the possibility of scarcity tactics there and to the need for caution.

Suppose, however, we accomplish this trick of using the rising tide of arousal as a signal to calm ourselves and to proceed with care. What then? Is there any other piece of information we can use to help make a proper decision in the face of scarcity? After all, merely recognizing that we ought to move carefully doesn't tell us the direction in which to move; it only provides the necessary context for a thoughtful decision.

Fortunately there is information available on which we can base thoughtful decisions about scarce items. It comes, once again, from the chocolate chip cookie study, where the researchers uncovered something that seems strange but rings true regarding scarcity: Even though the scarce cookies were rated as significantly more desirable, they were not rated as any better-tasting than the abundant cookies. So, despite the increased yearning that scarcity caused (the raters said they wanted to have more of the scarce cookies in the future and would pay a greater price for them), it did not make the cookies taste one whit better. Therein lies an important insight. The joy is not in the experiencing of a scarce commodity but in the possessing of it. It is important that we not confuse the two. Whenever we confront the scarcity pressures surrounding some item, we must also confront the question of what it is we want from the item. If the answer is that we want the thing for the social, economic, or psychological benefits of possessing something rare, then, fine; scarcity pressures will give us a good indication of how much we would want to pay for it—the less available it is, the more valuable to us it will be. However, very often we don't want a thing for the pure sake of owning it. We want it, instead, for its utility value; we want to eat it or drink it or touch it or hear it or drive it or otherwise use it. In such cases it is vital to remember that scarce things do not taste or feel or sound or ride or work any better *because* of their limited availability.

Although this point is simple it can often escape us when we experience the heightened desirability that scarce items naturally possess. I can cite a family example. My brother Richard supported himself through school by employing a compliance trick that cashed in handsomely on the tendency of most people to miss that simple point. In fact, his tactic was so effective in this regard that he had to work only a few hours each weekend for his money, leaving the rest of the time free for his studies.

Richard sold cars, but not in a showroom or on a car lot. He would buy a couple of used cars sold privately through the newspaper on one weekend, and adding nothing but soap and water, would sell them at a decided profit through the newspaper on the following weekend. To do this, he had to know three things. First, he had to know enough about cars to buy those that were offered for sale at the bottom of their blue book price range but that could be legitimately resold for a higher price. Second, once he got the car, he had to know how to write a newspaper ad that would stimulate substantial buyer interest. Third, once a buyer arrived, he had to know how to use the scarcity principle to generate more desire for the car than it perhaps deserved. Richard knew how to do all three. For our purposes, though, we need to examine his craft with just the third.

For a car he had purchased on the prior weekend, he would place an ad in the Sunday paper. Because he knew how to write a good ad, he usually received an array of calls from potential buyers on Sunday morning. Each prospect who was interested enough to want to see the car was given an appointment time—*the same appointment time.* So, if six people were scheduled, they were all scheduled for, say, 2:00 that afternoon. This little device of simultaneous scheduling paved the way for later compliance because it created an atmosphere of competition for a limited resource.

Typically, the first prospect to arrive would begin a studied examination of the car and would engage in standard car-buying behavior, such as pointing out any blemishes or deficiencies and asking if the price were negotiable. The psychology of the situation changed radically, however, when the second buyer drove up. The availability of the car to either prospect suddenly became limited by the presence of the other. Often the earlier arrival, inadvertently stoking the sense of rivalry, would assert his right to primary consideration. "Just a minute now, I was here first." If he didn't assert that right, Richard would do it for him. Addressing the second buyer, he would say, "Excuse me, but this other gentleman was here before you. So, can I ask you to wait on the other side of the driveway for a few minutes until he's finished looking at the car? Then, if he decides he doesn't want it or if he can't make up his mind, I'll show it to you."

Richard claims it was possible to watch the agitation grow on the first buyer's face. His leisurely assessment of the car's pros and cons had suddenly become a now-or-never, limited-time-only rush to a decision over a contested resource. If he didn't decide for the car—at Richard's asking price—in the next few minutes, he might lose it for good to that . . . that . . . lurking newcomer over there. The second buyer would be equally agitated by the combination of rivalry and restricted availability. He would pace about the periphery of things, visibly straining to get at this suddenly more desirable hunk of metal. Should 2:00 appointment number one fail to buy or even fail to decide quickly enough, 2:00 appointment number two was ready to pounce.

If these conditions alone were not enough to secure a favorable purchase decision immediately, the trap snapped securely shut as soon as the third 2:00 appointment arrived on the scene. According to Richard, stacked-up competition was usually too much for the first prospect to bear. He would end the pressure quickly by either agreeing to Richard's price or by leaving abruptly. In the latter instance, the second arrival would strike at the chance to buy out of a sense of relief coupled with a new feeling of rivalry with that . . . that . . . lurking newcomer over there.

All those buyers who contributed to my brother's college education failed to recognize a fundamental fact about their purchases: The increased desire that spurred them to buy had little to do with the merits of the car. The failure of recognition occurred for two reasons. First, the situation that Richard arranged for them produced an emotional reaction that made it difficult for them to think straight. Second, as a consequence, they never stopped to think that the reason they wanted the car in the first place was to use it, not merely to have it. The competition-for-a-scarce-resource pressures Richard applied affected only their desire to have the car in the sense of possessing it. Those pressures did not affect the value of the car in terms of the real purpose for which they had wanted it.

Should we find ourselves beset by scarcity pressures in a compliance situation, then, our best response would occur in a two-stage sequence. As soon as we feel the tide of emotional arousal that flows from scarcity influences, we should use that rise in arousal as a signal to stop short. Panicky, feverish reactions have no place in wise compliance decisions. We need to calm ourselves and regain a rational perspective. Once that is done, we can move to the second stage by asking ourselves why we want the item under consideration. If the answer is that we want it primarily for the purpose of owning it, then we should use its availability to help gauge how much we would want to spend for it. However, if the answer is that we want it primarily for its function (that is, we want something good to drive or drink or eat), then we must remember that the item under consideration will function equally well whether scarce or plentiful. Quite simply, we need to recall that the scarce cookies didn't taste any better.

SUMMARY

- According to the scarcity principle, people assign more value to opportunities when they are less available. The use of this principle for profit can be seen in such compliance techniques as the "limited number" and "deadline" tactics, wherein practitioners try to convince us that access to what they are offering is restricted by amount or time.
- The scarcity principle holds for two reasons. First, because things that are difficult to attain are typically more valuable, the availability of an item or experience can serve as a shortcut cue to its quality. Second, as things become less accessible, we lose freedoms. According to psychological reactance theory, we respond to the loss of freedoms by wanting to have them (along with the goods and services connected to them) more than before.
- As a motivator, psychological reactance is present throughout the great majority of the life span. However, it is especially evident at a pair of ages: the terrible twos and the teenage years. Both of these times are characterized by an emerging sense of individuality, which brings to prominence such issues as control, rights, and freedom. Consequently, individuals at these ages are especially sensitive to restrictions.
- In addition to its effect on the valuation of commodities, the scarcity principle also applies to the way that information is evaluated. Research indicates that the act of limiting access to a message causes individuals to want to receive it more and to become more favorable to it. The latter of these findings—that limited information is more persuasive—seems the more surprising. In the case of censorship, this effect occurs even when the message has not been received. When a message has been received, it is more effective if it is perceived as consisting of exclusive information.
- The scarcity principle is most likely to hold true under two optimizing conditions. First, scarce items are heightened in value when they are newly scarce. That is, we value those things that have become recently restricted more than those that were restricted all along. Second, we are most attracted to scarce resources when we compete with others for them.
- It is difficult to steel ourselves cognitively against scarcity pressures because they have an emotion-arousing quality that makes thinking difficult. In defense, we might try to be alert to a rush of arousal in situations involving scarcity. Once alerted, we can take steps to calm the arousal and assess the merits of the opportunity in terms of why we want it.

STUDY QUESTIONS

Content Mastery

1. What is the relationship between the scarcity principle and Brehm's theory of psychological reactance?

2. What makes the terrible twos and the teenage years especially susceptible to reactance effects?

3. How might modern social science explain the deaths of Shakespeare's famous characters, Romeo and Juliet?

4. What are the standard reactions of a potential audience to banned information?

5. What does the chocolate chip cookies study by Worchel, Lee, and Adewole (1975) indicate about the circumstances that maximize the effects of the scarcity principle?

Critical Thinking

1. During the 1983 and 1984 Christmas holiday seasons, the most sought-after toy in this country was the Cabbage Patch Kid doll, which was in very limited supply. From what you know about the scarcity principle, explain why people are reported to have spent as much as $700 at public auctions to secure a doll that cost $25 when available in stores.

2. Ovid said, "Easy things nobody wants, but what is forbidden is tempting." Explain his meaning in psychological terms.

3. Recall my brother Richard's approach to selling used cars. He never lied to anyone, yet some of his friends accused him of questionable ethics. What do you think? Was his technique ethically acceptable or objectionable? Why?

4. For more than a decade, the major message of a massive advertising campaign for Virginia Slims cigarettes has been that modern women "have come a long way" from the old days when they were required by social norms to be subdued, proper, and obedient. No longer, imply these ads, should a woman have to feel bound by chauvinistic and outmoded constraints on her independence. No matter what your view of the basic message, use your knowledge of psychological reactance to help explain the following fact: During the lengthy duration of this campaign, the percentage of cigarette smokers has risen in only one U.S. demographic group—teenage women.

5. How does the ad that opens this chapter reflect the topic of the chapter?

8

Instant Influence

Primitive Consent
for an Automatic Age

// companies / customers / suppliers / partners / everyone / everywhere / prepare to merge

Welcome to the City of e.

SAP™ is proud to deliver the first true, virtual city. A digital marketplace where more than 10,000 companies collaborate in one big free trade zone of uninterrupted e-business. // It's a place where you can find suppliers you never knew existed, work with partners you've never even met, and capitalize on opportunities you never thought you'd have. //

mySAP.com

It's your own personalized Web environment, where the solutions you need are always at your fingertips. Where companies of all sizes, in all industries, can conduct one-step business. // If you've got a business, we've got a city. The City of e. Get there through mySAP.com or call 800-283-1SAP.

SAP

Every day in every way, I'm getting better.
                                    —EMILÉ COUÉ

Every day in every way, I'm getting busier.
                                    —ROBERT CIALDINI

Back in the 1960s a man named Joe Pine hosted a rather remarkable TV talk show that was syndicated from California. The program was made distinctive by Pine's caustic and confrontational style with his guests—for the most part, a collection of exposure-hungry entertainers, would-be celebrities, and representatives of fringe political or social organizations. The host's abrasive approach was designed to provoke his guests into arguments, to fluster them into embarrassing admissions, and generally to make them look foolish. It was not uncommon for Pine to introduce a visitor and launch immediately into an attack on the individual's beliefs, talent, or appearance. Some people claimed that Pine's acid personal style was partially caused by a leg amputation that had embittered him to life; others said, no, that he was just vituperative by nature.

One evening rock musician Frank Zappa was a guest on the show. This was at a time in the 1960s when very long hair on men was still unusual and controversial. As soon as Zappa had been introduced and seated, the following exchange occurred:

Pine: I guess your long hair makes you a girl.

Zappa: I guess your wooden leg makes you a table.

PRIMITIVE AUTOMATICITY

Aside from containing what may be my favorite ad-lib, the dialogue between Pine and Zappa illustrates a fundamental theme of this book: Very often when we make a decision about someone or something we don't use all of the relevant available information. We use, instead, only a single, highly representative piece of the total. An isolated piece of information, even though it normally counsels us correctly, can lead us to clearly stupid mistakes—mistakes that, when exploited by clever others, leave us looking silly or worse.

At the same time, a complicating companion theme has been present throughout this book: Despite the susceptibility to stupid decisions that accompanies a reliance on a single feature of the available data, the pace of modern life demands that we frequently use this shortcut. Recall that early in Chapter 1, we compared this shortcut to the automatic responding of lower animals, whose elaborate behavior patterns could be triggered by the presence of a lone stimulus feature—a cheep-cheep sound, a shade of red breast feather, or a specific sequence of light flashes. The reason these lower animals must often rely on such solitary stimulus features of their environments is their restricted mental capacity. Their small brains cannot begin to register and process all of the relevant information in their environments. So these species have evolved special sensitivities to certain aspects of the information. Because those selected aspects of information are normally enough to cue a correct response, the system is usually very efficient: Whenever a mother turkey hears cheep, cheep, *click, whirr,* out rolls the proper maternal behavior in a mechanical fashion that conserves much of her limited brainpower for dealing with the other situations and choices she must face in her day.

We, of course, have vastly more effective brain mechanisms than do mother turkeys, or any other animal group, for that matter. We are unchallenged in the ability to take into account a multitude of relevant facts and, consequently, to make good decisions. Indeed, it is this information-processing advantage over other species that has helped make us the dominant form of life on the planet.

Still, we have our capacity limitations, too; and, for the sake of efficiency, we must sometimes retreat from the time-consuming, sophisticated, fully informed brand of decision making to a more automatic, primitive, single-feature type of responding. For instance, in deciding whether to say yes or no to a requester, we frequently pay attention to a single piece of the relevant information in the situation. In preceding chapters, we have explored several of the most popular of the single pieces of information that we use to prompt our compliance decisions. They are the most popular prompts precisely because they are the most reliable ones, those that normally point us toward the correct choice. That is why we employ the factors of reciprocation, consistency, social proof, liking, authority, and scarcity so often and so automatically in making our compliance decisions. Each, by itself, provides a highly reliable cue as to when we will be better off saying yes instead of no.

We are likely to use these lone cues when we don't have the inclination, time, energy, or cognitive resources to undertake a complete analysis of the situation. When we are rushed, stressed, uncertain, indifferent, distracted, or fatigued, we tend to focus on less of the information available to us. When making decisions under these circumstances, we often revert to the rather primitive but necessary single-piece-of-good-evidence approach.[1] All this leads to an unnerving insight: With the sophisticated mental apparatus we have used to build world eminence as a species, we have created an environment so complex, fast-paced, and information-laden that we must increasingly deal with it in the fashion of the animals we long ago transcended.

Sometimes the consequences can be calamitous. Remember the FBI's infamously misguided assault on Branch Davidian Church headquarters in Waco, Texas? According to an analysis by U.S. Justice Department consultants, during the

---

[1]For evidence of such perceptual and decisional narrowing, see Berkowitz and Buck (1967); Bodenhausen (1960); Cohen (1978); Easterbrook (1959); Gilbert and Osborne (1989); Hockey and Hamilton (1970); Keinan (1987); Kruglanski and Freund (1983); Mackworth (1965); Milgram (1970); Paulus, Martin, and Murphy (1992); Scammon (1977); Tversky and Kahneman (1974); and Webster, Richter, and Kruglansk (1996).

FBI's 51-day siege of the Branch Davidian's compound, the agency collected so much information that it had to ignore the vast majority of it. Said Professor Robert Louden, one of the Justice Department's consultants, "The FBI had such an intelligence information overload that . . . they just fell back on past practice—and since they didn't have any experience with religion, they treated it like a standard barricade" ("Overload of Advice," 1993). The disastrous outcome was that, when the FBI finally attacked, more than 80 sect members died in an act of faith- and fear-fueled self-emulation.

MODERN AUTOMATICITY

John Stuart Mill, the British economist, political thinker, and philosopher of science, died over 125 years ago. The year of his death (1873) is important because he is reputed to have been the last man to know everything there was to know in the world. Today, the notion that one of us could be aware of all known facts is laughable. After eons of slow accumulation, human knowledge has snowballed into an era of momentum-fed, multiplicative, monstrous expansion. We now live in a world where most of the information is less than 15 years old. In certain fields of science alone (physics, for example), knowledge is said to double every eight years. The scientific information explosion is not limited to such arcane arenas as molecular chemistry or quantum physics, but extends to everyday areas of knowledge where we strive to keep ourselves current—health, child development, nutrition. What's more, this rapid growth is likely to continue, since researchers are pumping their newest findings into an estimated 400,000 scientific journals worldwide.

Apart from the streaking advance of science, things are quickly changing much closer to home. According to yearly Gallup polls, the issues rated as most important on the public agenda are becoming more diverse and are surviving on that agenda for a shorter time (McCombs & Zhu, 1995). In addition, we travel more and faster; we relocate more frequently to new residences, which are built and torn down more quickly; we contact more people and have shorter relationships with them; in the supermarket, car showroom, and shopping mall, we are faced with an array of choices among styles and products that were unheard-of last year and may well be obsolete or forgotten by next year. Novelty, transience, diversity, and acceleration are acknowledged as prime descriptors of civilized existence.

This avalanche of information and choices is made possible by burgeoning technological progress. Leading the way are developments in our ability to collect, store, retrieve, and communicate information. At first, the fruits of such advances were limited to large organizations—government agencies or powerful corporations. With further developments in telecommunications and computer technology, access to such staggering amounts of information is falling within the reach of individual citizens. Extensive cable and satellite systems provide one route for that information into the average home.

Sipress

**Opting Out
of the Options**
Too many options can
prove wearisome.

© 1984, David Sipress, from
Wishful Thinking, © 1987,
by Harper and Row.

The other major route is the personal computer. In 1972, Norman Macrae, an editor of the The *Economist,* speculated prophetically about a time in the future:

> *The prospect is, after all, that we are going to enter an age when any duffer sitting at a computer terminal in his laboratory or office or public library or home can delve through unimaginable increased mountains of information in mass-assembly data banks with mechanical powers of concentration and calculation that will be greater by a factor of tens of thousands than was ever available to the human brain of even an Einstein. (Macrae, 1972)*

Just one decade later, *Time* magazine signaled that Macrae's future age had arrived by naming a machine, the personal computer, as its Man of the Year. *Time's* editors defended their choice by citing the consumer "stampede" to purchase small computers and by arguing that "America [and], in a larger perspective, the entire world will never be the same." Macrae's vision is presently being realized. Millions of ordinary "duffers" are sitting in front of computers with the potential to present and analyze enough data to bury an Einstein.

Modern day visionaries—like Bill Gates, chairman of Microsoft—agree with Macrae, asserting that we are creating an array of devices capable of delivering a universe of information "to anyone, anywhere, anytime" (Davidson, 1999). But notice something telling: Our modern era, often termed The Information Age, has never been called The Knowledge Age. Information does not translate directly into knowledge. It must first be processed—accessed, absorbed, comprehended, integrated, and retained.

SHORTCUTS SHALL BE SACRED

Because technology can evolve much faster than we can, our natural capacity to process information is likely to be increasingly inadequate to handle the abundance of change, choice, and the challenge that is characteristic of modern life. More and more frequently, we will find ourselves in the position of lower animals—with a mental apparatus that is unequipped to deal thoroughly with the intricacy and richness of the outside environment. Unlike the lower animals, whose cognitive powers have always been relatively deficient, we have created our own deficiency by constructing a radically more complex world. The consequence of our new deficiency is the same as that of the animals' long-standing one: when making a decision, we will less frequently engage in a fully considered analysis of the total situation. In response to this "paralysis of analysis," we will revert increasingly to a focus on a single, usually reliable feature of the situation.

When those single features are truly reliable, there is nothing inherently wrong with the shortcut approach of narrowed attention and automatic responding to a particular piece of information. The problem comes when something causes the normally trustworthy cues to counsel us poorly, to lead us to erroneous actions and wrongheaded decisions. As we have seen, one such cause is the trickery of certain compliance practitioners, who seek to profit from the mindless and mechanical nature of shortcut responding. If, as it seems, the frequency of shortcut responding is increasing with the pace and form of modern life, we can be sure that the frequency of this trickery is destined to increase as well.

What can we do about the expected intensified attack on our system of shortcuts? More than evasive action, I urge forceful counterassault; however, there is an important qualification. Compliance professionals who play fairly by the rules of shortcut responding are not to be considered the enemy; to the contrary, they are our allies in an efficient and adaptive process of exchange. The proper targets for counteraggression are only those individuals who falsify, counterfeit, or misrepresent the evidence that naturally cues our shortcut responses.

Let's take an illustration from what is perhaps our most frequently used shortcut. According to the principle of social proof, we often decide to do what other people like us are doing. It makes all kinds of sense since, most of the time, an action that is popular in a given situation is also functional and appropriate. Thus, an advertiser who, without using deceptive statistics, provides information that a brand of toothpaste is the largest selling has offered us valuable evidence about the quality of the product and the probability that we will like it. Provided that we are in the market for a tube of good toothpaste, we might want to rely on that single piece of information, popularity, to decide to try it. This strategy will likely steer us right, will unlikely steer us far wrong, and will conserve our cognitive energies for dealing with the rest of our increasingly information-laden, decision-overloaded environment. The advertiser who allows us to use effectively this efficient strategy is hardly our antagonist but rather our cooperating partner.

The story becomes quite different, however, when a compliance practitioner tries to stimulate a shortcut response by giving us a fraudulent signal for it. The enemy is an advertiser who seeks to create an image of popularity for a brand of toothpaste by, say, constructing a series of staged "unrehearsed interview" commercials in which an array of actors posing as ordinary citizens praises the product. Here, where the evidence of popularity is counterfeit, we, the principle of social proof, and our short-cut response to it, are all being exploited. In an earlier chapter, I recommended against the purchase of any product featured in a faked "unrehearsed interview" ad and urged that we send the product manufacturers letters detailing the reason and suggesting that they dismiss their advertising agency. I also recommended extending this aggressive stance to any situation in which a compliance professional abuses the principle of social proof (or any other weapon of influence) in this manner. We should refuse to watch TV programs that use canned laughter. If we see a bartender begin a shift by salting the tip jar with a bill or two, that bartender should get no tip from us. If, after waiting in line outside a nightclub, we discover from the amount of available space that the wait was designed to impress passersby with false evidence of the club's popularity, we should leave immediately and announce our reason to those still in line. In short, we should be willing to use boycott, threat, confrontation, censure, tirade, nearly anything, to retaliate.

I don't consider myself pugnacious by nature, but I actively advocate such belligerent actions because in a way I am at war with the exploiters. We all are. It is important to recognize, however, that their motive for profit is not the cause for hostilities; that motive, after all, is something we each share to an extent. The real treachery, and what we cannot tolerate, is any attempt to make their profit in a way that threatens the reliability of our shortcuts. The blitz of modern daily life demands that we have faithful shortcuts, sound rules of thumb in order to handle it all. These are no longer luxuries; they are out-and-out necessities that figure to become increasingly vital as the pulse quickens. That is why we should want to retaliate whenever we see someone betraying one of our rules of thumb for profit. We want that rule to be as effective as possible. To the degree that its fitness for duty is regularly undercut by the tricks of a profiteer, we naturally will use it less and will be less able to cope efficiently with the decisional burdens of our day. That we cannot allow without a fight. The stakes are far too high.

SUMMARY

- Modern life is different from any earlier time. Because of remarkable technological advances, information is burgeoning, choices and alternatives are expanding, knowledge is exploding. In this avalanche of change and choice, we have had to adjust. One fundamental adjustment has come in the way we make decisions. Although we all wish to make the most thoughtful, fully considered decision possible in any situation, the changing form and accelerating pace of modern life frequently deprive us of the proper conditions for such a careful analysis of all the relevant pros and cons. More and more, we are forced to resort to another decision-making approach—a shortcut approach in which the decision to comply (or agree or believe or buy) is made on the basis of a single, usually reliable piece of information. The most reliable and, therefore, most popular such single triggers for compliance are those described throughout this book. They are commitments, opportunities for reciprocation, the compliant behavior of similar others, feelings of liking or friendship, authority directives, and scarcity information.

- Because of the increasing tendency for cognitive overload in our society, the prevalence of shortcut decision making is likely to increase proportionately. Compliance professionals who infuse their requests with one or another of the triggers of influence are more likely to be successful. The use of these triggers by practitioners is not necessarily exploitative. It only becomes so when the trigger is not a natural feature of the situation but is fabricated by the practitioner. In order to retain the beneficial character of shortcut response, it is important to oppose such fabrication by all appropriate means.

STUDY QUESTIONS

Critical Thinking

1. Pick any three of the weapons of influence described in this book. Discuss in each case how the weapon could be used to enhance compliance in what you would consider an exploitative manner and in what you would consider a nonexploitative manner.

2. For each of the three weapons of influence you choose, describe the way you would defend yourself should the weapon be used against you in an exploitative fashion.

3. Describe the three most important lessons that you have learned about the influence process from this book.

References

Aaker, D. A. (1991). *Managing brand equity.* New York: Free Press.

Abrams, D., Wetherell, M., Cochrane, S., Hogg, M. A., & Turner, J. C. (1990). Knowing what to think by knowing who you are. *British Journal of Social Psychology, 29,* 97–119.

Adams, G. R. (1977). Physical attractiveness research: Toward a developmental social psychology of beauty. *Human Development, 20,* 217–239.

Allgeier, A. R., Byrne, D., Brooks, B., & Revnes, D. (1979). The waffle phenomenon: Negative evaluations of those who shift attitudinally. *Journal of Applied Social Psychology, 9,* 170–182.

Allison, S. T., Mackie, D. M., Muller, M. M., & Worth, L. T. (1993). Sequential correspondence biases and perceptions of change. *Personality and Social Psychology Bulletin, 19,* 151–157.

Allison, S. T., & Messick, D. M. (1988). The feature-positive effect, attitude strength, and degree of perceived consensus. *Personality and Social Psychology Bulletin, 14,* 231–241.

Altheide, D. L., & Johnson, J. M. (1977). Counting souls: A study of counseling at evangelical crusades. *Pacific Sociological Review, 20,* 323–348.

Anderson, S. M., & Zimbardo, P. G. (1984). On resisting social influence. *Cultic Studies Journal, 1,* 196–219.

Ardry, R. (1970). *The social contract.* New York: Atheneum.

Aronson, E. (1975, February). The jigsaw route to learning and liking. *Psychology Today,* pp. 43–50.

Aronson, E., Bridgeman, D. L., & Geffner, R. (1978a). The effects of a cooperative classroom structure on students' behavior and attitudes. In D. Bar-Tal & L. Saxe (Eds.), *Social psychology of education: Theory and research.* New York: Halstead Press.

Aronson, E., Bridgeman, D. L., & Geffner, R. (1978b). Interdependent interactions and prosocial behavior. *Journal of Research and Development in Education, 12,* 16–27.

Aronson, E., & Mills, J. (1959). The effect of severity of initiation on liking for a group. *Journal of Abnormal and Social Psychology, 59,* 177–181.

Aronson, E., Stephan C., Sikes, J., Blaney, N., & Snapp, M. (1978). *The jigsaw classroom.* Beverly Hills, CA: Sage Publications.

Asch, S. (1946). Forming impressions of personality. *Journal of Abnormal and Social Psychology, 41,* 258–290.

Ashmore, R. D., Ramchandra, V., & Jones, R. A. (1971, April). *Censorship as an attitude change induction.* Paper presented at the meeting of the Eastern Psychological Association, New York.

Asimov, I. (1975, August 30). The Miss America pagent. *TV Guide.*

Bachman, W., & Katzev, R. (1982). The effects on noncontingent free bus tickets and personal commitment on urban bus ridership. *Transportation Research, 16A(2),* 103–108.

Bandura, A., Grusec, J. E., & Menlove, F. L. (1967). Vicarious extinction of avoidance behavior. *Journal of Personality and Social Psychology, 5,* 16–23.

Bandura, A., & Menlove, F. L. (1968). Factors determining vicarious extinction of avoidance behavior through symbolic modeling. *Journal of Personality and Social Psychology, 8,* 99–108.

Barker, J. (1998, May 10). Judges on junkets. *The Arizona Republic,* pp. A1, A6, A7.

Benson, P L., Karabenic, S. A., & Lerner, R. M. (1976). Pretty pleases: The effects of physical attractiveness on race, sex, and receiving help. *Journal of Experimental Social Psychology, 12,* 409–415.

Benton, A. A., Kelley, H. H., & Liebling, B. (1972). Effects of extremity of offers and concession rate on the outcomes of bargaining. *Journal of Personality and Social Psychology, 24,* 73–83.

Berkowitz, L., & Buck, R. W. (1967). Impulsive aggression: Reactivity to aggressive cues under emotional arousal. *Journal of Personality and Social Psychology, 35,* 415–424.

Berry, S. H., & Kanouse, D. E. (1987). Physician response to a mailed survey: An experiment in timing of payment. *Public Opinion Quarterly, 51,* 102–114.

Berscheid, E., & Walster [Hatfield], E. (1978). *Interpersonal attraction.* Reading, MA: Addison-Wesley.

Bickman, L. (1974). The social power of a uniform. *Journal of Applied Social Psychology, 4,* 47–61.

Bierley, C., McSweeney, F K., & Vannieuwkerk, R. (1985). Classical conditioning preferences of stimuli. *Journal of Consumer Research, 12,* 316–323.

Blake, R., & Mouton, J. (1979). Intergroup problem solving in organizations: From theory to practice. In W. Austin & S. Worchel (Eds.), *The social psychology of intergroup relations.* Monterey, CA: Brooks/Cole.

Blass, T. (1991). Understanding behavior in the Milgram obedience experiment. *Journal of Personality and Social Psychology, 60,* 398–413.

Blass, T. (1999). The Milgram paradigm after 35 years: Some things we now know about obedience to authority. *Journal of Applied Social Psychology, 29,* 955–978.

Bodenhausen, G. V. (1990). Stereotypes as judgmental heuristics: Evidence of circadian variations in discrimination. *Psychological Science, 1,* 319–322.

Bodenhausen, G. V., Macrae, C. N., & Sherman, J. W. (1999). On the dialectics of discrimination: Dual processes in social sterotyping. In S. Chaiken & Y. Trope (Eds.), *Dual-process theories in social psychology* (pp. 271–290). New York: Guilford.

Bollen, K. A., & Phillips, D. P (1982). Imitative suicides: A national study of the effects of television news stories. *American Sociological Review, 47,* 802–809.

Bornstein, R. F., Leone, D. R., & Galley, D. J. (1987). The generalizability of subliminal mere exposure effects. *Journal of Personality and Social Psychology, 53,* 1070–1079.

Brehm, J. W. (1966). *A theory of psychological reactance.* New York: Academic Press.

Brehm, S. S. (1981). Psychological reactance and the attractiveness of unattainable objects: Sex differences in children's responses to an elimination of freedom. *Sex Roles, 7,* 937–949.

Brehm, S. S. & Brehm, J. W. (1981). *Psychological reactance.* New York: Academic Press.

Brehm, S. S., & Weintraub, M. (1977). Physical barriers and psychological reactance: Two-year-olds' responses to threats to freedom. *Journal of Personality and Social Psychology, 35,* 830–836.

Brewer, M. (1979). In-group bias in the minimal intergroup situation: A cognitive-motivational analysis. *Psychological Bulletin, 86,* 307–324.

Brock, T. C. (1968). Implications of commodity theory for value change. In A. G. Greenwald, T. C. Brock, & T. M. Ostrom (Eds.) *Psychological foundations of attitudes.* New York: Academic Press.

Brockner, J., & Rubin, J. Z. (1985). *Entrapment in escalating conflicts: A social psychological analysis.* New York: Springer-Verlag.

Broeder, D. (1959). The University of Chicago jury project. *Nebraska Law Review, 38,* 744–760.

Brownstein, R., & Katzev, R. (1985). The relative effectiveness of three compliance techniques in eliciting donations to a cultural organization. *Journal of Applied Social Psychology, 15,* 564–574.

Bruner, J. S., & Goodman, C. C. (1947). Value and need as organizing factors in perception. *Journal of Abnormal and Social Psychology, 42,* 33–44.

Budesheim, T. L., & DePaola, S. J. (1994). Beauty or the beast? The effects of appearance, personality, and issue information on evaluations of political candidates. *Personality and Social Psychology Bulletin, 20,* 339–348.

Burger, J. M., & Petty, R. E. (1981). The low-ball compliance technique: Task or person commitment? *Journal of Personality and Social Psychology, 40,* 492–500.

Burgess, T., & Sales, S. (1971). Attitudinal effects of "mere exposure": A reevaluation. *Journal of Experimental Social Psychology, 7,* 461–472.

Burn, S. W. (1991). Social psychology and the stimulation of recycling behaviors: The block leader approach. *Journal of Applied Social Psychology, 21,* 611–629.

Bushman, B. J. (1988). The effects of apparel on compliance. *Personality and Social Psychology Bulletin, 14,* 459–467.

Bushman, B. J., & Stack, A. D. (1996). Forbidden fruit versus tainted fruit: Effects of warning labels on attraction to television violence. *Journal of Experimental Psychology: Applied, 2,* 207–226.

Buss, D. M., & Kenrich, D. T. (1998). Evolutionary social psychology. In D. T. Gilbert, S. T. Fiske, & G. Lindzey, (Eds.), *The handbook of social psychology* (4th ed.) (Vol. 2, pp. 982–1026). Boston: McGraw-Hill.

Byrne, D. (1971). *The attraction paradigm.* New York: Academic Press.

Byrne, D., Rasche, L., & Kelley, K. (1974). When "I like you" indicates disagreement. *Journal of Research in Personality, 8,* 207–217.

Carducci, B. J., Deuser, P. S., Bauer, A., Large, M., & Ramaekers, M. (1989). An application of the foot-in-the-door technique to organ donation. *Journal of Business and Psychology, 4,* 245–249.

Castellow, W. A., Wuensch, K. L., & Moore, C. H. (1990). Effects of physical attractiveness of the plaintiff and defendant in sexual harassment judgments. *Journal of Social Behavior and Personality, 5,* 547–562.

Chaiken, S. (1979). Communicator physical attractiveness and persuasion. *Journal of Personality and Social Psychology, 37,* 1387–1397.

Chaiken, S. (1986). Physical appearance and social influence. In C. P. Herman, M. P. Zanna, & E. T. Higgins (Eds.), *Physical appearance, stigma, and social behavior: The Ontario Symposium* (Vol. 3, pp. 143–177). Hillsdale, NJ: Lawrence Erlbaum.

Chaiken, S., & Trope, Y. (Eds.) (1999). *Dual-process theories in social psychology.* New York: Guilford.

Chartrand, T. L., & Bargh, J. A. (1999). The chameleon effect: The perception-behavior link and social interaction. *Journal of Personality and Social Psychology, 76,* 893–910.

Chen, S., & Chaiken, S. (1999). The heuristic-systematic model in its broader context. In S. Chaiken & Y. Trope (Eds.), *Dual-process theories in social psychology* (pp. 73–96). New York: Guilford.

Church, A. H. (1993). Estimating the effect of incentives on mail survey response rates. *Public Opinion Quarterly, 57,* 62–79.

Cialdini, R. B., & Ascani, K. (1976). Test of a concession procedure for inducing verbal, behavioral, and further compliance with a request to give blood. *Journal of Applied Psychology, 61,* 295–300.

Cialdini, R. B., Borden, R. J., Thorne, A., Walker, M. R. Freeman, S., & Sloan, L. R. (1976). Basking in reflected glory: Three (football) field studies. *Journal of Personality and Social Psychology, 34,* 366–375.

Cialdini, R. B., Cacioppo, J. T., Bassett, R., & Miller, J. A. (1978). Low-ball procedure for producing compliance: Commitment then cost. *Journal of Personality and Social Psychology, 36,* 463–476.

Cialdini, R. B., Vincent, J. E., Lewis, S. K., Catalan, J., Wheeler, D., & Darby, B. L. (1975). Reciprocal concessions procedure for inducing compliance: The door-in-the-face technique. *Journal of Personality and Social Psychology, 31,* 206–215.

Cioffi, D., & Garner, R. (1996). On doing the decision: The effects of active versus passive choice on commitment and self-perception. *Personality and Social Psychology Bulletin, 22,* 133–147.

Clark, M. S. (1984). Record keeping in two types of relationships. *Journal of Personality and Social Psychology, 47,* 549–557.

Clark, M. S., & Mills, J. (1979). Interpersonal attraction in exchange and communal relationships. *Journal of Personality and Social Psychology, 37,* 12–24.

Clark, M. S., Mills, J. R., & Corcoran, D. M. (1989). Keeping track of needs and inputs of friends and strangers. *Personality and Social Psychology Bulletin, 15,* 533–542.

Clark, M. S., Mills, J., & Powell, M. (1986). Keeping track of needs in communal and exchange relationships. *Journal of Personality and Social Psychology, 51,* 333–338.

Clark, M. S., & Waddell, B. (1985). Perceptions of exploitation in communal and exchange relationships. *Journal of Personal and Social Relationships, 2,* 403–418.

Clark, R. D., III, & Word, L. E. (1972). Why don't bystanders help? Because of ambiguity? *Journal of Personality and Social Psychology, 24,* 392–400.

Clark, R. D., III, & Word, L. E. (1974). Where is the apathetic bystander? Situational characteristics of the emergency. *Journal of Personality and Social Psychology, 29,* 279–287.

Cohen, A. (1999, May 31). Special report: Troubled kids. *Time,* p. 38.

Cohen, M., & Davis, N. (1981). *Medication errors: Causes and prevention.* Philadelphia: G. F. Stickley Co.

Cohen, S. (1978). Environmental load and the allocation of attention. In A. Baum, J. E. Singer, & S. Valins (Eds.), *Advances in environmental psychology* (Vol. 1). New York: Halstead Press.

Collins, J. (1998, November 9). Distinct? Or extinct? *Time,* p. 110.

Conway, M., & Ross M. (1984). Getting what you want by revising what you had. *Journal of Personality and Social Psychology, 47,* 738–748.

Cook, D. (1984). *Charles de Gaulle: A biography.* New York: Putnam.

Cook, S. W. (1990). Toward a psychology of improving justice. *Journal of Social Issues, 46,* 147–161.

Craig, K. D., & Prkachin, K. M. (1978). Social modeling influences on sensory decision theory and psychophysiological indexes of pain. *Journal of Personality and Social Psychology, 36,* 805–815.

Darley, J. M., & Latané, B. (1968). Bystander intervention in emergencies: Diffusion of responsibility. *Journal of Personality and Social Psychology, 8,* 377–383.

Davidson, P. (1999, June 16). Gates speaks softly of antitrust laws. *USA Today,* p. B2.

Davies, J. C. (1962). Toward a theory of revolution. *American Sociological Review, 27,* 5–19.

Davies, J. C. (1969). The J-curve of rising and declining satisfactions as a cause of some great revolutions and a contained rebellion. In H. D. Graham & T. R. Gurr (Eds.), *Violence in America.* New York: Signet Books.

Deci, E. L., & Ryan, R. M. (1985). *Intrinsic motivation and self-determination in human behavior.* New York: Plenum.

DeDreu, C. K. W., & McCusker, C. (1997). Gain-loss frames and cooperation in two-person social dilemmas: A transformational analysis. *Journal of Personality and Social Psychology, 72,* 1093–1106

De Paulo, B. M., Nadler, A., & Fisher, J. D. (Eds.). (1983). *New directions in helping: Vol. 2, Help seeking.* New York: Academic Press.

Deutsch, M., & Gerard, H. B. (1955). A study of normative and informational social influences upon individual judgment. *Journal of Abnormal and Social Psychology, 51,* 629 636.

DeVries, D. L., & Slavin, R. E. (1978). Teams games tournaments (TGT): Review of ten classroom experiments. *Journal of Research and Development in Education, 12,* 28–38.

Dion, K. K. (1972). Physical attractiveness and evaluation of children's transgressions. *Journal of Personality and Social Psychology, 24,* 207–213.

Doob, A. N., & Gross, A. E. (1968). Status of frustrator as an inhibitor of horn-honking response. *Journal of Social Psychology, 76,* 213–218.

Downs, A. C., & Lyons, P. M. (1990). Natural observations of the links between attractiveness and initial legal judgments. *Personality and Social Psychology Bulletin, 17,* 541–547.

Drachman, D., deCarufel, A., & Inkso, C. A. (1978). The extra credit effect in interpersonal attraction. *Journal of Experimental Social Psychology, 14,* 458–467.

Driscoll, R., Davis, K. E., & Lipetz, M. E. (1972). Parental interference and romantic love: The Romeo and Juliet effect. *Journal of Personality and Social Psychology, 24,* 1–10.

Dukes, W. F., & Bevan, W. (1952). Accentuation and response variability in the perception of personally relevant objects. *Journal of Personality, 20,* 457–465.

Eagly, A. H., Ashmore, R. D., Makhijani, M. G., & Longo, L. C. (1991). What is beautiful is good, but . . . : A meta-analytic review of research on the physical attractiveness stereotype. *Psychological Bulletin, 110,* 109–128.

Eagly, A. H., Wood, W., & Chaiken, S. (1978). Causal inferences about communicators and their effect on opinion change. *Journal of Personality and Social Psychology, 36,* 424–435.

Easterbrook, J. A. (1959). The effects of emotion on cue utilization and the organization of behavior. *Psychological Review, 66,* 183–201.

Efran, M. G., & Patterson, E. W. J. (1976). *The politics of appearance.* Unpublished manuscript, University of Toronto.

Eibl-Eibesfeldt, I. (1975). *Ethology: The biology of behavior* (2d ed.). New York: Holt, Rinehart & Winston.

Emswiller, T., Deaux, K., & Willits, J. E. (1971). Similarity, sex, and requests for small favors. *Journal of Applied Social Psychology, 1,* 284–291.

Eron, L. D., & Huesmann, L. R. (1985). The role of television in the development of prosocial and antisocial behavior. In D. Olweus, M. Radke-Yarrow, & J. Block (Eds.), *Development of prosocial and antisocial behavior.* Orlando, FL: Academic Press.

Evans, F. B. (1963). *American Behavioral Scientists, 6*(7), 76–79.

Fazio, R. H., Blascovich, J., & Driscoll, D. (1992). On the functional value of attitudes. *Personality and Social Psychology Bulletin, 18,* 388 401.

Fazio, R. H., Sherman, S. J., & Herr, P. M. (1982). The feature-positive effect in the self-perception process. *Journal of Personality and Social Psychology, 42,* 404–411.

Feinberg, R. A. (1986). Credit cards as spending facilitating stimuli. *Journal of Consumer Research, 13,* 348–356.

Feinberg, R. A. (1990). The social nature of the classical conditioning phenomena in people. *Psychological Reports, 67,* 331–334.

Fenigstein, A., Scheier, M. F., & Buss, A. H. (1975). Public and private self-consciousness: Assessment and theory. *Journal of Consulting and Clinical Psychology, 43,* 522–527.

Festinger, L. (1954). A theory of social comparison processes. *Human Relations, 7,* 117–140.

Festinger, L. (1957). *A theory of cognitive dissonance.* Stanford: Stanford University Press.

Festinger, L., Riecken, H. W., & Schachter, S. (1964). *When prophecy fails.* New York: Harper & Row.

Fiske, S. T., & Neuberg, S. L. (1990). A continuum of impression formation: Influences of information and motivation on attention and interpretation. In M. P. Zanna (Ed.), *Advances in experimental social psychology* (Vol. 23, pp. 1–74). New York: Academic Press.

Fleming, T. (1997, November 23). 13 things you never knew about the American Revolution. *Parade,* pp. 14–15.

For women, all's pheromones in love, war. (1999, March 7). *The Arizona Republic,* p. E19.

Foster, E. (1991, January 28). Lobbyists circle over capitol. *The Arizona Republic,* pp. A1, A6.

Foushee, M. C. (1984). Dyads and triads at 35,000 feet: Factors affecting group process and aircraft performance. *American Psychologist, 39,* 885–893.

Fox, M. W. (1974). *Concepts in ethology: Animal and human behavior.* Minneapolis: University of Minnesota Press.

Freedman, J. L. (1965). Long-term behavioral effects of cognitive dissonance. *Journal of Experimental Social Psychology, 1,* 145–155.

Freedman, J. L., & Fraser, S. C. (1966). Compliance without pressure: The foot-in-the door technique. *Journal of Personality and Social Psychology, 4,* 195–203.

Frenzen, J. R., & Davis, H. L. (1990). Purchasing behavior in embedded markets. *Journal of Consumer Research, 17,* 1–12.

Fromkin, H. L., & Brock, T. C. (1971). A commodity theory analysis of persuasion. *Representative Research in Social Psychology, 2,* 47–57.

Fuller, R. G. C., & Sheehy-Skeffington, A. (1974). Effects of group laughter on responses to humorous materials: A replication and extension. *Psychological Reports, 35,* 531–534.

Furnham, A. (1996). Factors relating to the allocation of medical resources. *Journal of Social Behavior and Personality, 11,* 615–624.

Gaertner, S. L., Dovidio, J. F., Rust, M. C., Neir, J. A., Banker, B. S., Ward, C. M., Mottola, G. R., & Houlette, M. (1999). Reducing intergroup bias: Elements of intergroup cooperation. *Journal of Personality and Social Psychology, 76,* 388–402.

Ganzberg, M. (1964, March 27). *New York Times,* p. 1.

Garner, R. L. (1999). *What's in a name: Persuasion perhaps?* Unpublished manuscript, Sam Houston State University.

George, W. H., Gournic, S. J., & McAfee, M. P (1988). Perceptions of postdrinking female sexuality. *Journal of Applied Social Psychology, 18,* 1295–1317.

Gerard, H. B. (1983). School segregation: The social science role. *American Psychologist, 38,* 869–877.

Gerard, H. B., & Mathewson, G. C. (1966). The effects of severity of initiation on liking for a group: A replication. *Journal of Experimental Social Psychology, 2,* 278–287.

Gergen, K., Ellsworth, P., Maslach, C., & Seipel, M. (1975). Obligation, donor resources, and reactions to aid in three cultures. *Journal of Personality and Social Psychology, 31,* 390–400.

Gigerenzer, G., & Goldstein, D. G. (1996). Reasoning the fast and frugal way: Models of bounded rationality. *Psychological Review, 103,* 650–669.

Gilbert, D. T., & Osborne, R. E. (1989). Thinking backward: Some curable and incurable consequences of cognitive business. *Journal of Personality and Social Psychology, 57,* 940–949.

Glass, S. (1997, December). The Hollywood hustle. *George,* pp. 90–94.

Gleick, E. (1997, February 10). Marine blood sports. *Time,* p. 30.

Goethals, G. R., & Reckman, R. F. (1973). The perception of consistency in attitudes. *Journal of Experimental Social Psychology, 9,* 491–501.

Gonzales, M. H., Davis, J. M., Loney, G. L., Lukens, C. K., & Junghans, C. M. (1983). Interactional approach to interpersonal attraction. *Journal of Personality and Social Psychology, 44,* 1192–1197.

Goodenough, U. W. (1991). Deception by pathogens. *American Scientist, 79,* 344–355.

Gordon, R. E., & Gordon, K. (1963). *The blight on the ivy.* Englewood Cliffs, NJ: Prentice-Hall.

Gorn, G. J. (1982). The effects of music in advertising on choice behavior: A classical conditioning approach. *Journal of Marketing, 46,* 94–101.

Gould, M. S., & Shaffer, D. (1986). The impact of suicide in television movies. *The New England Journal of Medicine, 315,* 690–694.

Green, F. (1965). The "foot-in-the-door" technique. *American Salesmen, 10,* 14–16.

Greenberg, M. S., & Shapiro, S. P. (1971). Indebtedness: An adverse effect of asking for and receiving help. *Sociometry, 34,* 290–301.

Greenwald, A. F., Carnot, C. G., Beach, R., & Young, B. (1987). Increasing voting behavior by asking people if they expect to vote. *Journal of Applied Psychology, 72,* 315–318.

Gregory, S. W., & Webster, S. (1996). A nonverbal signal in voices of interview partners effectively predicts communication accommodation and social status perceptions. *Journal of Personality and Social Psychology, 70,* 1231–1240.

Gruner, S. J. (1996, November). Reward good consumers. *Inc.,* p. 84.

Grush, J. E., (1980). Impact of candidate expenditures, regionality, and prior outcomes on the 1976 Democratic presidential primaries. *Journal of Personality and Social Psychology, 38,* 337–347.

Grush, J. E., McKeough, K. L., & Ahlering, R. F. (1978). Extrapolating laboratory exposure experiments to actual political elections. *Journal of Personality and Social Psychology, 36,* 257–270.

Hammermesh, D., & Biddle, J. E. (1994). Beauty and the labor market. *The American Economic Review, 84,* 1174–1194.

Harper, C. R., Kidera, C. J., & Cullen, J. F. (1971). Study of simulated airplane pilot incapacitation: Phase II, subtle or partial loss of function. *Aerospace Medicine, 42,* 946–948.

Heider, F. (1946). Attitudes and cognitive organization. *Journal of Psychology, 21,* 107–112.

Heilman, M. E. (1976). Oppositional behavior as a function of influence attempt intensity and retaliation threat. *Journal of Personality and Social Psychology, 33,* 574–578.

Higgins, E. T., Lee, J., Kwon, J., & Trope, Y. (1995). When combining intrinsic motivations undermines interest. *Journal of Personality and Social Psychology, 68,* 749–767.

Higham, P. A., & Carment, D. W. (1992). The rise and fall of politicians. *Canadian Journal of Behavioral Science,* 404–409.

Hill, G. W. (1982). Group versus individual performance: Are N + 1 heads better than one? *Psychological Bulletin, 91,* 517–539.

Hockey, G. R. J., & Hamilton, P. (1970). Arousal and information selection in short-term memory. *Nature, 226,* 866–867.

Hofling, C. K., Brotzman, E., Dalrymple, S., Graves, N., & Pierce, C. M. (1966). An experimental study of nurse-physician relationships. *Journal of Nervous and Mental Disease, 143,* 171–180.

Hölldobler, B. (1971). Communication between ants and their guests. *Scientific American, 198,* 68–76.

Hornstein, H. A., Fisch, E., & Holmes, M. (1968). Influence of a model's feeling about his behavior and his relevance as a comparison other on observers' helping behavior. *Journal of Personality and Social Psychology, 10,* 222–226.

Howard, D. J. (1990). The influence of verbal responses to common greetings on compliance behavior: The foot-in-the-mouth effect. *Journal of Applied Social Psychology, 20,* 1185–1196.

Howard, D. J., Gengler, C., & Jain, A. (1995). What's in a name? A complimentary means of persuasion. *Journal of Consumer Research, 22,* 200–211.

Howard, D. J., Gengler, C., & Jain, A. (1997). The name remembrance effect. *Journal of Social Behavior and Personality, 12,* 801–810.

Hunt, J. M., Domzal, T. J., & Kernan, J. B. (1981). Causal attribution and persuasion: The case of disconfirmed expectancies. In A. Mitchell (Ed.), *Advances in consumer research* (Vol. 9). Ann Arbor, MI: Association for Consumer Research.

James, J. M., & Bolstein, R. (1992). Effect of monetary incentives and follow-up mailings on the response rate and response quality in mail surveys. *Public Opinion Quarterly, 54,* 442–453.

Johnson, C. S. (1972). *Fraternities in our colleges.* New York: National Interfraternity Foundation.

Johnson, D. W., & Johnson, R. T. (1983). The socialization and achievement crisis: Are cooperative learning experiences the solution? In L. Bickman (Ed.), *Applied social psychology annual* (Vol. 4). Beverly Hills, CA: Sage Publications.

Jones, E. E., & Harris, V. E. (1967). The attribution of attitudes. *Journal of Experimental Social Psychology, 3,* 1–24.

Jones, E. E., & Wortman, C. (1973). *Integration: An attributional approach.* Morristown, NJ: General Learning Corp.

Joule, R. V. (1987). Tobacco deprivation: The foot-in-the-door technique versus the low-ball technique. *European Journal of Social Psychology, 17,* 361–365.

Kahn, B. E., & Baron, J. (1995). An exploratory study of choice rules favored for high-stakes decisions. *Journal of Consumer Psychology, 4,* 305–328.

Kahneman, D., Slovic, P., & Tversky, A. (Eds.). (1982). *Judgment under uncertainty: Heuristics and biases.* New York: Cambridge University Press.

Kamisar, Y. (1980). Police interrogation and confession: Essays in law and policy. Ann Arbor: University of Michigan Press.

Katzev, R., & Johnson, T. (1984). Comparing the effects of monetary incentives and foot-in-the-door strategies in promoting residential electricity conservation. *Journal of Applied Psychology, 14,* 12–27.

Katzev, R., & Pardini, A. (1988). The comparative effectiveness of token reinforcers and personal commitment in promoting recycling. *Journal of Environmental Systems, 17,* pp. 93–113.

Keinan, G. (1987). Decision making under stress: Scanning of alternatives under controllable and uncontrollable threats. *Journal of Personality and Social Psychology, 52,* 639–644.

Kelman, H. C., & Hamilton, V. L. (1989). *Crimes of obedience.* New Haven, CT: Yale University Press.

Kenrick, D. T., Gutierres, S. E., & Goldberg, L. L. (1989). Influence of popular erotica on judgments of strangers and mates. *Journal of Experimental Social Psychology, 25,* 159–167.

Kenrick, D. T., & Keefe, R. C. (1992). Age preferences in mates reflect sex differences in human reproductive strategies. *Brain and Behavioral Sciences, 15,* 75–133.

Kerr, N. L., & MacCoun, R. J. (1985). The effects of jury size and polling method on the process and product of jury deliberation. *Journal of Personality and Social Psychology, 48,* 349–363.

Ketelaar, T. (1995, June). *Emotions as mental representations of gains and losses: Translating prospect theory into positive and negative affect.* Paper presented at the meeting of the American Psychological Society, New York, NY.

Kissinger, H. (1982). *Years of upheaval.* Boston: Little, Brown.

Knishinsky, A. (1982). *The effects of scarcity of material and exclusivity of information on industrial buyer perceived risk in provoking a purchase decision.* Unpublished doctoral dissertation, Arizona State University, Tempe.

Knouse, S. B. (1983). The letter of recommendation: Specificity and favorability information. *Personal Psychology, 36,* 331–341.

Knox, R. E., & Inkster, J. A. (1968). Postdecisional dissonance at post time. *Journal of Personality and Social Psychology, 8,* 319–323.

Kraut, R. E. (1973). Effects of social labeling on giving to charity. *Journal of Experimental Social Psychology, 9,* 551–562.

Kruglanski, A. E., & Freund, T. (1983). The freezing and unfreezing of lay inferences: Effects on impressional primacy, ethnic stereotyping, and numerical anchoring. *Journal of Experimental Social Psychology, 19,* 448–468.

Kulka, R. A., & Kessler, J. R. (1978). Is justice really blind? The effect of litigant physical attractiveness on judicial judgment. *Journal of Applied Social Psychology, 4,* 336–381.

Kunz, P. R., & Woolcott, M. (1976). Season's greetings: From my status to yours. *Social Science Research, 5,* 269–278.

Kurtzburg, R. L., Safar, H., & Cavior, N. (1968). Surgical and social rehabilitation of adult offenders. *Proceedings of the 76th Annual Convention of the American Psychological Association, 3,* 649–650.

Lack, D. (1943). *The life of the robin.* London: Cambridge University Press.

Langer, E. J. (1989). Minding matters. In L. Berkowitz (Ed.), *Advances in experimental social psychology* (Vol. 22). New York: Academic Press.

Langer, E., Blank, A., & Chanowitz, B. (1978). The mindlessness of ostensibly thoughtful action: The role of "placebic" information in interpersonal interaction. *Journal of Personality and Social Psychology, 36,* 635–642.

Latané, B., & Darley, J. M. (1968a). Group inhibition of bystander intervention in emergencies. *Journal of Personality and Social Psychology, 10,* 215–221.

Latané, B., & Darley, J. M. (1968b). *The unresponsive bystander: Why doesn't he help?* New York: Appleton-Century-Crofts.

Latané, B., & Nida, S. (1981). Ten years of research on group size and helping. *Psychological Bulletin, 89,* 308–324.

Latané, B., & Rodin, J. (1969). A lady in distress: Inhibiting effects of friends and strangers on bystander intervention. *Journal of Experimental Social Psychology, 5,* 189–202.

Laughlin, P. R. (1980). Social combination processes in cooperative problem-solving groups in verbal intellective tasks. In M. Fishbein (Ed.), *Progress in social psychology.* Hillsdale, NJ: Lawrence Erlbaum.

Leakey, R., & Lewin, R. (1978). *People of the lake.* New York: Anchor Press/Doubleday.

Lefkowitz, M., Blake, R. R., & Mouton, J. S. (1955). Status factors in pedestrian violation of traffic signals. *Journal of Abnormal and Social Psychology, 51,* 704–706.

Leippe, M. R., & Elkin, R. A. (1987). When motives clash: Issue involvement and response involvement as determinants of persuasion. *Journal of Personality and Social Psychology, 52,* 269–278.

Lepper, M. R., & Greene, D. (Eds). (1978). *The hidden costs of reward.* Hillsdale, NJ: Lawrence Erlbaum.

Levine, L. E. (1983). Mine: Self-definition in two-year-old boys. *Developmental Psychology, 19,* 544–549.

Lewis, M., & Brooks-Gunn, J. (1979). *Social cognition and the acquisition of self.* New York: Plenum.

Liebert, R., & Baron, R. A. (1972). Some immediate effects of televised violence on children's behavior. *Developmental Psychology, 6,* 469–475.

Lloyd, J. E. (1965). Aggressive mimicry in *Photuris:* Firefly *femme fatales. Science, 149,* 653–654.

Locke, K. S., & Horowitz, L. M. (1990). Satisfaction in interpersonal interactions as a function of similarity in level of dysphoria. *Journal of Personality and Social Psychology, 58,* 823–831.

Lott, A. J., & Lott, B. E. (1965). Group cohesiveness as interpersonal attraction: A review of relationships with antecedent and consequent variables. *Psychological Bulletin, 64,* 259–309.

Lynn, M. (1989). Scarcity effect on value: Mediated by assumed expensiveness. *Journal of Economic Psychology, 10,* 257–274.

Lynn, M., & McCall, M. (1998). *Beyond gratitude and gratuity.* Unpublished manuscript, Cornell University, School of Hotel Administration, Ithaca, NY.

Lynn, M., & Shurgot, B. A. (1984). Responses to lonely hearts advertisements: Effects of reported physical attractiveness, physique, and coloration. *Personality and Social Psychology Bulletin, 10,* 349–357.

Lytton, J. (1979). Correlates of compliance and the rudiments of conscience in two-year-old boys. *Canadian Journal of Behavioral Science, 9,* 242–251.

Mack, D., & Rainey, D. (1990). Female applicants' grooming and personnel selection. *Journal of Social Behavior and Personality, 5,* 399–407.

MacKenzie, B. (1974, June 22). When sober executives went on a bidding binge. *TV Guide.*

Mackworth, N. H. (1965). Visual noise causes tunnel vision. *Psychonomic Science, 3,* 67–68.

Macrae, N. (1972, January 22). Multinational business. *The Economist.*

Magruder, J. S. (1974). *An American life: One man's road to Watergate.* New York: Atheneum.

Mahler, M. S., Pine, F., & Bergman, A. (1975). *The psychological birth of the infant.* New York: Basic Books.

Major, B., Carrington, P. I., & Carnevale, P. J. D. (1984). Physical attractiveness and self-esteem: Attributions for praise from an other-sex evaluator. *Personality and Social Psychology Bulletin, 10,* 43–50.

Manis, M., Cornell, S. D., & Moore, J. C. (1974). Transmission of attitude relevant information through a communication chain. *Journal of Personality and Social Psychology, 30,* 81–94.

Markus, H., & Kitayama, S. (1991). Culture and the self: Implications of cognition, emotion, and motivation. *Psychological Bulletin, 98,* 224–253.

Maruyama, G., Miller, N., & Holtz, R. (1986). The relation between popularity and achievement: A longitudinal test of the lateral transmission of value hypothesis. *Journal of Personality and Social Psychology, 51*, 730–741.

Mauro, R. (1984). The constable's new clothes: Effects of uniforms on perceptions and problems of police officers. *Journal of Applied Social Psychology, 14*, 42–56.

Mauss, M. (1954). *The gift.* (I. G. Cunnison, Trans.). London: Cohen and West.

Mazis, M. B. (1975). Antipollution measures and psychological reactance theory: A field experiment. *Journal of Personality and Social Psychology, 31*, 654–666.

Mazis, M. B., Settle, R. B., & Leslie, D. C. (1973). Elimination of phosphate detergents and psychological reactance. *Journal of Marketing Research, 10*, 390–395.

McCall, M., & Belmont, H. J. (1996). Credit card insignia and restaurant tipping: Evidence for an associative link. *Journal of Applied Psychology, 81*, 609–613.

McCombs, M., & Zhu, J. (1995). Capacity, diversity, and volatility of the public agenda. *Public Opinion Quarterly, 59*, 495–525.

McGuinnies, E., & Ward, C. D., (1980). Better liked than right: Trustworthiness and expertise as factors in credibility. *Personality and Social Psychology Bulletin, 6*, 467–472.

Meeus, W. H. J., & Raaijmakers, Q. A. W. (1986). Administrative obedience: Carrying out orders to use psychological-administrative violence. *European Journal of Social Psychology, 16*, 311–324.

Melamed, B. F., Yurcheson, E., Fleece, L., Hutcherson, S., & Hawes, R. (1978). Effects of film modeling on the reduction of anxiety-related behaviors in individuals varying in level of previous experience in the stress situation. *Journal of Consulting and Clinical Psychology. 46*, 1357–1374.

Meyerwitz, B. E., & Chaiken, S. (1987). The effect of message framing on breast self-examination attitudes, intentions, and behavior. *Journal of Personality and Social Psychology, 52*, 500–510.

Milgram, S. (1963). Behavioral study of obedience. *Journal of Abnormal and Social Psychology, 67*, 371–378.

Milgram, S. (1970). The experience of living in cities. *Science, 13*, 1461–1468.

Milgram, S. (1974). *Obedience to authority.* New York: Harper & Row.

Milgram, S., Bickman, L., & Berkowitz, O. (1969). Note on the drawing power of crowds of different size. *Journal of Personality and Social Psychology, 13*, 79–82.

Milgram, S., & Sabini J. (1975). *On maintaining norms: A field experiment in the subway.* Unpublished manuscript, City University of New York.

Miller, A. G., Collins, B. E., Brief, D. E. (Eds.) (1995). Perspectives on obedience to authority: The legacy of the Milgram experiments. *Journal of Social Issues, 51* (3).

Miller, N., Campbell, D. T., Twedt, H., & O'Connell, E. J. (1966). Similarity, contrast, and complementarity in friendship choice. *Journal of Personality and Social Psychology, 3*, 3–12.

Miller, R. L., Seligman, C., Clark, N. T., & Bush, M. (1976). Perceptual contrast versus reciprocal concession as mediators of induced compliance. *Canadian Journal of Behavioral Science, 8*, 401–409.

Mills, J., & Clark, M. S. (1982). Exchange and communal relationships. In L. Wheeler (Ed.), *Review of personality and social psychology* (Vol. 3). Beverly Hills, CA: Sage Publications.

Mita, T. H., Dermer, M., & Knight, J. (1977). Reversed facial images and the mere exposure hypothesis. *Journal of Personality and Social Psychology, 35*, 597–601.

Moriarty, T. (1975). Crime, commitment, and the responsive bystander. *Journal of Personality and Social Psychology, 31,* 370–376.

Morrow, L. (1991, September 2). The Russian revolution, *Time,* p. 20.

Murphy, S. T., & Zajonc, R. B. (1993). Affect, cognition and awareness. *Journal of Personality and Social Psychology, 64,* 723–739.

Murray, D. A., Leupker, R. V., Johnson, C. A., & Mittlemark, M. B. (1984). The prevention of cigarette smoking in children: A comparison of four strategies. *Journal of Applied Social Psychology, 14,* 274–288.

Newcomb, T. (1953). An approach to the study of communicative acts. *Psychological Review, 60,* 393–404.

News. (1988). *Stanford Business School Magazine, 56,* 3.

Nosanchuk, T. A., & Lightstone, J. (1974). Canned laughter and public and private conformity. *Journal of Personality and Social Psychology, 29,* 153–156.

O'Connor, R. D. (1972). Relative efficacy of modeling, shaping, and the combined procedures for modification of social withdrawal. *Journal of Abnormal Psychology, 79,* 327–334.

O'Leary, S. G. (1995). Parental discipline mistakes. *Current Directions in Psychological Science, 4,* 11–13.

Olson, J. C. (1977). Price as an informational cue: Effects of product evaluations. In A. G. Woodside, J. N. Sheth, & P. D. Bennett (Eds.), *Consumer and industrial buying behavior.* New York: North-Holland.

Oskamp, S., & Schultz, P. W. (1998). *Applied Social Psychology.* Englewood Cliffs, NJ: Prentice-Hall.

Overload of advice likely misled FBI (1993, October 8). *Arizona Republic,* p. A13.

Packard, V. (1957). *The hidden persuaders.* New York: D. McKay Co.

Paese, P. W., & Gilin, D. A. (2000). When an adversary is caught telling the truth. *Personality and Social Psychology Bulletin, 26,* 75–90.

Pallak, M. S., Cook, D. A., & Sullivan, J. J. (1980). Commitment and energy conservation. *Applied Social Psychology Annual, 1,* 235–253.

Pardini, A., & Katzev, R. (1983–1984). The effect of strength of commitment on newspaper recycling. *Journal of Environmental Systems, 13,* 245–254.

Paulhus, D. L., Martin, C. L., & Murphy, G. K. (1992). Some effects of arousal sex stereotyping. *Personality and Social Psychology Bulletin, 18,* 325–330.

Peiponen, V. A. (1960). Verhaltensstudien am blaukehlchen [Behavior studies of the bluethroat]. *Ornis Fennica, 37,* 69–83.

Peters, D. P., & Ceci, S. J. (1982). Peer-review practices of the psychological journals: The fate of published articles, submitted again. *The Behavioral and Brain Sciences, 5,* 187–195.

Petty, R. E., & Cacioppo, J. T., & Goldman, R. (1981). Personal involvement as a determinant of argument-based persuasion. *Journal of Personality and Social Psychology, 41,* 847–855.

Petty, R. E., & Wegener, D. T. (1999). The elaboration likelihood model: Current status and controversies. In S. Chaiken & Y. Trope (Eds.), *Dual-process theories in social psychology* (pp. 41–72). New York: Guilford.

Phalen, C. W., Chairperson. (1951). [Panel discussion of N.I.C. Public Relations Committee]. *Yearbook.* New York: National Interfraternity Conference.

Phillips, D. P. (1974). The influence of suggestion on suicide: Substantive and theoretical implications of the Werther effect. *American Sociological Review, 39,* 340–354.

Phillips, D. P. (1979). Suicide, motor vehicle fatalities, and the mass media: Evidence toward a theory of suggestion. *American Journal of Sociology, 84,* 1150–1174.

Phillips, D. P. (1980). Airplane accidents, murder, and the mass media: Towards a theory of imitation and suggestion. *Social Forces, 58,* 1001–1024.

Phillips, D. P. (1983). The impact of mass media violence on U. S. homicides. *American Sociological Review, 48,* 560–568.

Phillips, D. P., & Cartensen, L. L. (1986). Clustering of teenage suicides after television news stories about suicide. *The New England Journal of Medicine, 315,* 685–689.

Phillips, D. P., & Cartensen, L. L. (1988). The effect of suicide stories on various demographic groups, 1968–1985. *Suicide and Life-Threatening Behavior, 18,* 100–114.

Quote without comment. (1975, January). *Consumer Reports,* p. 62.

Rao, A. R., & Monroe, K. B. (1989). The effect of price, brand name, and store name on buyer's perceptions of product quality. *Journal of Marketing Research, 26,* 351–357.

Razran, G. H. S. (1938). Conditioning away social bias by the luncheon technique. *Psychological Bulletin, 35,* 693.

Razran, G. H. S. (1940). Conditional response changes in rating and appraising sociopolitical slogans. *Psychological Bulletin, 37,* 481.

Regan, D. T., & Kilduff, M. (1988). Optimism about elections: Dissonance reduction at the ballot box. *Political Psychology, 9,* 101–107.

Regan, R. T. (1971). Effects of a favor and liking on compliance. *Journal of Experimental Social Psychology, 7,* 627–639.

Ridley, M. (1997). *The origin of virtue: Human instincts and the evolution of cooperation.* London: Penguin Books.

Riley, D., & Eckenrode, J. (1986). Social ties: Subgroup differences in costs and benefits. *Journal of Personality and Social Psychology, 51,* 770–778.

Ritts, V., Patterson, M. L., & Tubbs, M. E. (1992). Expectations, impressions, and judgments of physically attractive students: A review. *Review of Educational Research, 62,* 413–426.

Rogers, M., Hennigan, K., Bowman, C., & Miller, N. (1984). Intergroup acceptance in classroom and playground settings. In N. Miller & M. B. Brewer (Eds.), *Groups in contact: The psychology of desegregation.* New York: Academic Press.

Rosen, S., & Tesser, A. (1970). On the reluctance to communicate undesirable information: The MUM effect. *Sociometry, 33,* 253–263.

Rosenfield, D., & Stephan, W. G. (1981). Intergroup relations among children. In S. Brehm, S. Kassin, & F. Gibbons (Eds.), *Developmental social psychology.* New York: Oxford University Press.

Rosenfeld, P., Kennedy, J. G., & Giacalone, R. A. (1986). Decision-making: A demonstration of the postdecision dissonance effect. *Journal of Social Psychology, 126,* 663–665.

Rosenthal, A. M. (1964). *Thirty-eight witnesses.* New York: McGraw-Hill.

Ross, A. S. (1971). Effects of increased responsibility on bystander intervention: The presence of children. *Journal of Personality and Social Psychology, 19,* 306–310.

Ross, C. (1979, February 12). Rejected. *New West,* pp. 39–43.

Rothman, A. J., Martino, S. C., Bedell, B. T., Detweiler, J. B., & Salovey, P. (1999). The systematic influence of gain- and loss-framed messages on interest in and use of different types of health behavior. *Personality and Social Psychology Bulletin, 25,* 1355–1369.

Rothman, A. J., & Salovey, P. (1997). Shaping perceptions to motivate healthy behavior: The role of message framing. *Psychological Bulletin, 121,* 3–19.

Ruback, B. R., & Juieng, D. (1997). Territorial defense in parking lots: Retaliation against waiting drivers. *Journal of Applied Social Psychology, 27,* 821–834.

Rubinstein, S. (1985, January 30). What they teach used car salesmen. *San Francisco Chronicle.*

Scammon, D. L. (1977). Information overload and consumers. *Journal of Consumer Research, 4,* 148–155.

Schein, E. (1956). The Chinese indoctrination program for prisoners of war: A study of attempted "brainwashing." *Psychiatry, 19,* 149–172.

Schindler, R. M. (1998). Consequences of perceiving oneself as responsible for obtaining a discount. *Journal of Consumer Psychology, 7,* 371–392.

Schlenker, B. R., Dlugolecki, D. W., & Doherty, K. (1994). The impact of self-presentations on self-appraisals and behavior. The power of public commitment. *Personality and Social Psychology Bulletin, 20,* 20-33.

Schmidtke, A., & Hafner, H. (1988). The Werther effect after television films: New evidence for an old hypothesis. *Psychological Medicine, 18,* 665–676.

Schultz, P. W. (1999). Changing behavior with normative feedback interventions: A field experiment on curbside recycling. *Basic and Applied Social Psychology, 21,* 25–36.

Schwarz, N. (1984). When reactance effects persist despite restoration of freedom: Investigations of time delay and vicarious control. *European Journal of Social Psychology, 14,* 405–419.

Segal, H. A. (1954). Initial psychiatric findings of recently repatriated prisoners of war. *American Journal of Psychiatry, III,* 358–363.

Settle, R. B., & Gordon, L. L. (1974). Attribution theory and advertiser credibility. *Journal of Marketing Research, 11,* 181–185.

Shappell, L. (1995, April 2). Injuries create havoc for Hornets. *The Arizona Republic,* p. C11.

Sheldon, K. M., Ryan, R. M., Rawsthorne, L. J., & Ilardi, B. (1997). Trait self and true self, *Journal of Personality and Social Psychology, 73,* 1380–1393.

Shepperd, J. A., & Strathman, A. J. (1989). Attractiveness and height. *Personality and Social Psychology Bulletin, 15,* 617–627.

Sherif, M., Harvey, O. J., White, B. J., Hood, W. R., & Sherif, C. W. (1961). *Intergroup conflict and cooperation: The Robbers' Cave experiment.* Norman, OK: University of Oklahoma Institute of Intergroup Relations.

Sherman, S. J. (1980). On the self-erasing nature of errors of prediction. *Journal of Personality and Social Psychology, 39,* 211–221.

Slavin, R. E. (1983). When does cooperative learning increase student achievement? *Psychological Bulletin, 94,* 429–445.

Smith, G. H., & Engel, R. (1968). Influence of a female model on perceived characteristics of an automobile. *Proceedings of the 76th Annual Convention of the American Psychological Association, 3,* 681–682.

Smith, R. E., & Hunt, S. D. (1978). Attributional processes in promotional situations. *Journal of Consumer Research, 5,* 149–158.

Smyth, M. M., & Fuller, R. G. C. (1972). Effects of group laughter on responses to humorous materials. *Psychological Reports, 30,* 132–134.

Spangenberg, E. R., & Greenwald, A. G. (2001). Self-prophesy as a method for increasing participation in socially desirable behaviors. In W. Wosinska, R. B. Cialdini, D. W. Barrett, and J. Reykowski (Eds.), *The practice of social influence in multiple cultures.* Mahwah, NJ: Lawrence Erlbaum.

Staff. (1993). Analysis of flight data and cabin voice tapes for Korean Air Lines flight KE-007. *Aviation Week and Space Technology, 138* (25), 17.

Stanne, M. B., Johnson, D. W., & Johnson, R. T. (1999). Does competition enhance or inhibit motor performance: A meta-analysis. *Psychological Bulletin, 125,* 133–154.

Stelfox, H. T., Chua, G., O'Rourke, K., & Detsky, A. S. (1998). Conflict of interest in the debate over calcium-channel antagonists. *New England Journal of Medicine, 333,* 101–106.

Stephan, W. G. (1978). School desegregation: An evaluation of predictions made in *Brown vs. Board of Education. Psychological Bulletin, 85,* 217–238.

Stewart, J. E., II. (1980). Defendant's attractiveness as a factor in the outcome of trials. *Journal of Applied Social Psychology, 10,* 348–361.

Stogdill, R. (1948). Personal factors associated with leadership. *Journal of Psychology, 25,* 35–71.

Styron, W. (1977). A farewell to arms. *New York Review of Books, 24,* 3–4.

Suedfeld, P., Bochner, S., & Matas, C. (1971). Petitioner's attire and petition signing by peace demonstrators: A field experiment. *Journal of Applied Social Psychology, 1,* 278–283.

Swap, W. C. (1977). Interpersonal attraction and repeated exposure to rewards and punishers. *Personality and Social Psychology Bulletin, 3,* 248–251.

Tajfel, J. (1981). *Human groups and social categories.* London: Cambridge University Press.

Taylor, R. (1978). Marilyn's friends and Rita's customers: A study of party selling as play and as work. *Sociological Review, 26,* 573–611.

Tedeschi, J. T., Schlenker, B. R., & Bonoma, T. V. (1971). Cognitive dissonance: Private ratiocination or public spectacle? *American Psychologist, 26,* 685–695.

Teger, A. I. (1980). *Too much invested to quit.* Elmsford, NY: Pergamon.

Tesser, A., Campbell, J., & Mickler, S. (1983). The role of social pressure, attention to the stimulus, and self-doubt in conformity. *European Journal of Social Psychology, 13,* 217–233.

Thompson, L. (1990). An examination of naive and experienced negotiators. *Journal of Personality and Social Psychology, 59,* 82–90.

Tiger, L., & Fox, R. (1989). *The imperial animal.* New York: Holt.

Toufexis, A. (1993, June 28). A weird case, baby? Uh huh! *Time,* p. 41.

Triandis, H. C. (1995). *Individualism and collectivism.* Boulder, CO: Westview Press.

Tversky, A., & Kahneman, D. (1974). Judgment under uncertainty: Heuristics and biases. *Science, 185,* 1124–1131.

Tversky, A., & Kahneman D. (1981). The framing of decisions and the psychology of choice. *Science, 211,* 453–458.

Vallacher, R. R., & Wegner, D. M. (1985). *A theory of action.* Hillsdale, NJ: Lawrence Erlbaum.

Walker, M. G. (1967). *Organizational type, rites of incorporation, and group solidarity: A study of fraternity hell week.* Unpublished doctoral dissertation, University of Washington, Seattle.

Warnick, D. H., & Sanders, G. S. (1980). The effects of group discussion on eyewitness accuracy. *Journal of Applied Social Psychology, 10,* 249–259.

Warriner, K., Goyder, J., Gjertsen, H., Horner, P., & McSpurren, K. (1996). Charities, no; lotteries, no; cash, yes. *Public Opinion Quarterly, 60,* 542–562.

Watson, T. J., Jr. (1990). *Father, son, & Co.* New York: Bantam Books.

Webster, D. W., Richter, L., & Kruglanski, A. W. (1996). On leaping to conclusions when feeling tired. *Journal of Experimental Social Psychology, 32,* 181–195.

West, S. G. (1975). Increasing the attractiveness of college cafeteria food: A reactance theory perspective. *Journal of Applied Psychology, 60,* 656–658.

White, M. (1997, July 12). Toy rover sales soar into orbit. *Arizona Republic,* pp. E1, E9.

Whiting, J. W. M., Kluckhohn, R., & Anthony A. (1958). The function of male initiation ceremonies at puberty. In E. E. Maccoby, T. M. Newcomb, & E. L. Hartley (Eds.), *Readings in social psychology.* New York: Henry Holt and Co.

Whitney, R. A., Hubin, T., & Murphy, J. D. (1965). *The new psychology of persuasion and motivation in selling.* Englewood Cliffs, NJ: Prentice-Hall.

Wicklund, R. A., & Brehm, J. C. (1974) cited in Wicklund, R. A. *Freedom and reactance.* Hillsdale, NJ: Lawrence Erlbaum.

Wilson, D. K., Kaplan, R. M., & Schneiderman, L. J. (1987). Framing of decisions and selection of alternatives in health care. *Social Behaviour, 2,* 51–59.

Wilson, D. K., Purdon, S. E., & Wallston, K. A. (1988). Compliance to health recommendations: A theoretical overview of message framing. *Health Education Research, 3,* 161–171.

Wilson, P. R. (1968). The perceptual distortion of height as a function of ascribed academic status. *Journal of Social Psychology, 74,* 97–102.

Wilson, T. D., Dunn, D. S., Kraft, D., & Lisle, D. J. (1989). Introspection, attitude change, and behavior consistency. In L. Berkowitz (Ed.), *Advances in experimental social psychology* (Vol. 22). San Diego, CA: Academic Press.

Wolf, S., & Montgomery, D. A. (1977). Effects of inadmissible evidence and level of judicial admonishment to disregard on the judgments of mock jurors. *Journal of Applied Social Psychology, 7,* 205–219.

Woodside, A. G., & Davenport, J. W. (1974). Effects of salesman similarity and expertise on consumer purchasing behavior. *Journal of Marketing Research, 11,* 198–202.

Wooten, D. B., & Reed, A. (1998). Informational influence and the ambiguity of product experience: Order effects on the weighting of evidence. *Journal of Consumer Research, 7,* 79–99.

Worchel, S. (1979). Cooperation and the reduction of intergroup conflict: Some determining factors. In W. Austin & S. Worchel (Eds.), *The social psychology of intergroup relations.* Monterey, CA: Brooks/Cole.

Worchel, S., & Arnold, S. E. (1973). The effects of censorship and the attractiveness of the censor on attitude change. *Journal of Experimental Social Psychology, 9,* 365–377.

Worchel, S., Arnold, S. E., & Baker, M. (1975). The effect of censorship on attitude change: The influence of censor and communicator characteristics. *Journal of Applied Social Psychology, 5,* 222–239.

Worchel, S., Lee, J., & Adewole, A. (1975). Effects of supply and demand on ratings of object value. *Journal of Personality and Social Psychology, 32,* 906–914.

Wright, S. C., Aron, A., McLaughlin-Volpe, T., & Ropp, S. A. (1997). The extended contact effect: Knowledge of cross-group friendships and prejudice. *Journal of Personality and Social Psychology, 73,* 73–90.

Young, F. W. (1965). *Initiation ceremonies.* New York: Bobbs-Merrill.

Zajonc, R. B. (1968). The attitudinal effects of mere exposure. *Journal of Personality and Social Psychology Monographs, 9,* (2, Part 2).

Zajonc, R. B., Markus, H., & Wilson, W. R. (1974). Exposure effects and associative learning. *Journal of Experimental Social Psychology, 10,* 248–263.

Zellinger, D. A., Fromkin, H. L., Speller, D. E., & Kohn, C. A. (1974). *A commodity theory analysis of the effects of age restrictions on pornographic materials.* (Paper No. 440). Lafayette, IN: Purdue University, Institute for Research in the Behavioral, Economic and Management Sciences.

Zimmatore, J. J. (1983). Consumer mindlessness: I believe it, but I don't see it. *Proceedings of the Division of Consumer Psychology,* American Psychological Association Convention, Anaheim, CA.

Index

ABC, 224–226
Abraham, 185
Abrams, Robert, 211
Adams, Scott, 190
Advertising, 101, 120, 136, 164–165, 188,
      196–197, 207, 216, 223–224, 229, 239
Airline accidents, 9–10, 122, 124–127, 139
American Cancer Society, 62
American Disabled Veterans, 30
Amway Corporation, 28–29, 71
Animals, 2–5, 10–11, 100–101, 186–187, 190
Anthony, A., 75–76
Aronson, Elliot, 79–80, 155, 158
Asimov, Isaac, 170
Asking, 4, 74
Association principle, 161–174
Auctions, 224–227
Authority principle, 179–201
      advertising and, 188, 196–197
      blind obedience and, 185–188
      clothes and, 193–195
      con artists and, 188, 191, 193, 194–195
      defenses against, 196–200
      experts and, 8, 9–10
      food and, 187, 188, 193, 196–197,
         198–199
      in medicine, 186, 188, 191–192, 196–197
      obedience studies, 179–184, 185, 187,
         191–192, 193–196
      power of, 180–184
      titles and, 8, 9–10, 188–193
      trappings and, 195–196
Automaticity
      consistency principle and, 55–61
      fixed-action patterns, 3–6, 16–17
      modern, 236–237
      primitive, 234–236
      of reciprocation rule, 20
      of stereotypes, 6, 7, 11, 12
Automobile accidents, suicide and, 122,
      124–127
Automobile sales
      commitment principle and, 61–62
      contrast principle, 16
      liking principle and, 147–148, 152, 164,
         175
      low-ball technique in, 85–86
      positive association and, 164
      used-car tactics, 61–62, 229–230

Bandura, Albert, 101–102
Bank examiner scheme, 194–195
Bargain sales, 224
Baron, Robert, 103n
Barry, Dave, 137
Bassett, Rod, 86–87
Bickman, Leonard, 193–195
Blood donations, 44
Boiler-room operations, 211
Boot camp initiations, 80
Branch Davidian Church, 235–236
Brehm, Jack, 209
Brock, Timothy, 218
Brunswick, 43
BUG free sample device, 28–29
Butler, Samuel, 84
Bystander inaction, 111–119, 138–140

Cabbage Patch Kids, 61
Cacioppo, John, 86–87
Calley, William, 184n
Canned laughter, 99–100, 134
Captainitis, 9–10
Carter, Jimmy, 26
Castro, Fidel, 69
CBS Television, 226, 228
Ceci, Stephen, 192
Celebrities, 165–167, 169–174, 187–188,
      196–197
Censorship, 215–218
Charitable organizations, 23–25, 30–33,
      36–39, 44, 62–63, 65–67, 164
Children. See also Schools; Teenagers
      authority principle and, 189
      camp experiences, 156–157
      freedoms and, 221–222
      reciprocation rule and, 36–37, 47
      scarcity principle and, 210–212
      similarity principle and, 120–121
      social proof and, 103–104, 120–121
      stage parents and, 173
Chivas Regal Scotch Whiskey, 6n
Claquing, 134–136
Clinton, Bill, 26, 187
Close-outs, 224
Clothing, authority and, 193–195
Clothing industry, 12
Cohen, Michael, 186
Colgate Total, 207

Commitment principle, 61–96
  cults and, 106
  defenses against, 90–95
  extra effort and, 75–80
  hazing practices and, 76–79, 81
  inner change and, 84–87
  inner choice and, 80–84
  liking and, 144–146, 168
  public commitments and, 72–74
  public good and, 87–90
  self-image and, 69–70, 84
  written commitments and, 61–62, 63–65, 67–72
Commodity theory, 218
Compliments, liking principle and, 152–153
Con artists, 188, 191, 193–195, 211
Concentration camps, 184*n*
Concessions, 36–46, 49
Consistency principle, 53–96. *See also* Commitment principle
Contact, liking principle and, 154–157
Contrast principle, 12–16, 40–43, 49, 160–161, 200
Controlled responding, 8–10
Cooperation, liking principle and, 154–157, 158–161
Copycat suicides, 122, 124–127
Costner, Kevin, 173–174
Courtship rituals, 3, 5, 10–11, 11*n*, 13*n*, 34–35, 53–54, 212–214, 216
Credit card use, 164–165
Cults, 23–25, 105–111, 235–236

Dances with Wolves (movie), 173
Darley, John, 113–116
Davies, James C., 219, 220
Davis, Neil, 186
Deadline tactic, 207–208
Dean, John, 42
Defenses
  against authority principle, 196–200
  against commitment and consistency, 90–95
  against liking principle, 174–175
  against reciprocation rule, 46–49
  against scarcity principle, 228–230
  against social proof, 134–140
DeGaulle, Charles, 74*n*
Desegregation, 154–156, 158, 220
Deutsch, Morton, 72–73
Diller, Barry, 224–226
Discount coupons, 7*n*, 223

Door-in-the-face technique, 38–46
Door-to-door sales
  commitment procedures for charity drives, 62
  endless chain technique in, 49, 146–147
  foot-in-the-door technique, 65–68
  reciprocation rule and, 28–29
  rejection-then-retreat strategy in, 39–40
  written commitments and, 71
Drubeck brothers, 12

Eibesfeldt, Eibl, I., 29–30
Endless chain technique, 49, 146–147
Ent, Uzal, 10
Environmental issues, 87–90, 214
Escobar, Andres, 170*n*
Ethiopia, reciprocation rule and, 21
Ethology, 2–4
Exclusive information, 217–218
Expensive = good principle, 6, 8, 12
Experimental juries, 217
Experts, 8, 9–10

Faraday, Michael, 54
FBI, 235–236
"Feeding frenzy" phenomenon, 224–227
Feinberg, Richard, 164, 165*n*
Festinger, Leon, 54, 105, 107–110
First Amendment, 215–216
Fixed-action patterns, 3–6, 16–17
Flawed items, 205
Fleming, Thomas, 219–220
Food
  association principle and, 164–165, 167
  authority principle and, 187, 188, 193, 196–197, 198–199
  free samples of, 27–28
  restaurant reservations and, 74
  restaurant tips and, 25, 164–165, 198–199
  scarcity principle and, 204, 218–219, 222, 223–224, 228–229
Foot-in-the-door technique, 65–68
Fox, M. W., 2
Fox, R., 20–21
Fraser, Scott, 65–67
Free choice, 209–212
Freedman, Jonathan, 65–67, 82–84
Free-information-and-inspection gambit, 47–49
Free samples, reciprocation rule and, 27–30
Free speech, 215–216
Fromkin, Howard, 218

Gates, Bill, 237
General Foods, 71–72
Genovese, Catherine, 111–114
Gerard, Harold, 72–73
Gifts. *See* Reciprocation rule
Girard, Joe, 147–148, 152, 175
Glasnost, 221
Goethe, Johann von, 123–124
Good Cop/Bad Cop routine, 160–161
Gorbachev, Mikhail, 221, 222
Gore, Al, 166
Gouldner, Alvin, 20
Graf, Steffi, 170, 171
Graham, Billy, 101
Grammer, Karl, 11n
Green, Donna, 214
Gun laws, 214

Hare Krishna Society, 23–25, 31–32
Harris, James, 69
Hazing practices, 76–79, 81
Health Care Financing Administration, U.S.,
  186, 191
Heider, Fritz, 54
Hidden Persuaders (Packard), 27–28
Hiring situations, liking principle and, 149
Hoarding behavior, 214
Hobbes, Thomas, 185
Home party sales, 144–146, 168
Homicide, 126–129, 133
Howard, Daniel, 62–63

Impression management, 99–100, 134–136
Information, 47–49, 217–218, 237
Initiation rites, 75–80, 81
Instant influence, 234–240
Insurance, 151, 217

Jigsaw classroom, 158
Johnson, Lyndon, 26
Jones, Edward, 69
Jones, Jim, 30, 130–133
Jonestown mass suicide, 30, 130–133
Jordan, Michael, 187
Judgmental heuristics, 8
Juette, Astrid, 11n
Jujitsu, 12–16, 27–30, 174
Jury trials, 62, 217
Justice Department, U.S., 235–236

Katzev, Richard, 90n
Kelley, G. Warren, 43

Kerr, Peter, 211
King, Larry, 187
Kissinger, Henry, 70
Kluckhohn, R., 75–76
Kosinski, Jerzy, 192

Labor negotiation, 39
Langer, Ellen, 4
Langford, David L., 163
Large-then-small-request sequence, 43–44
LaRue, Frederick, 41, 42–43
Latané, Bibb, 113–116
Laugh tracks, 99–100, 134
Leakey, Richard, 20
Leno, Jay, 166
Liddy, G. Gordon, 41, 42, 43
Liebert, Robert, 104n
Liking principle, 22–23, 145–176
  in automobile sales, 147–148, 152, 164, 175
  compliments and, 152–153
  conditioning and association in, 161–174
  contact and cooperation in, 154–161, 174
  defenses against, 174–175
  endless chain method of sales and, 49,
    146–147
  Good Cop/Bad Cop routine, 160–161
  physical attractiveness and, 148–150, 174
  in race relations, 154–156, 158–159
  similarity and, 150–152, 170
  Tupperware parties and, 144–146, 168
Limited-number tactic, 205–207
Lost-wallet study, 120, 121–122
Louden, Robert, 236
Louie, Diane, 30
Low-ball technique, 85–90
Luncheon technique, 167

MacKenzie, Bob, 226
Macrae, Norman, 237
Magic Writing Pad, 72–73
Magruder, Jeb Stuart, 41, 42
Mars, Franklin, 165
MasterCard, 164
Mating rituals, 3, 5, 10–11, 11n
Mauss, Marcel, 31
MCI Friends and Family Calling Club, 147
Medication Errors (Cohen and Davis), 186
Medicine, 27, 186, 188, 191–192, 196–197,
  205
Microsoft, 237
Mihaly, Orestes J., 211
Milgram, Stanley, 31n, 179–185, 195–196

Miller, John, 86–87
Mills, Judson, 79–80
Mimicry, 10–11
Mitchell, John, 41, 42
Monkeys, 186–187
Morrow, Lance, 221
Muskie, Edmund, 41
My Lai massacre, 184*n*

Namedropping, 173
Nazis, 184*n*
NBC, 225–226
Negotiation opponent, 45
Newcomb, Theodore, 54
Nixon, Richard, 41–43

Obedience studies, 179–184, 185, 187,
   191–192, 193–196
O'Brien, Lawrence, 41, 42
O'Connor, Robert, 103–104
Olympics sponsorships, 165, 165*n*

Packard, Vance, 27–28
Paralysis of analysis, 238
Pavlov, Ivan, 167–168
People's Temple mass suicide, 30, 130–133
Perceptual contrast principle. *See* Contrast
   principle
Perestroika, 221
Personal computers, 237
Pest exterminator companies, 48*n*
Peters, Douglas, 192
Phillips, David, 123–130
Physical attractiveness, 11*n,* 13*n,* 148–150,
   174
Pine, Joe, 234
Pluralistic ignorance phenomenon, 111–119,
   138–140
Police, Good Cop/Bad Cop routine, 160–161
Political essay contests, 63–64, 67–72, 81–82
Politics
   association principle and, 165–167
   authority principle and, 187, 189, 190*n*
   liking principle and, 154, 165, 166
   reciprocation rule and, 26–27
   revolutions and, 219–222
   scarcity principle and, 215–216, 219–222
Porcher, 134–136
Poseidon Adventure, The (movie), 224–226,
   228
Praise, liking principle and, 152–153
Precious mistakes, 205

Prisoner-of-war camps, collaboration in,
   63–64, 67–72, 81–82
Procter & Gamble, 71–72, 223
Profiteers, 6, 8, 10–12
Psychological reactance, 208–218
Public commitments, 72–74

Race relations, 154–156, 158–159, 220–221
Razran, Gregory, 167–168
Reactance, psychological, 208–218
Real estate market, 14–16, 224
Reciprocation rule, 20–50, 167
   charitable organizations and, 23–25, 30,
      31–33, 36–39, 44
   concessions and, 36–46
   defense against, 46–49
   liking and, 144
   power of, 22–30
   in rejection-then-retreat strategy, 38–46, 49
   tips and, 25, 198–199
   unequal exchanges and, 33–36
   uninvited debts and, 20–21, 30–33
Regan, Dennis, 22–23, 24, 31, 33
Rejection-then-retreat strategy, 38–46, 49
Responsibility, 45, 82, 111–119, 138–140
Revolutions, 219–222
Reynolds, Joshua, 55
Riecken, Henry, 105, 107–110
Rites of passage, 75–80
Robert, Cavett, 101
Romeo and Juliet effect, 212–214, 216
Rosenthal, A. M., 112, 113
Rosten, Leo, 12
Rothman, Alexander, 205
Ryan, Leo R., 130

Sabin, Robert, 135
Sabini, John, 31*n*
Sadat, Anwar, 70
Sales, 224
Sales motivation analysts, 13–16
Salovey, Peter, 205
Samples, reciprocation rule and, 27–30
Sanka, 188, 196–197
Satisfaction, in rejection-then-retreat, 45–46
Saturday Night Fever (movie), 227
Sauton, 134–136
Scarcity principle, 204–231
   advertising and, 207, 216, 223–224, 229
   auctions and, 224–227
   censorship and, 215–218
   defenses against, 228–230

food and, 204, 218–219, 222, 223–224, 228–229
limited-number tactic, 205–207
in medicine, 205
optimal conditions for, 218–227
power of, 204–208
psychological reactance and, 208–218
revolutions and, 219–222
Romeo and Juliet effect, 212–214, 216
shortcuts and, 208–209
time deadline tactic, 207–208
Schachter, Stanley, 105, 107–110
Schein, Edgar, 63–64
Schools, 154–156, 158, 216–217, 220
Seasonal buying patterns, 58–61
Segal, Henry, 68
Seles, Monica, 169–170, 171
Self, William, 226
Self-image, 69–70, 84, 173
Sexual attractiveness, 11n, 13n
Sexual obligation, 34–35
Shaklee Corporation, 146–147
Sherif, Muzafer, 156–157, 158
Sherman, Steven J., 62
Shortcuts, 3–12, 16–17, 208–209, 234–236, 238–239
Similarity, 119–133, 150–152, 170
Sipress, David, 237
Smuggling, 214
Social proof, 99–141
    in advertising, 101, 120, 136, 239
    bystander inaction and, 111–119, 138–140
    cults and, 105–111
    defenses against, 134–140
    homicide and, 126–129, 133
    impression management and and, 99–100, 134–136
    liking and, 144
    lost-wallet study and, 120, 121–122
    power of, 101–105
    shortcuts and, 238–239
    similarity and, 119–133
    suicide and, 122, 124–133
    uncertainty and, 111–119, 132–133
Solomon, Thomas (TJ), 129
Sorrows of Young Werther, The (Goethe), 123–124
Soviet Union, former, 221, 222
Sports, 168–172, 187
Stanko, Jack, 61–62
Stereotypes, 6, 7, 11, 12
Storke, Bill, 225

Styron, William, 80
Suicide, 30, 122–127, 130–133
Supreme Court, 220
Surprise, 31n, 196
Survey completion rates, 25, 151

Talking the top of the line strategy, 43–44
Tamraz, Roger, 26
Teenagers, 128, 129, 212–214, 216. *See also* Children; Schools
Telephone solicitation, 62–63
Television, 99–101, 103n, 120, 136, 224–226. *See also* Advertising
Testimonials, 71–72, 120, 136
Thonga people, 75–76, 79
Thorne, Avril, 172
Tienanmen Square massacre, 81–82
Tiger, L., 20–21
Time-limit tactic, 207–208
Tips, 25, 164–165, 198–199
Titles, authority principle and, 8, 9–10, 188–193
Toy manufacturers, 58–61
Transcendental Meditation (TM), 55–58
Travolta, John, 227
Trigger feature, 3–6, 9
Tupperware Home Parties Corporation, 144–146, 168
Turkeys, 2–4, 100–101

Uncertainty, social proof and, 111–119, 132–133
Used-car sales, 61–62, 229–230

Van Kampen, Jakob, 111n
Vartan Bhanji, 20n

Watergate scandal, 41–43
Watson, John, Jr., 10
Weather reports, 161–162, 163
Weight-reduction clinics, 73–74
Werther effect, 123–124
West, Louis Jolyon, 131
Whiting, J. W. M., 75–76
Willson, S. Brian, 184
Wood, Robert, 226, 228
Worchel, Stephen, 218–219

Yamuda, Tom, 165
Young, Robert, 188, 196–197

Zappa, Frank, 234
Zero tolerance, 80

Credits

Text and Figure Credits

p. 125: Figure 4.1. From "The Influence of Suggestion on Suicide: Substantive and Theoretical Implications of the Werther Effect," by David E. Phillips, *American Sociological Review,* Vol. 39, 1974, Figure 1, p. 343. Reprinted by permission of the American Sociological Society and the author.

p. 127: Figure 4.2. Reprinted from *Social Forces,* Vol. 58, June 1980, pp. 1005, 1012. "Airplanes, Accidents, Murder, and the Mass Media: Toward a Theory of Imitation and Suggestion," by David E. Phillips. Copyright © 1980 by the University of North Carolina Press.

p. 137: Figure 4.4. "Stay Tuned Folks: Consumers from Mars Are on Next," by Dave Barry. From *The Arizona Republic,* May 12, 1991. Reprinted by permission of Knight-Ridder Tribune News Service.

p. 163: Figure 5.1. "Weathermen Pay Price for Nature's Curve Balls," by David L. Langford. From *The Arizona Republic,* December 18, 1981. Reprinted by permission of The Associated Press.

p. 211: Figure 7.1. "Officials Warn Public of Frauds by Phone," by Peter Kerr, *The New York Times,* May 14, 1983. Copyright © 1983 by The New York Times Company. Reprinted by permission.

Photo and Advertisement Credits

p. 1: Chapter 1 opener. Copyright © 1999. Advertisement reprinted by permission of Palm Computing, Inc.; p. 5: © George Holton/ Photo Researchers; p. 19: Chapter 2 opener. Advertisement reprinted by permission of Life and Health Insurance Foundation for Education (LIFE); pp. 24, 129, 222, 225: © AP/ Wide World Photos; p. 28: © Alan Carey/ The Image Works; p. 52: Chapter 3 opener. Copyright © 1999 General Motors Corp. Used with permission of GM Media Archives; p. 60: © Ted Thai/ Time Magazine; p. 66: © Mark Antman/ The Image Works; p. 77: (top) © Luuk Kramer; (bottom) © Deborah Copaken/ Liaison Agency; p. 98: Chapter 4 opener. Advertisement reprinted by permission of Toyota Motor Sales, U.S.A., Inc. and Tim Damon of Damon Productions, Inc; p. 102: Advertisement reprinted by permission of The U.S. Department of the Treasury, Savings Bonds Marketing Office, Washington, D.C.; p. 115: © Jan Halaskal/ Photo Researchers; p. 123: © R. Kalman/ The Image Works; p. 132: © Philippe Ladrue/ CORBIS Sygma; p. 143: Chapter 5 opener. Advertisement reprinted by permission of Jim Petrillo, owner of Crew Restaurants; p. 145: © Pat Watson/ The Image Works; p. 159: © Cameramann/ The Image Works; p. 166: © AFP/ CORBIS; p. 171: (top) © Associated Press; (bottom) © Liaison Agency; p. 172: © Otto Greule/ Focus West; p. 178: Chapter 6 opener. Advertisement reprinted by permission of Bozwell Worldwide, Inc., as agent for the National Fluid Milk Processor Promotion Board, copyright © 1999; p. 181: © 1965 by Stanley Milgram. From the film "Obedience," distributed by Pennsylvania State University, Audio Visual Services; p. 187: © Cynthia Johnson/ Liaison Agency; p. 203: Chapter 7 opener. Copyright © 1999, Nissan. Nissan and the Nissan logo are registered trademarks of Nissan. Reprinted by permission; p. 207: Advertisement reprinted by permission of Colgate–Palmolive Company. Copyright © 1999, Colgate–Palmolive; p. 227: © Shooting Star; p. 233: Chapter 8 opener. This print advertisement is part of the "City of e" campaign to support SAP America's Internet strategy. Reprinted by permission.